SOMETHING'S THE MATTER WITH AMY

Something's the Matter with Amy

Christy Gerrell

Copyright © 2025 Christy Gerrell

All rights reserved.

No part of this book may be reproduced, stored in a retrieval system, or transmitted by any means, electronic, mechanical, photocopying, recording, or otherwise, without written permission from the author.

ISBN (Paperback): 979-8-9921204-9-3

Dedicated to my beautiful daughter:
Amy Haven Lynn Bac — with a love that will last
throughout eternity.

We miss you Amy, wait for us,
we'll join you in heaven soon.

All our love,
Mommy

PROLOGUE

Ephesians 2:10: For we are God's handiwork, created in Christ Jesus to do good works, which God prepared in advance for us to do…

She was a happy surprise. She was an unmade wish that had come true. She was a long-held desire that until the moment that she was held in the loving arms of her parents, her Mommy and Daddy didn't know that she was their every desire.

They named her Amy. She was almost nine pounds at birth, and she had a head full of dark, thick hair, and huge deep dark brown eyes that dominated her beautiful little face, and those huge eyes would continue to dominate her beautiful little face all of her life. One glance from her, and her parents could almost see the angel that she was within her eyes, those beautiful dark eyes that were the window to Amy's soul

When the nurses handed her to her Mommy, her Mommy did what new mother's do and counted all of her little fingers and all of her little tiny toes and with a happy smile, her Mommy looked up at her Daddy and her Mommy told her Daddy over and over again thank you for the gift of this child, this little girl that looked more like an angel straight out of heaven rather than a baby in her mother's arms.

Her Daddy looked at her Mommy and he laughed, his laughter sounding almost like the chimes of a church bell ringing as he told her Mommy that Mommy had given him this child and that he was the one that was thankful. And her father was thankful, even while he changed the first diaper of his new little girl and that diaper was muddy.

She wasn't an ordinary baby. She was born in silence. No cry came from her at birth, and as the doctor held her up for her Mommy to see the moment after she was born, the baby gave to her mother a smile, one eye closing as the smile touched her baby face in a way that made the mother think the little baby was giving her mommy a wink of the eye.

The doctor assured the delighted parents that the smile was not a smile; it couldn't be, the doctor had said, newborn babies don't smile. But always her Mommy knew, that first meeting between mother and daughter, they did in fact exchange smiles and the two would often exchange smiles in the coming years of Amy's life. That was the course that the baby set for her life with her Mommy, a mother that would become this baby's lifelong best friend and biggest supporter.

So began the life of little Amy Haven Lynn Bac. A little girl born to a father that was career military and to a mother that was going to stay home and raise her to know God and to never take life for granted. And Amy's life would be filled with love, with a mother that had an endless amount of patience with her and a father that would do what he needed and what he must do to provide for his child and to try and save his child's life.

Chapter One

Colossians 3:19: Husbands, love your wives and do not be harsh with them

March 10th 2000 Eglin Air Force Base, Florida

She stood beside him dressed in a simple white dress with pink flowers adorning the dress, yet the flowers were not overpowering, nor did the flowers take away from the simple beauty of the white dress. She felt small standing next to him and she knew in that instant that she was small. His hand took a firm hold of her hand and she looked down seeing his long and lean fingers, feeling the muscles in his hand and the strength that he had as he held tightly to her, his flesh warm and all too real as she clung to him suddenly terrified in what she was doing.

She looked up at him, she had to tilt her head back to do so as he was a good foot taller than she was and a fear consumed her as she wanted to turn and run and she wanted to run far and fast away from this man that she was in the very process of marrying.

Instead of running, she swallowed hard and she swallowed fast and she blinked hard to stop the tears that threatened to fall from falling. A few deep breaths, a forced calmness in her actions she heard herself replying to the question asked of her with a timid and hesitant, "I do."

The man standing beside her had already spoken those two words and more words were being said, but she wasn't hearing those words. Inside of her mind she was in a panic state because she had done this before and the result had been disastrous, more than disastrous. It had taken years for her to find a safe place, a place where bad things didn't happen to you because you were always wrong. A place where kindness was offered and kindness was shown and being right or wrong really didn't matter so much just surviving the day was all that was important.

This woman about to marry for another time had learned to accept herself. She learned to accept that we all have faults, she might have more than most, but then again, she might not have more than most. Her name was Christy; she was thirty-eight years old. To the world, she was a nobody and she liked being a nobody. She had been born an identical twin and blessed with an older brother and later a younger brother. Her father had been a Forest Ranger and her early life would be one defined as one of growing up on Government owned land that was far from big cities and sometimes even far from small towns.

As a little girl, as a very small child, this young woman about to be married again had seen her mother stumble and fall. As a child, Christy thought nothing of her mother's clumsy ways. And her mother had more things going on that would go unnoticed by a small child. Her mother Sara often wrecked the car, her father was often not happy that her mother had wrecked the car, but it couldn't be helped, accidents happen and they're called accidents for a reason.

Sara was a very beautiful woman; she was full of life and smiles and sometimes tears. She wasn't someone her children ever really knew well, not because her children didn't want to know their mother, but because their mother wasn't well and certainly not strong. Maybe Sara had always been weak, no one will ever know as she's long dead.

Standing here now Christy thought of her mother and she tried to remember Sara as her mother. She then accepted that we all have faults and her mother was no more perfect than she was. For Christy, it was too much that Sara had died. And the reality was that Sara had died misunderstood and Sara was misunderstood by her daughter, a daughter that had wanted to be close to her mother, a daughter that had tried to be close to her mother, but never had a real chance to be so.

"Christy," he spoke her name and she found herself able to grab a deep breath and she looked up at him and she knew, here before her stood kindness. Here before her was a man that saw her as something to cherish and to care for, not something to degrade or put down. The reality was that in all the time that she had known this man, he had always and only spoken kindly to her.

He loved her, she thought as she looked up into his dark brown eyes and she knew that he loved her despite her faults. He wanted to be with her even though she wasn't the kind of person that saw herself as lovable and honestly, she wasn't loved, until she met him.

"They have cake," he said with a smile and she turned with him and saw all the food spread out on a table in the bank where she worked. It was horribly dark outside and the rain was coming down heavy and hard and she knew they couldn't leave here, not in this storm and too, she didn't want him running outside in that rain in his uniform, a uniform that was clean and pressed and ready for him to wear on Monday morning when he went to work.

The cake was cut and she watched him carefully, she watched him almost with fear wondering what she had done. She had been safe. She had escaped an unhappy relationship where she had been both physically and emotionally degraded; degraded in a way that no one should be treated in this life by another human being ever. And she had sworn never to be in a relationship again where she might risk being harmed and yet here she was, here she was with this man that was now her husband. And he was not just any man, she thought in a frantic way, but a man that was twice her size and a man that was career military, a man that knew how to fight; a man that knew how to win.

She found herself backed into a corner watching him. She found herself afraid of him when he had done nothing in the time that she had known him to make her feel afraid of him. In fact, he'd done everything to protect her and she clearly knew that despite her fear.

Christy heard his laughter from across the room. She saw the two deep dimples in his cheek and she felt herself begin to relax as she remembered when he had taken her home to his family in Texas. He had been careful of her, gentle in his way and protective, making her feel not just loved, but safe and that trip had taken place months ago.

In her mind, standing here on her wedding night, Christy went back to her childhood, back to her mother, back to the words that were said to her as a child and words that would haunt her all of her life. "A child whose own mother doesn't love her, no one else ever will." Her mother had gone away, her mother had walked off and her mother had left four small children.

Sara's children didn't know, they didn't understand, and they would be grown before the knowledge of their mother became real and their mother would be dead. Sara hadn't been well; in fact, Sara had been showing signs of her illness since before she had given birth to Christy. An illness that was thought to be Multiple Sclerosis, yet had many more devastating signs and symptoms not attached to that disease.

"I didn't know," Christy whispered to herself as she watched her tall and handsome husband interact with her co-workers and beyond the windows in the near darkness, the rain poured down, the thunder roared and the lightning flashed. This was typical weather in the later afternoon in Destin, Florida and they were only two blocks from the beach. "I didn't know," she whispered to herself again and in her mind she tumbled back into a time of her childhood.

Things weren't good in the household that she grew up in. They were not a poor family, her father earned a good living, but still things weren't good. Her mother would wander away, Christy knew this because she'd heard stories from various family members. Once when she had been a baby, her mother had taken her and her siblings to Panama City Beach and roamed off becoming lost, the children left to fend for themselves. After that event and several others, Sarah had been locked away in the State Mental Hospital in Chattahoochee, Florida and sadly diagnosed as a paranoid schizophrenic.

Sara would stay in that hospital until she was rescued by a doctor that wrote that she was suffering from some form of physical disease and that she was not nor had she ever been mentally ill. This happened in an era where there was almost nothing known of degenerative diseases. This happened in a time when someone with epilepsy was viewed as demon possessed and often severe epileptics were locked away or hidden by their families. Too often, children were locked away that weren't well, and the fact of our history wasn't positive as children that were deformed or labeled as retarded were locked in tool sheds or in attics if a mental hospital wasn't available to the child and this was deemed acceptable by our society as a whole.

Christy closed her eyes thinking that now, in this year of two thousand things had changed. If her mother Sara were alive in this day and age there would be supportive help. There would be medications and there would be a community that she could belong to of others that were suffering a disease such as she was suffering. And in all likelihood, Christy's mother would be having tests such as Magnet Resonance Imagining or a CAT scan or even blood testing that could diagnose Sara, and that diagnosis would come with a list of things to expect that would happen over the course of the disease.

But for Sara, there would be no such testing, there would be no community to accept her, a community where others were suffering as she was. Instead, Sara would come home from Chattahoochee and have to find some way to cope with her illness, some way to raise four small children and cook and clean and live every minute of the day when for her, the world wasn't in balance and there were times that she faded away, times that the car was wrecked and times that she would fall and get hurt and even a time clear today in Christy's mind.

The Andy Griffith show had been playing on the TV, a small black and white TV placed under the window that looked out onto the screened porch. Sara had been in the kitchen pouring a cup of coffee, Christy nearby her mother and seeing the coffee pouring over the rim of the cup, the coffee burning her mother's hand and she was frightened, something wasn't right, her mother didn't look well. The crashing of the coffee pot to the floor was loud and Christy heard her sister scream from the open kitchen doorway as their mother fell to the floor and jerked and jerked and jerked while lying on that cold hard floor.

No one told Sara's children that she was ill. What Christy had been told was that Sara was a fat lazy cow that didn't want to take care of her children. On nights that tuna salad was served for dinner, Christy didn't know it was because Sara had burned the dinner that she had prepared because she 'got lost inside of herself again and forgot.' There were tears, Christy would remember those tears always as Sara cried often and often Sara explained to her children that it was her fault, that she was bad.

A stool had been made by a grandfather, a stool that small children used to put clothes in the washing machine for their mother. The oldest brother turned the washer on and the oldest brother stood on the stool below the clothes line with Sara's little twin girls handing him the wet clothes to hang on the clothes line to dry. As Sara coped with her illness, her children adapted as well often doing things to protect their mother from the cruel words that were said of her.

Coming back to the present, Christy saw her husband and she wondered in a near breath taking moment, 'would he change? Would he become mean someday?' If anyone knew that the world was full of mean people, it was Christy. She had grown up knowing what mean was, though as a child, she had accepted the mean words being said of her mother, she had believed those words and very likely at the time she had even supported those mean words.

"She's not sick," the voice in her mind took Christy back, back to being that little girl that didn't know or understand what was happening in her family. "She's just seeking attention. She's lazy and no good and worthless."

"If she were seeking attention," Christy whispered to herself as she watched her new husband having a drink to celebrate their marriage, "she died seeking that attention and she never was given any positive attention."

Sara was judged by everyone, Christy thought on of her mother. Sara was said to have been things no one would want to be accused of being and those accusations were made by people that were supposed to have loved Sara. It's easy to be critical, and hard to be kind, Sara had told Christy when she had been a little girl sitting on the picnic table while her mother put a perm in her hair.

Christy's memories of her mother were different and often conflicting. She remembered her mother having walked away often and having left the family, that was true and that had happened. She also remembered her mother tucking her into bed at night, brushing her hair and holding her close when she was ill. Sara hadn't been all bad, though most of Christy's life after Sara had gone away; Christy had been assured by one and all that Sara was very bad.

"A child whose own mother doesn't love her, no one else ever will," these words echoed again loud and long and clear in Christy's mind as she looked up and saw the man that she had married was coming toward her with a drink for her in his hand. She didn't drink alcoholic beverages, she never had and she never would because if anyone knew that alcohol could turn someone that was mean into someone that was meaner, it was Christy. She had grown up with that as a huge part of her knowledge.

"No," she said to the drink and no was what she would always say to alcoholic drinks.

"Aren't you going to have some cake?" she heard him ask as he looked up at her seeing her standing alone and in the corner of the room. She shook her head and she saw his face change. The look that he gave to her was not the playful look that he often gave to her, but a concerned look, a look that told her he was worried for her. As he knew of her past, he also knew that her fear of men was real and she had a valid reason for that fear, but not of him. He would see that she never feared him either in hitting her or in using words to tear her down. And he had learned in his courtship of Christy that words could harm someone as quickly as a beating with fists could, maybe the words could harm more as the bruises healed but words, once spoke, could not be taken back and would always be remembered.

He knew, Chad thought to himself as he saw her standing alone in that corner of the room. He knew that she was afraid and he knew further that she might be afraid of him in this moment. He knew that she had been in a difficult relationship in her past and he knew that she had been hurt in that relationship. And Chad knew more than anyone else, he knew everything of his new wife, because she had shown him her medical records, records that showed spiral breaks of her arm; records that showed much more harm had been done than just the breaking of a bone. Men were supposed to be gentle of women, men weren't to ever physically degrade a woman.

Until he had seen those medical records, Chad hadn't known of any man that would treat a wife the way that his new wife had been treated in her previous relationship. She had been physically degraded and she had been broken and she had been left with scars that he feared a lifetime on earth wouldn't heal. Scars that only heaven would see banished. Scars this woman nor any woman should bear.

She was fun to be with, he thought now as he looked at her looking at him. She was agreeable and she fell in beside him in whatever he wanted to do, be it going for a ride on the island or to work on his RX-7. She never complained and she was always what he thought of as sweet. He also had learned early on that she could organize him as she had helped him unpack his new home. She was someone that he was comfortable with and she was someone he could see himself growing old with.

He closed his eyes lost in his thoughts, the cake forgotten as he stood only a few feet from her and he remembered weeks ago when his things had arrived from Germany where he had been based to his new townhome outside of Eglin Air Force Base. He and Christy had been unpacking his belongings and she had lifted out a glass teapot, a teapot that he had gotten while based in England several years earlier and without warning, she had dropped that teapot and it had shattered at her feet.

Chad remembered seeing her face as she looked up at him. The fear was easy to see and he remembered the way that she had backed up and away from him and she had kept saying that she was sorry and he didn't want her to be sorry then nor now. He had another teapot and he didn't care about the teapot, he cared about her not being afraid and he was holding her in his arms in his memory and now his eyes opened and he went to her pulling her into his arms and he knew, they would be all right, she would be safe forever and they would both be all right. He would see to that.

Until her, until he had met her Chad had been alone. He had come from a big and loving family, he had been embraced by everyone that knew him, but he had never belonged to just one person. He had never had that one special partner in his life, the one that was his best friend and his lover and would be with him in every step that he took in life. Then he had met her and they fit together despite his being over six feet tall and her being a foot shorter than he was. She belonged with him and he belonged with her. They were alike, and yet they were nothing alike and he smiled now knowing that they would complement one another.

Christy clung to him, his arms around her and she took several long deep breaths suddenly knowing that here with him there would be no cursing her, there would be no back of the hand hitting her across the face. There would be no twisting of her arm and there would be no walking away with anger and fury left behind and her in tears, tears and in sorrow that seemed to have lasted forever, but with him were now at an end.

She closed her eyes and forced the memories that hurt her from her mind. She closed her eyes and listened and the silence around them, a silence that told her that the rain had stopped and that was often the way that it was here on the island right on the Gulf of Mexico. The rain would come on suddenly fast and furious only to end just as suddenly and it would be within the hour as though it hadn't rained at all only a puddle of water standing in a pothole in the road to give knowledge that it had rained hard early in the evening.

"Can we go Chad?" she asked him and he pulled away taking a hold of her hand. They thanked her co-workers for the party and for the wedding, though Chad and Christy had eloped, they had been married in the bank where she worked. A few photographs were made to remember the moment by, a bit of cake taken quickly and a mad dash to leave the crowd and be the couple that they now were.

"I'll meet you at the house," Chad called out to his new wife after opening her car door so that she could get in before he turned and ran to his own car parked nearby. "If we hurry we can watch JAG while we change clothes."

"I'll follow you," Christy waved to him as he got into his own car and she backed out of the bank parking lot coming behind Chad's car and turning onto Highway 98. Within a few minutes they had gone over the Destin Bridge and then over the Brooks Bridge and finally a right turn and they were headed for the small city of Shalimar where Chad's townhome was and where they would live together as a couple, where they would bring home their newborn daughter, a daughter that they would name Amy.

Chapter Two

John 10: 27-28: My sheep hear my voice, and I know them, and they follow me: and I give unto them eternal life; and they shall never perish; neither shall any man pluck them out of my hand...

Christy wasn't young; in fact she was probably what most would consider old at the age of thirty-nine. And Chad, he was seven years younger than she was though standing side by side the couple looked to be the same age. They were what most people would consider them to be; a well matched couple. Chad was playful and happy and easy to tease, Christy was reserved and a homebody that needed a man like Chad that would inspire her to go places and to try new things. Both of them were non confrontational. Christy left problems behind and never faced them head on. Chad pretended the problem didn't exist and went on with his life ignoring all problems leaving the problem to either fix itself or to be forgotten in time.

Some might refer to both Chad and Christy as passive, and maybe that word could apply, but they were passive only in the fact that they didn't argue or fuss or fight with anyone nor with one another. There were no raised voices in their home, there were no arguments ever. They agreed on everything and if they didn't agree, the one or the other would plead his case with pros and cons and they'd work it out with smiles and kisses.

The subject of children had come up while they were dating and Christy had advised Chad that they get a dog. But as they already had a dog, that was a moot point. And as it was, they married on the tenth of a month and on the fifteenth of that very month, Chad left, the military sending him away for a few months and he couldn't tell Christy where he was going or how long he was going to be away.

The goodbye on the morning of the fifteenth wasn't easy, but Chad made certain it wasn't hard by being playful and making a joke of where he couldn't tell his wife that he was going. The truck carrying the troops pulled away and Christy found herself standing alone. She was in a new town only a mile from the base, she had a new job at a bank where she'd only been working a month and she had made no friends. She knew none of the neighbors as she had just moved in with Chad and she didn't yet have a military ID.

Being alone wasn't easy. Being alone in a new place was frightening and she had nothing to do but work and watch TV with the dog. The days were short as work seemed to fly by and the nights were long as she played the music on the CD player that Chad had left behind. The music was his favorite, 'Lord of the Dance' and soon the music became her favorite as well.

Her wedding ring had been specially ordered and it came a week after Chad had left. Alone and lonely, she slipped her wedding band onto her finger, the band special as it had an emerald instead of a diamond as the centerpiece. Within a few minutes of her having done this, the phone rang and it was Chad, he was settled in and he was cold. It was the middle of March and wherever he was he needed his coat sent to him right away. He spoke long enough to give Christy a military address in New York and assured her that he wasn't in New York and he had to go, he would send her an email soon and call later on the weekend. And the weekday calls from him; if there were weekday calls from him, were short and bittersweet, the weekends were when the long calls took place.

In the year 1999 and 2000 it cost anywhere from a quarter to a dime a minute to talk long distance on the phone. Cell phones were becoming popular, but even they had a cost per minute so phone calls were precious to receive and the phone calls didn't last very long and were not often made. Email or ICQ, an instant messaging system was used and often that system suffered delays that were aggravating. But Chad and Christy used the system until he came home for a week in May.

May 4th 2000 Eglin Air Force Base, Florida

The plane was late; Christy thought as she chewed on her fingernail and looked at the board lit up showing the time of arrival of all flights due in from Atlanta, Georgia. There were several women in the area where she was standing and like her, they were all dressed up in sundresses and sandals with their hair done.

"Is your husband a part of the 36th squadron?" a young and beautiful woman standing near her asked and Christy nodded her head in a shy way uncertain how to answer this question. She was new to the military way of life and she wasn't certain if she were allowed to tell what squadron her husband was in to someone that she didn't know. "I've seen you around our townhome complex," the woman spoke on and Christy turned and looked the woman full in the face suddenly aware that this woman lived only two doors down from Chad's townhome.

"I'm Christy," she introduced herself and saw the woman smile as they shook hands as though they were men.

"Jodi," the woman answered and Christy found herself relaxing when she heard over the speaker announcing the number of Chad's flight. He had arrived home. "Let's go greet our men," Jodi laughed as they joined the small crowd of women moving toward the gate where the 36th squadron of men were coming from, the men almost in a single line formation with Chad the tallest in the crowd and easy for Christy to spot.

"I'm home," he said throwing one arm over her shoulder and pulling her close. They wasted no time visiting with the other men that were in his squadron nor did they visit with those men's wives. Chad had a mission and that mission was to get his luggage and go home to spend time with his new wife.

"How's your back?" Christy asked him as she held on to him, both of her arms wrapped around his waist and he looked down at her and gave her what she would come to know was a playful smile before he answered her.

"My back is fine," he said and she knew that he was fine when he slung his luggage into the trunk of her car.

"What are we going to do?" Chad heard his wife ask him this question as he went into the house and he didn't answer her, instead he chased her up the stairs where he caught her and he showed her that his back wasn't hurting him and that he loved her and that he knew that she loved him.

Christy had no idea that first time that she met Chad at the airport that she would often be meeting Chad at the airport for years to come. And that first night home after two months gone the subject of babies came up and there was no teasing of getting a dog in their conversation. There was the attitude of if that happens then we'll be God blessed. If that doesn't happen, we'll cling to one another. As a couple they both decided to let God be in control and they would just love one another. With the soundtrack of "Lord of the Dance" playing in the house and Christy no longer alone, dinner was made late in the night and dinner was eaten even later in the night and life was deemed good as they made plans to go to the Island the next day to swim and enjoy the short time they had together.

Before he left again for parts unknown to his wife, Chad saw that Christy had a military ID and that she knew the way to the commissary and the Base Exchange. He had no idea that his wife never went anywhere she hadn't been before alone. In fact, he had no real concept of the fact that Christy was a homebody who read her books and kept to herself until he came home the last week of June. And when he came home, he saw that she didn't get out much, she wasn't outgoing as he was. Chad seemed to make it his mission in life to pull her out of her shell, to show her the world and to have her see the world through his eyes instead of her own eyes which he knew for Christy, she was afraid of the world and he also knew that for Christy, she had reason to fear the world.

Late June 2000 Eglin Air Force Base, Florida

The townhome they were renting was being sold and after talking it over in great detail, as a couple they decided not to buy the place. Instead, they moved to another townhome right around the corner to rent. A townhome that was identical to the one that they were living in so the move was made easy. Life was changing and for Chad, he was home, he was getting a chance to spend time with his wife and enjoy Florida as he was new to this area having spent eight years overseas while first in the military.

The jar had slipped from her hand as she stood in the pantry and she looked at the mess on the floor at her feet. Prego Spaghetti sauce and broken glass were in a puddle in the entrance way of the pantry, the noise of the jar crashing on the floor echoing in the kitchen was loud and frightening to someone that tried never to make a mistake or a mess.

"What happened?" Chad yelled down the long hallway to the kitchen as he hurried to the kitchen to see if his wife was hurt. Within seconds he found his wife safe, the jar of Prego was not so safe. "What'd ya do?" he asked in a serious way and he saw his wife looking up at him chewing on her lower lip. "Who's going to clean up this mess?" he asked quickly, his words sounding harsh when he hadn't meant for his words to sound harsh and he saw her, his wife, close her eyes and turn her face away from him as though she feared he would hit her and in that instance, Chad saw the fear his innocent question had caused his wife.

"I'm sorry," she was saying quickly and he watched her drop to her knees and pick up the broken glass putting that glass in the trash can. He also heard the fear in her voice and within a second he knew that she was crying.

"Hey you," he said in a gentle way as he pulled the trash can closer to where they were and he began to help her clean up the mess. "Hey," he said again and he saw his wife lift her face up and their eyes met and he had no doubt that she was afraid he would hurt her because she had dropped a jar and Chad would never hurt anyone and certainly not someone over a broken jar of Prego sauce.

Her previous partner had done a number on her, Chad thought as he watched her clean up the mess and he held the trash can for her as she put in paper towels that were soaked in red sauce. He had seen his wife flinch several times when he had raised his voice while talking to someone on the phone. He had further seen that he could control her with the tone of his voice or with a certain look that he gave to her. She was afraid of her own shadow and she had a very low opinion of herself. She was weak and he knew within days of meeting her that she was a fragile person and maybe that was what drew him to her. Chad thought on as he watched Christy stand up with the mop in hand and clean the floor. His wife was often afraid and he knew that his wife was afraid of him. He didn't like that she was afraid of him.

"I leave in seven days but the good news is I'll only be gone twenty seven days this time," he spoke to her as she rung the mop out in the bucket and the pantry floor was clean as though no sauce had ever spilled on that floor. "I'll be home by the fourth of August."

He was talking to make conversation. He was talking to her in a normal way hoping that if they lived life normally that soon she would come to know that with him, she would always be safe.

"But you won't leave for another week?" Christy asked him as she poured the dirty water from the mop bucket into the toilet and flushed coming out of the bathroom to find her husband standing only a foot away from her.

"I leave in a week," he confirmed as he raised his eyebrows and she saw him smile. "Only a week."

Three hours later, after they were showered and dressed, Chad took his wife to Sonic for dinner, the spaghetti that might have been meant for their dinner forgotten in an afternoon that they spent together not worrying about Chad's back or broken jars on pantry floors and they wondered, would God bless them with a baby soon?

The knock sounded at the front door and she was amazed that she heard the knocking on the door because her husband was having some sort of fit on their back porch. "Are you okay?" Jodi asked when Christy pulled the door open and within a second Christy saw that Jodi felt that she was in some sort of danger.

"I'm fine," Christy answered Jodi's question while holding the door open and seeing Jodi walk in looking past her and down the hall and beyond the hall to the back porch.

"He doesn't sound fine," Jodi said speaking of Chad. "I thought he was hitting you."

Christy burst into laughter at this statement because the simple truth was, when Chad started cursing and yelling at the washing machine, Christy had been terrified out of her mind and had actually locked herself in the downstairs bathroom until she was certain that it wasn't her he was cursing and yelling at.

"He's not hitting me," she answered Jodi and led the way down the long hallway. "He's hitting the washing machine. The thing broke this morning and Chad seems to be under the impression that if he calls our washing machine every dirty word in the world, that somehow he will make the machine work again."

"Well," Jodi said looking out the backdoor at Chad kick the washing machine and use more swear words. "All he's doing is destroying the machine. He just put a dent in the front of it and I don't think that will help it work."

"Piece of ___," Chad said turning to see Jodi standing in his back doorway and his wife had moved into the kitchen and he saw that Christy was looking at him with wide and frightened eyes. "It was used when I got it," he spoke to Jodi flashing her one of his deep dimpled grins with no idea in the world of who she might be or what she was doing in his home. "I'll order another one from the same place I got that one," he frowned in confusion. "Who are you?" he finally asked Jodi after having spoken to her with no knowledge of who she was or what she was doing in his house.

"I'm Jodi," she said and turned to look at Christy with a worried frown on her pretty face. "You're certain you're okay with this guy?"

"Hey," Chad looked from the woman he didn't know to his wife. "You think I'd hit or hurt my wife?" he saw Jodi turn and face him and with a bold nod of her head Jodi said yes in a firm voice.

"Anyone that would beat up a washing machine,"

"I'd never hit her or any woman," Chad interrupted Jodi and looked quickly at his wife standing in the kitchen unmoving. "Hey you," he changed the tone of his voice to gentle and kind as he often spoke to her in that way. "I'd only yell at a washing machine and kick a washing machine. Never a person." Chad was moving into the kitchen and pulling his wife into his arms speaking on of how he would never ever hurt anyone in this life, he wasn't that sort of man and while saying this, neither Chad nor Christy saw Jodi slip out the front door, the young woman assured that Christy was safe with Chad.

He was gone again only this time he wouldn't be gone long and Christy spent her time fixing the new townhome they were living in now as it wasn't as nice as the old townhome. The walls needed a fresh coat of paint and the carpet needed cleaning, but even after cleaning the carpet, the flooring still looked like what it was, old and used and worn out.

She kept to herself, once in a while she would babysit for Jodi's small child or another neighbors children just to keep busy. She took the dog on long walks and she knew the neighbors by sight and the neighborhood. The place was mostly a military community, young, middle aged and retired and in this place Christy felt safe alone and without Chad.

Not yet married for five months and it was her third time picking him up at the airport but this early August day was different. He wasn't going to be leaving again for a while, he was home to stay and they could focus on one another and on being together and just living life as a couple. Chad was content, Christy was content, life was good as they laid together watching TV or held hands walking in the Base Exchange or just drove around the flight line. Life was slow and lazy and peaceful in those dog days of summer and there was a lot of time to just be still and quiet.

And then God stepped in and life changed. She was now forty years old and she thought at first that her missed cycle was the telling of her age. A quick stop at Eckerd Drug Store on the way home from work where she bought every pregnancy kit on the shelf would soon let her know if she and Chad were going to become parents.

On that drive home she thought of him, of Chad. He was a good man, a loving and gentle and kind man. But Chad was also strong willed and determined. He put his mind to something and that something was done. He was also a perfectionist and everyone knew when Chad was in the room, he commanded attention and

Christy was a nervous silly mouse, at least that's how she viewed herself.

The truth was that Chad was changing her. Chad was making her more outgoing. She'd gone to a function at the officers club and she had managed to fit in and not make a fool of herself. She was getting to know the neighbors and they were getting to know her and she was starting to find her own space in the world with Chad beside her and supporting her. Things that had been hard in the past were becoming things that she could handle with ease. She had found a safe place and she never wanted to leave this safe place.

She laid the pregnancy test kits on the bathroom counter and she looked at them over and over and over again thinking she would test now as they all clearly stated they could be used anytime of the day, not just first thing in the morning. She shook her head hard and put the kits under the bathroom sink walking away and thinking that Chad had only been home a month and ten days, could she really be pregnant that quick? The answer seemed simple to her and she thought of that answer over and over again in her head as she cooked dinner – no, there was no way a forty year old woman could get pregnant fast.

He was late coming home and dinner was done. She went to the downstairs bathroom and she looked in the mirror for a long time wondering what she would do if she were going to have a baby. Could they live only on his salary with the military? She and Chad had never talked that out. They had left everything to God and she knew in this instance that she couldn't worry about money. God was in control and they had decided as a couple to put their faith in Him to guide them into their future, no matter what that future might be.

"I feel like its Friday the thirteenth," Chad spoke as he came in the front door. "Everything seemed to go wrong at work," and as he spoke his wife came out of the bathroom hearing again of a co-worker that seemed determined to make Chad's life as miserable as possible. "I cannot please this guy and he blames me for things that aren't in my control. He even blames me for doing a job that he assigned to another troop."

They sat down at the table and began to eat dinner, Chad not seeing that his wife was more silent than usual. She sat there hearing him talk and hearing his frustration and she knew, tonight was not the night to take a pregnancy test; she would do so another time. If she told him she was late with her cycle, he might get excited, and then if the test was negative, he would be sad. He was already upset over the co-worker, it was best to keep what she suspected to herself for the time being at least.

He watched her loading the dishwasher telling her of his day and asking how her day went and he never noticed that she was keeping something to herself. He never noticed that she was nervous and anxious over what was in the bathroom under the sink and he pulled her up the stairs completely unaware that their lives might be heading for a change, a huge change that included another mouth to feed in their home. At the moment, they were together, the husband holding his wife and alone with his wife and the wife anxious and clinging to him uncertain of what their future might hold and she hoped that the future held more than a dog in the house.

Chapter Three

Hebrews 12:15: See to it that no one falls short of the grace of God and that no bitter root grows…

The hour was late; Christy thought as she left the bed and went toward the bathroom. A quick glance at the clock on the dresser as she left the room let her know that the hour wasn't late at all, the hour was early as it was nearing four in the morning. She closed the bathroom door and turned on the light. With shaking hands she pulled out the Eckerd Drug Store bag and laid it on the counter wondering if now was the right time to take the pregnancy test. As the bag held three different test kits, she knew she could take one, if it was negative, the others could possibly be used at a later date.

Downstairs was a grandfather clock and she heard the bonging noises and knew that it was four in the morning. She put the test kit on the counter and waited counting to sixty three full times before she looked at the kit and she saw the two pink lines. "I'm going to have a baby," she whispered and closed her eyes thanking God. She wanted a baby. She loved children. This was one of the greatest things to ever happen in her life and within a moment she was smiling and crying and whispering thanks to God.

"Chad," she shook him and he moaned, but he didn't wake up. They had three more hours they could sleep before they had to get up and here she stood over him shaking him awake. "Chad, I need you," she pleaded with him to wake up and he sat up in the bed opening his eyes.

"I heard you the first time you told me to wake up," he rubbed his eyes and reached for his glasses. "I didn't hear anyone breaking into the house," he said this while looking at his wife and he frowned when she handed him something and he took that something looking at it and then back at her. "What's this?" he demanded to know and he saw her worried frown.

"A pregnancy test kit," she answered him and Christy saw his eyes grow wide as he looked down at the lines and back up at her. "We're going to have a baby."

Within a few minutes; at a little after four in the morning, Chad, called his mother and woke her up telling her their news. He was only on the phone for a few minutes before he turned to his wife and pulled her back into bed, both of them giggling like little school children as he whispered that he wanted a little girl and she assured him that she would have a little boy like him, with his big brown eyes and her perfect nose.

"Then it's decided," he had laughed with the coming dawn, "a baby with my eyes and your nose."

If Chad and Christy had only known then that yes, their child would be born gaining the best of each of them, but that the best of each of them wouldn't stop what was going to come, what was going to happen, what was going to wreck havoc on their lives.

At the grand old age of forty Christy was expecting crisis after crisis in her pregnancy and so were her doctors. The first three months were very calm and she worked full time loving life and happy with Chad home. No trips to the airport and a peace and calm in her life that she had never known. Chad took care of her and she cooked and cleaned and went to work. They were old and set in their ways after only seven months of marriage.

The headaches came on slowly as did the struggle to breathe. The struggle to breathe was frightening and made the headaches seem mild in comparison. Asthma, Christy knew and at first she thought to just be calm and say nothing as the medication might affect the baby she was carrying. Until one night she and Chad were watching the movie, "The Green Mile" with Tom Hanks and Christy kept coughing, the coughing became worse and worse.

"I don't know what to do," Chad had said in a hushed and worried tone as the movie was halfway over and his wife was gasping and wheezing and didn't sound well in the least.

"I think we need to go to the ER," she managed to tell him despite the coughing and she left it to him to get her purse as it took all of her effort to walk, to breathe and to get into the car.

At the ER there was no wait. They walked in and the receptionist yelled out a patient was in distress and within minutes Christy was using the nebulizer and being given Prednisone. It took three treatments before she was finally breathing with ease and the doctor came in telling her that she wasn't going home, she was going up to labor and delivery.

"I'm only five months along," she had spoken in a frantic voice and felt Chad take a hold of her hand.

"Your blood pressure is too high, we need to monitor you and we need to keep you until you've seen the pulmonologist for your asthma," the doctor said as he wrote on the chart in his hands.

"I've been asthmatic since childhood and it's been well controlled all my adult life," Christy said looking from the doctor to Chad. "I've never had high blood pressure. In fact, I've been the opposite and had low blood pressure."

"It's high now, you're going up to labor and delivery," the doctor said this to her in a way that left no doubt she wasn't going home and that she might be in a little trouble, her little baby might be in a lot of trouble.

And so began the difficult pregnancy. Between the asthma and the blood pressure being way too high, bed rest was ordered and she had to leave her job. Everything had fallen onto Chad to do now, she wasn't a wife, she wasn't a cook; she wasn't working. She was resting in bed or on the sofa day in and day out hoping that soon the blood pressure would stabilize and life would go back to some sense of normal for her and she could know peace that her baby was safe inside of her.

Christmas came and went, Chad and Christy drove to Shreveport to be with his family and she lay in the car the whole trip only standing to get out and use the restroom. She was small as she was only just five months along. Her blood pressure continued to be high on the trip and she was careful of what she ate, careful of how long she sat up and careful of sleeping ten hours a night even on Christmas night.

When they arrived home to Eglin Air Force Base on the twenty-eighth of December, there was a voice mail on their answering machine directing Christy to call her OB-gyn office as soon as possible. The message was left the day that she and Chad had left for Shreveport.

Within an hour the couple had been told that the levels of PAPP-A and HCG in Christy's blood tests were an indicator there might be a problem with the baby. They got into the car and drove to the hospital where an ultrasound was done. The doctor doing the ultrasound was young and he said the baby might be a boy and he couldn't tell if the baby had what was seen in Down Syndrome on an ultrasound or not.

"What are we going to do?" Christy asked Chad as they waited for the OB-gyn to come into the room and talk with them. First the asthma and then the blood pressure and now this, she was too old to be having a baby and right now Christy was more afraid of losing the baby than anything else.

"I want to send you both over to Keesler Air Force Base for further testing," the doctor said to them as she entered the room and sat down across from them. "The baby has a good strong heartbeat, your asthma is controlled at this time, your blood pressure is still higher than we'd like, so stay off your feet all you can and never pass a sink without getting a drink." And with this advice they were given a date to go to Keesler for a 3D ultrasound and an amniocentesis.

"Chad," he came up the stairs and into their bedroom seeing his wife sitting at the desk and looking at the huge monitor of their desktop computer. "This amnio is dangerous," she said to him and he joined her at the desk looking over her shoulder at the computer monitor. "The baby is at an increased risk of death having this test done Chad."

"Do we have to have the test?" he didn't ask this of her, he knew this was a question for the doctor and yet his wife answered.

"It says here on this baby center website that a 3D ultrasound, if done properly, can detect some fluid buildup in the baby that has Down Syndrome." She turned and looked at her husband now reading the site and she moved over so that he could come and sit beside her.

"We'd put the baby at risk with this amniocentesis, risk of death by miscarriage," he looked at his wife and saw her shaking her head.

"I don't want to lose our baby Chad," he heard her whimpering cry in the words and he put his arm around her pulling her close.

"Then we won't lose our baby Christy," he spoke in his firm and authoritative way. "We don't have to have this test," he spoke in a low voice and in a thoughtful way. "No one is holding a gun to our head making us do anything."

"Chad, if the baby has Down Syndrome we're still keeping our baby," Christy looked up at him and he saw her fear and her worry that he might not want a baby with Down Syndrome.

"We can't give the baby back at this late date," he put his hand on her well rounded tummy and laughed in a nervous way, the laugh meant to calm his wife's fears. "We aren't giving our baby up no matter what. Besides, that dude that did the ultrasound thought it was a boy. I kind of like the idea of a son."

"I thought you wanted a girl," Christy said this in surprise as she looked still up into his deep dark eyes that at times appeared black instead of brown. "A little girl with your brown eyes and my perfect nose."

"A little boy with my perfect brown eyes and your pretty nose," he teased and hugged her closer. "Let's just wait and see what the doctors at Keesler say. And you're supposed to be on bed rest and it's late. Time to get you tucked in while I watch some Highlander on USA."

"Are you watching that downstairs or up here?" Christy asked him as she climbed into their bed wishing she could go down and be with him, she wanted to always be with him.

"I'll watch it up here. Give me five minutes to turn the lights off downstairs," Chad spoke this as he ran from the room knowing his show was starting in three minutes. "It's a good thing I have long legs," he called up the stairwell as he hurried back to the room turning on the small TV. "Did I tell you I saw all of these when I was in Europe?" he climbed into bed with his wife and saw her nodding her head. "My time in Europe would have been better if I had been married to you."

For a long few moments Christy remembered her past life before Chad. She remembered her life was nothing as it was now and as she closed her eyes, tucked up in his arms with the theme song of Highlander playing on the TV and she wished that she had been with him in Europe as well.

Keesler Air Force Base, Gulfport, Mississippi
January 17, 2001

The drive from Northwest Florida to Southern Mississippi had been hard on Christy, not because of the asthma and the high blood pressure, both of those problems had become stable, but because of the worry over the amniocentesis. She didn't want to do anything that might cost her this baby. The little thing was active, almost in constant motion inside of her and she and Chad had chosen his name already.

He would be named after his Great Grandfather, a man that Chad admired that had been a Lieutenant Colonel in the United States Air Force for thirty years, a man that had inspired Chad's career. "Shawn Andrew Bac," Christy whispered her baby's name to him and she heard Chad laugh beside her in the front seat of the car as they went to the airport to pick up his mother. Cheryl Bac was flying in to support them during the testing and too, Christy was anxious to show Cheryl the baby things she and Chad were buying for the new baby's bedroom in their townhome.

"Shawn for John," Chad said leaning back in the seat as he saw his mother waiting at the curb outside the airport terminal waving her hand when she saw him. "So will we call him Shawn or Andrew?" Chad asked as his mother got into his car before he pulled out into traffic heading to the base.

"Drew," Christy said seeing Cheryl turn in the seat and look at her and Christy could see her mother-in-law was wondering at the conversation. "We've decided to name the baby Shawn Andrew," she said with a smile and saw Cheryl smile as well. "And we'll call him Drew."

"A baby with three names," Cheryl said and all three occupants in the car laughed. "Well, what will you name the baby if it's a girl?"

"It's not a girl mom," Chad spoke in a certain and sure way. "And his name is Drew."

"Shawn Andrew," Christy said with a smile as Chad pulled into the Base Exchange parking lot.

"How's your blood pressure?" Cheryl asked Christy as they walked into the store and Christy turned worried eyes on to Chad.

"So far it's been okay, but I need to drink more water and stay off my feet all that I can," she saw her husband hurry to the counter of a Subway inside the food court of the Exchange and he ordered her a glass of water and made her sit down.

"I just got out of the car," Christy complained to her worried husband. "I want to show your mother the Winnie-the-Pooh bedding I've chosen."

"I'll show her," Chad said and Christy frowned while shaking her head hard.

"They have three different styles Chad and I want the blue set with Pooh holding the balloon." Christy stood up with her cup of water and saw Chad frowning at her.

"I can find a blue pooh set with a balloon. Mom can help me," Chad insisted, neither of them seeing that Chad's mother had gone inside the store and was searching for the bedding.

"Your mother isn't here," Christy pointed out to her husband after he forced her to sit back down.

"Great," Chad said leaving his wife in the chair outside of the Subway sandwich shop. "Mom's not supposed to go in there without me. She's not military."

All Christy could do was wait and be still. Chad was right, she needed to stay sitting, she had to put her baby's health and wellbeing first and who cared if they picked out the right pooh bedding or not? As long as the baby was born safe, that's all that mattered. She and Chad had wanted to become parents, and the cost was cheap, it just meant being still and at the end of the day a tall glass of water was consumed by the pregnant mother and the mother-in-law managed to find and to purchase the right bedding for the new baby that was set to be named Shawn Andrew Bac and to be called Drew.

"I would strongly advise that you have the amniocentesis," the doctor said to Christy as she lay on the table watching the screen where her unborn baby would show up any moment as the ultrasound was being done by the doctor. "You'll almost be forty-one years old when this baby comes, your blood levels are concerning and you're having several problems. The amnio won't take long and the risk isn't that great," the doctor spoke on encouraging a test that for Christy, was frightening.

"Look," Chad sat up and spoke in his military take charge way. "Even if the baby does have something wrong with him, we're not giving him back. We're keeping him amnio or no amnio. He's ours so the test, for us, wouldn't give us anything more than what we want now, which is our baby."

"Her," the doctor said and Chad frowned.

"Excuse me?" Chad spoke this as he sat up straight.

"The baby is a girl," the doctor said and Christy turned and gave her husband a worried look as he said a very filthy word and in front of the doctor and his mother.

"I thought you wanted a little girl," she said to him a few seconds later and he looked at her and the frown on his face was awful.

"I did want a little girl until I thought it was a little boy, my fighter pilot." Chad heard the doctor laughing and he turned from looking at Christy to giving his full attention to the doctor. "What's so funny?" he asked and saw the doctor looking at him.

"Girls nowadays are fighter pilots too," the doctor stood and printed out a photograph of the 3D ultrasound showing the baby sucking on her thumb. "I think you're both wrong to not do further testing. This baby is at risk and knowledge is power."

"We can gain that knowledge," Chad spoke in a patient way. "Nothing is stopping us from being prepared for a special needs child."

"We decided to let God give us this baby before we became pregnant," Christy spoke as she sat up handing the photograph of their little girl to her mother-in-law. "God's will be done."

Once in the car and heading to the airport so that Cheryl could catch her flight home, Christy sat staring at the photograph of her baby and thinking that no matter what, she and Chad were strong enough to be good parents. Together they were a team and they'd be a team of three when this baby came.

"So, the name Shawn Andrew won't do," Cheryl spoke as she looked at Christy.

"I was thinking of Haven Lynn," Christy said to her husband and her mother-in-law. "Haven is Chad's middle name and it means heaven and Lynn for you," she looked to Cheryl and saw the older woman smiling.

"Lynn is good," Chad said from the driver seat as he pulled into the airport. "But I don't want my middle name for the baby's first name. Think of something else Christy."

"But I like Haven," Christy said seeing Cheryl getting out of the car at the airport terminal.

"You have no other name in mind?" Cheryl asked as she reached for her bags and Christy got out of the car to hug her goodbye.

"Amy," Chad heard his wife saying. "It means love and we already love her."

"I like that name," Chad said looking into his wife's eyes and reaching for her hand. "Amy Bac."

"Amy Lynn Bac," Cheryl said before she turned to hurry and catch her flight. "Drive home safely, call me when you get there."

"Call us when you land in Houston," Chad called back to his mother before helping his wife into the car knowing that they had a long drive home. "I'm going to be the father of a little girl."

"A little girl named Amy," Christy spoke with a smile. "And she'll have your brown eyes,"

"And your perfect nose," Chad laughed pulling out into traffic and knowing it would be late before he got his wife home.

Chapter Four

Eglin Air Force Base, Florida
May 2001

She was swollen and miserable. Standing next to her husband that was a foot taller than she was they looked like an odd couple, him long and lanky and her short and fat. "I look like I swallowed a watermelon," Christy complained as she looked in the full length mirror. "Those photographs of us together during your reenlistment ceremony make me look like I'm half your size in height and twice as wide as you."

"You look fine," Chad said as he pulled up the photos on his desktop computer. "You're just full of my baby."

"Our baby is due anytime now," Christy said as she pulled on her socks and then her shoes. "I made it Chad. I'm a week out of reaching my due date." Her husband smiled not looking back at her as he was looking through the photographs of his reenlistment. In the photographs his arms were around his wife and he was looking down into her eyes thinking that soon Christy would make him a daddy and their baby would make her a mommy.

Fourteen years Chad had been in the Air Force and now he had been married for more than a year. He was growing into the old man that he wanted to become and soon he would be a father. He had taken a class on base that had taught him how to be a father.

He had to change the baby doll's diaper and he had given the baby doll a bath. And he had failed at doing both, drowning the baby and holding the baby wrong causing the neck to break. At the time he had laughed, but now that the time was getting near that his child was going to be born, Chad felt confident that he would be fine, basically because Christy had passed the class with flying colors.

"No changing diapers for me," Chad said as he stood from the computer and kissed his wife on the top of the head. "Diapers are your duty, mine is to stand back far away and watch you." He laughed at his own words knowing they would hold true to those words, he was not a diaper changing man. "And you have an appointment this morning."

"I'm having twice a week stress tests now," Christy said as she stood up and waddled to their bedroom doorway. "And today the doctor wants to examine me. I'm putting too much protein out in my urine and she's very concerned. And this blood pressure issue I'm having, well I'm tired of stressing over something that has control of me and that I have no control over."

"Soon this will be behind us," Chad said in confidence. "And no more bed rest for you and no more asthma attacks that require hospitalization. After our baby comes, it's going to be smooth flying for the three of us. I'll have my little fighter pilot and within a year she'll be speaking in Klingon."

"So we're having a Trekkie instead of a baby?" Christy laughed knowing her husband loved Star Trek and she liked the show as well. "I'll just be glad to have this behind me and this little one in my arms. And Monday mornings are always hectic at the base hospital. I need to get going," she said knowing she'd be late if she didn't leave for the hospital now.

"I'll drive the Amigo," Chad said as that jeep like vehicle had a standard transmission and he didn't want his wife driving a stick shift this far along in her pregnancy. Chad was afraid that Christy was in trouble, she was swollen from the preeclampsia and he could hear her wheezing as she hurried down the staircase. "It's easier on you to drive the Monte Carlo," he called down the stairwell seeing her turn and look up at him. He could see by the look that she gave to him that he was right and Christy knew he was right as he tossed her his car keys and she tossed him her keys knowing they were parting for the day. "Love you," he called after her as he still wasn't in his full uniform and he had to hurry and dress or he'd be late.

"Love you more!" Chad heard his wife calling back to him never dreaming that this was the last time she'd be home for a whole week and that her, her baby and Chad would soon be in trouble.

Christy stopped by the hospital lab and sat still waiting for her name to be called so she could have her blood drawn and be on her way upstairs to the maternity ward for the stress test she was having to go through every week. Now she was facing it twice a week as her blood pressure was higher than it had been and in frustration, she wondered why this was happening to her. She wasn't really that fat, she was well rounded with her baby and she had never in her life had high blood pressure until now.

"You look about to burst," Jodie said to her and Christy looked at her friend with a huge smile.

"I am," she confirmed and felt a twinge of pain. "I've not told Chad but I'm dilated to one centimeter, the doctor told me on Friday. "I'm having pains but they're not consistent."

Jodi sat down in the chair beside Christy and the two women faced one another, the concern on Christy's face was obvious to her friend. "Maybe you'll have the baby today and the troubles will be behind you."

"I just keep praying that the baby will be healthy," Christy felt the tears in her eyes. "This hasn't been easy. The baby doesn't move often. Last week three days passed and I didn't feel her moving and the doctor took several minutes to find her heartbeat on Friday. The doctor finally did an ultrasound to confirm the heartbeat."

"Well my blood pressure would have been higher than yours were that me Christy," Jodi leaned back in the chair not knowing what else to say in the way of comfort.

"They called my name," Christy stood up and reached down for her purse. "I'm going up to the maternity ward for another stress test and then home to bed."

"I'll bring dinner over to you and Chad tonight," Jodi stood with her and gave Christy a fast hug. "Low sodium and no salt is on the menu tonight."

"See you later," Christy turned and hurried to the lab technician feeling the baby kick, not a hard kick, but the baby kicked and that was a moment of relief for her.

"Here comes wheezy," the nurse made a joke as Christy entered the room on the maternity ward where the stress tests were given. The nurse making this joke was a Lieutenant Colonel and because of her rank, the woman knew that she could say what she wanted and no one could say anything back to her. Christy also knew the woman was worse than a Drill Sergeant and treated the expecting mothers as though they were the lowest of troops.

"The asthma doesn't have me," Christy said putting her purse down by an empty bed. "I have the asthma."

"Yes, you do," the Lieutenant Colonel confirmed as she watched Christy lay on the bed and lift her shirt ready to be hooked up to the monitor. "And you look pale and swollen."

"That's because I am pale and swollen," Christy laughed but she wasn't laughing because her words were funny, the laugh was a nervous laugh and one that the nurse knew was showing the expecting mother's fears.

"They just called with her lab results," a nurse Christy knew to be a civilian stuck her head in the door to call out. "I already made certain the doctor knows, she's on her way up."

The look the Lieutenant Colonel gave to the civilian nurse made Christy's heart stop for a second, she knew that whatever the lab results were, they were not good.

"We have a good and healthy heartbeat," the Lieutenant Colonel said to Christy in a calming way that was unusual for this nurse and Christy knew that too.

"My baby is in trouble," Christy said and saw the compassion filled Civilian Nurse come to her side.

"The Doctor will know what to do," both nurses said at the same time, the Lieutenant Colonel going to her desk and sitting down at her computer.

She had no doubt the nurse at the desk was looking at her lab results, and if she had a doubt it vanished when the nurse looked up at her with a worried frown. This was bad, whatever this was and touching her stomach, feeling her baby move, Christy did what she always did when she was afraid. Christy prayed, she pleaded with God to keep her baby safe and she pleaded with God to allow her and her baby to grow old together.

"We need to talk," the doctor came into the room and to where Christy was, the midwife was following the doctor and they both stopped by the edge of the bed.

Christy looked at the two women and she knew that she hadn't felt comfortable with the doctor since she had first started seeing the woman. But the mid-wife and Christy had formed a bond and there was a friendship there. Because of the rapport between her and the mid-wife she immediately looked to that kind and care-worn faced woman.

"This baby needs to come as soon as possible," the doctor said. "Because you're asthmatic we can't use Pitocin so we're going to have to use another drug and it'll take longer." The doctor continued to talk and Christy could only sit still and listen and take in what she understood and put herself in God's hands.

Things moved quickly. Within thirty minutes her clothes were gone, she was in a gown, in a room on the labor and delivery floor and she had been told that she was still dilated at one centimeter. The midwife had dialed the phone after she had been examined and she called Chad at his office and waited for him to answer. He hadn't answered and afraid to leave a message, Christy hung up intending to call back later.

"They don't want to do a Cesarean section because of the asthma," the midwife stood by Christy's bed and explained. The doctor had examined her and left and Christy was relieved, the woman made her nervous, the midwife did not. "I'm going to be honest with you," the midwife talked on. "Your blood pressure is too high, you're at risk of a seizure or worse and the baby is at risk as well. It's Monday and we need the little one to come now, today. But the team doesn't want to operate on you with the asthma as bad as it is."

"Will I lose the baby if she's not born today?" Christy asked of the midwife seeing the civilian nurse come into the room.

"We're more worried about you at this point," the midwife said as she turned to the nurse. "I'm going to be on the floor, call me if there's any change." Christy watched the midwife walk pass the nurse and she knew, she wasn't afraid, she was terrified.

"The good news is you're having contractions," the nurse said with a smile as she started an IV in Christy's left arm. "The screen there," she pointed to a television like screen by the bed. "When you're having a contraction the lines go up like they are now. You're not having strong contractions but you're starting, that's a good thing."

"I don't want to lose my baby," Christy almost cried knowing that she could cry with this nurse.

"Well then, you won't lose your baby," the nurse said in a firm and cheerful voice. "Let's try and call your husband again." She reached and handed Christy the phone before turning to clean up the bedside table and start the IV fluids the doctor had ordered.

"Chad," she said his name in a voice that didn't sound like her own when he answered the phone. "I need you," she started to cry and heard his heavy breathing on the other end.

"Are you home yet?" Chad asked his wife standing up in front of his desk.

"No," he heard his wife crying harder into the phone. "I'm admitted to labor and delivery and the doctor has me frightened."

"I'm on my way," Chad said to her and he hung up his phone reaching quickly to turn off his desktop work computer before grabbing his hat and hurrying for the elevator. "I might be a father soon," he called back to his commanding officer and was given permission to leave with several of his fellow troops calling out to him and wishing him good luck.

He didn't like hospitals. He didn't like doctors. He didn't like labs and shots and tests, Chad thought as he waited on the elevator that would take him to the second floor delivery ward and his wife. He hoped that Christy would have the baby today and they would be home tomorrow starting their new life together and he grinned from ear to ear thinking of the Winnie-the-Pooh decorated room at their townhouse and proud that he now knew the name of every Disney Princess.

Chad was ready. He was ready, willing and able to be a father. All he needed now was the baby. "And I'm never changing a diaper," he said with confidence to himself as he got off the elevator seeing the nurse that he couldn't stand was in the hallway looking at him and he knew by her look that she had heard him. The Lieutenant Colonel was a tough nurse and he knew that she was. He moved by her and her look followed him, Chad then followed that gesture with one of his signature smiles, a smile that he used to charm others as he had deep dimples and he knew how to use those dimples well.

"You'll change diapers," the Lieutenant Colonel said to him as he continued to smile at her confident that his wife had that chore on her chore list and off of his chore list.

"What room is she in?" he asked the nurse and she lost her tough stance and came to him.

"She's not well," the nurse warned him. "Her blood pressure is too high and she's wheezing like a broke down freight train. The team here doesn't want to take the baby with your wife in the condition that she's in. Keep her calm and be supportive. It's vital that we all work together for her benefit."

"I didn't know she was in trouble," Chad turned to go to his wife.

"The baby is in trouble too," the nurse touched his arm and he looked at her now very aware that he needed to be afraid and a man like Chad wasn't frightened easily.

She was sitting up in the bed crocheting lace on a blanket that she had made when he came into the room and he saw she had the hot rollers in her hair and her makeup on. "Where ya going?" he asked as he touched a curler and heard her giggle.

"Nowhere silly man," she giggled some more putting her blanket aside. "I don't want the baby to see me looking a mess when she gets here."

"Oh," Chad said completely at a loss as to what to say as he was certain Christy was teasing him.

She looked at her husband and she wanted to tell him the truth. She had put on her makeup and was doing her hair because she thought she was going to die. The concern and worry from all the doctors and nurses coming in and out of her room had her terrified. The baby only moved a few times a day and Christy could hear her breathing and she knew, this way that she was breathing was not normal. Many times she was actually gasping and the nebulizer was now by the bedside and the nurse was preparing it for her to use.

"They put me back on the Prednisone," Christy fought the tears in her eyes and Chad hugged her.

"We're gonna be okay baby," he spoke in his reassuring way when he wasn't certain they were going to be okay.

"She's having contractions," the kind civilian nurse interrupted the couple and pointed to the monitor. "They're coming more evenly and they're getting stronger. We might have a baby by this time tomorrow." The nurse's words caused Christy to look up at the clock and she saw it was nearly noon; she wanted the baby to come now.

Within the hour the doctor would breeze back into the room, do another routine exam and casually state Christy was still at one centimeter and leave the room as though the doctor were in a hurry. The midwife was very different. She came in often and sat by the bed and talked to the couple often watching the monitor for changes in the baby's heart rate. In the following days the midwife became a friend, the midwife was the one Christy wanted to deliver her baby.

Chapter Five

Matthew 5:3: Blessed are the poor in spirit; for theirs is the kingdom of heaven…

Monday had seemed like a day that wouldn't end for Chad and Christy Bac and their unborn baby. The nurses would run in often as the baby's heart rate would drop but within a single moment, the monitor would tell that the baby was rebounding and everything was good.

Tuesday was a repeat of Monday though Christy's wheezing became more stable, but as her breathing became easier her blood pressure increased. Late Tuesday night, with nothing but ice chips since Sunday night, Christy was ready for this baby to come, but this baby seemed determined to stay put.

"You cannot go to sleep," Christy held her breath as another pain hit her and she saw Chad hugging a pillow on the sofa bed beneath the window.

"I can't stay awake anymore baby," he moaned and saw his wife throw an empty paper cup at him.

"If I don't sleep, you don't sleep," she insisted and heard him moan as he changed the channel to the USA network and they both relaxed seeing a repeat episode of JAG on.

"You might as well try and sleep," the night nurse came in to say and Christy looked at the monitor showing her contractions. Like this, in this pain, she couldn't sleep.

"Has there been any change?" she pleaded of the nurse and saw the woman's head shaking after examining Christy. "I'm still at one centimeter with this?" Christy pointed to the monitor and the nurse gave her a look of sympathy.

"The good news is the baby's heart rate is fine," the nurse put another cup of ice chips on the bedside table before leaving the room. "And your husband can snore," she added before closing the door.

"And he's lucky because I'm going to let him sleep," Christy spoke to no one other than herself as she laid back and tried to rest feeling the tightness within telling her that her baby should come soon, but for some reason, she wasn't progressing. A quick glance at the monitor and seeing her blood pressure and she knew, this baby needed to come.

Thursday night was the worst night. Her blood pressure was at an all time high, she was wheezing still after two nebulizer treatments and she was stuck at one centimeter. The baby's heart rate was good, the doctor was very upbeat over how the baby was doing inside of Christy, it was Christy that wasn't doing so good.

The talk of the Cesarean became the main topic of conversation among the doctors. None of them wanted to use the anesthesia on Christy with her asthma as it was, not even an epidural was being considered. The baby was stuck, Christy was stuck and Chad was stuck knowing moments where he wasn't in charge and he had no control and he decided that he didn't like these moments.

Friday morning dawned with Christy seeing her blood pressure and deciding she was going to die today. She put in the hot rollers again, put on her makeup and decided she'd die looking better than a swollen mess. The nurse came in and agreed that she needed a spa day and that nurse painted her finger nails with a clear polish before helping her into a clean hospital gown.

"The baby's heart rate isn't where they'd like it to be," the midwife came in the room saying this and giving Christy a weak smile. "The baby's still good but she needs to get out of you in order for you to be well and in order for the baby to be well. But no one wants to do a c-section due to your asthma."

"Who decides to do the c-sections?" Christy asked looking at her husband and seeing him frowning at her. "Me or the doctor?"

"The doctor doesn't want to do the c-section, she wants to keep waiting," the midwife said this as the doctor came into the room. The woman looked mad and Christy couldn't understand why this woman was giving her an angry look. The truth was Christy was as frustrated as everyone else in the room, she too wanted her baby born safely, she wanted that event far more than this angry looking doctor.

"I want the c-section," Christy spoke up and the doctor looked even more furious.

"Well, I won't do it," and with those words, that doctor left the room.

"She's just going to let me and my baby die?" Christy asked the midwife when another doctor came into the room.

"The baby has to come, for both your sakes," the doctor spoke to Christy and she had a calm demeanor, much nicer than the mad faced doctor. "We have no choice," the doctor said sitting down in a chair in front of Christy and ignoring Chad. "You're high risk as is the baby, but we've tried everything for the past five days to get things moving along and you're failing to move. Because of your asthma, you'll have a harder time breathing, and you're at great risk."

She knew, Christy knew the doctors were expecting her to die due to the asthma and she knew if it meant her baby lived, then what needed to be done needed to be done now. "I understand,"

Christy said knowing that her husband didn't understand. The look of hope on his face gave her hope. "When?"

"This afternoon," the doctor stood and nodded to the nurse and the midwife.

"I'll stay by your side," the midwife said taking hold of Christy's hand. "I won't leave you alone and if it's hard to breathe, we'll breathe together."

Within two hours the anesthesiologist had come into the room, a friend of the midwife the two women stood talking while Christy was prepared for surgery.

"I've not eaten since Sunday night," she spoke in a teasing way to her husband. "Maybe after this baby comes I'll have lost weight."

"You'll lose the weight," Chad had teased back half heartedly as he was listening to the midwife talking. He knew his wife was in trouble, he knew the baby was in trouble, but he had high hopes in the medical facility they were in and he kept his hopes high as they took his wife away from him to prepare her for surgery and he too went to prepare for this surgery as within a few minutes he was suited up and looking more like a doctor than a sergeant and ready to go for the c-section to begin.

Prayers can pull you through anything. Christy had learned that early on in life and she closed her eyes now as they readied her and her baby for a birthday, a day that Christy wanted to keep in her memory for the rest of her life as one of the very best days of her life and she quickly and easily spoke the Lord's Prayer.

The midwife was true to her word and never left Christy's side. The epidural went in with ease. Christy was comfortable and if the truth were known, this was easier than jogging seven miles on a hot summer day. She wheezed in her breathing, but she breathed with an ease in that wheezing. They had prepared her saying that she would be battling to breathe and she would even feel like an elephant was sitting on her chest but that never happened. What happened was she was running a race and she was running fast and her breathing was as it would be in a race.

The baby was big, someone said and Christy tried to see the baby. Within a minute someone held the newborn up over the sheet and Christy saw a head full of dark hair and huge deep dark eyes, eyes like her husband Chad had.

"Is she all right?" Christy pleaded to know as the baby looked at her and she looked at the baby.

"She looks good," the midwife said. "She looks real good."

"She smiled at me," Christy cried out and heard Chad cry out with her.

"She did, she really did," Chad said in an excited voice. "She winked at me too."

"Newborns don't smile," they heard the nurse that was a Lieutenant Colonel say as she took their baby and cleaned the little girl up ordering Chad to put to use the camera that he had in his hand.

"She's fat Christy," he called out to his wife and heard her wheezing laughter in response to his words.

"She's nineteen inches long and eight pounds and eight ounces born at four seventeen on a Friday afternoon May eighteenth," the Lieutenant Colonel called out to Christy.

"Short and fat like me," Christy said closing her eyes and hearing the doctors talking. They had to remove her bladder to get the baby out, the newborn was that big and one of the doctor's said that she hoped the parents had clothes for a six month old baby as the little girl wasn't going to fit in newborn clothes. The tone in the doctor's voice wasn't very kind.

The midwife heard the exchange between the doctors and she looked at Christy. If she expected this new mother to speak up the midwife would know in a moment that Christy was the kind of person that avoided confrontation at all cost. The main reason that Christy was the way that she was had to do with her convictions.

The bible teaches us to turn the other cheek. It further teaches us to do unto others as we'd have them do unto us. Nowhere in the bible does it say if someone is unkind to you, you're to be unkind back. In fact, the bible goes on to tell us to love our neighbors and our enemies. Christy held strong to her faith and she held strong to what she knew was right and it was right to be nice, to set the example of being kind to others and they would follow that example. Anger begets anger.

"I have clothes for a three month old," Christy forced a smile onto her face and spoke this where everyone could hear; the smile on her face was in her words and tone of voice.

"Better a big baby than a small baby," the midwife chimed in to say and Christy saw her husband now holding the baby in his arms all wrapped up in a blanket with a pink hat on her head. The Lieutenant Colonel was taking his picture and he was smiling and she knew he was smiling even though there was a mask covering his face.

She was able to see the baby for a long few moments, the baby held in the midwife's arms as the doctors finished putting her back together. She touched her little girl and took these few precious moments to have her first mother daughter conversation.

"You and me and Daddy are going to be the three Musketeers. All for one and one for all." Christy said to the baby amazed that the baby was looking at her and the newborn's eyes blinked slowly and it was almost as if the baby understood what the mother was saying. "You'll never want for anything," she spoke on seeing the baby's exaggerated blink again. "You'll grow up loved and cared for. You're our Princess Pooh Bear and you'll be the love of our lives."

"And she's silent," the midwife said and Christy looked at the woman that had stayed by her side throughout this long labor and delivery.

"I've never seen a newborn this silent," the Lieutenant Colonel said coming to stand at Christy's head.

"She won't always be silent," Christy predicted. "She's a girl and girls talk a lot."

"She smiled again," Chad said and Christy saw the smile too as did everyone in the room.

"This baby really looks to be smiling," the midwife said in a happy voice.

"It's not a smile," one of the doctors said as she pulled away from Christy. "It's a grimace, the thing is probably hungry."

"Do not refer to this baby as a thing," the midwife said and stood up holding Christy and Chad's baby closer than she had been.

"The mother has to go to recovery and the baby needs to go to the Pediatrician, he's waiting on her," the doctor said as the doctor that did the surgery looked down at Christy.

"You did great," she said and Christy knew that they all had done well. The baby was here safely and that's all she cared about. "Daddy," the doctor spoke to Chad, "you can go with the nurse and the baby. Mom's going to recovery for an hour. We need to monitor her breathing."

"I love you Amy Lynn Bac," Christy called out to her baby as the nurse left the room holding her newborn with Chad walking beside the nurse. "She's here. My new best friend just came into the world today." Christy smiled and she smiled for a long time.

"Oh no," Christy sat up in the hospital bed seeing the late evening sunlight pouring through the hospital room window. What met her eyes was comical, and yet was also very serious.

The Lieutenant Colonel stood near the clear plastic baby bassinet with Chad on the other side. The hard hearted nurse held out huggies wipes toward Chad and Christy saw her husband violently shaking his head. "A baby's first bowel movement is meconium, it's sterile," the nurse laughed and laughed harder at the expression on Chad's face.

"It doesn't look sterile," Chad met Christy's eyes from across the room. "It looks like sticky, disgusting black mud."

"Well, I'd say it was more like tar," the Lieutenant Colonel nearly threw the wipes at Chad. "Get busy. Someone has to clean up this baby and since you're the Daddy – have a go."

"Oh no," Chad backed away and into the wall pressing himself tightly against the wall. "I'll throw up."

"Then throw up," the nurse advised looking quickly in the direction Chad was looking – at Christy. "Oh no, she just got here from recovery, she's not able to help you. You're on your own."

"Please, I can't," Chad shook his head seeking help and pity to spare him this chore. Had he looked up, he would have seen the base social worker and two other nurses standing in the doorway of the room, those three ladies all knew he had failed the newborn class by being playful with the baby doll and drowning the doll after breaking the poor doll's neck.

"He really can't do this," Christy said seeing Chad gag as he attempted to step near to their newborn baby.

"He certainly can and he certainly will," the hardhearted nurse said and Chad, always one to obey commands from an officer, stepped up and did what had to be done making faces and gagging, even at one point choking as he cleaned the baby of her first bowel movement. Christy also noted that he had put on not one pair of gloves, but two pair.

"And he survived," the Lieutenant Colonel said to Chad as he backed up with the baby clean and went to a sink to wash his hands.

"That was disgusting," he said several times hearing the nurses and the social worker standing in the doorway laughing at him.

"You need to take the baby to your wife," the Lieutenant Colonel ordered him and Chad turned around looking from the baby to the nurse that had given him another command.

"I have to pick that thing up?" Chad pointed to the now crying baby and shook his head so hard that he very nearly fell down. "I've done all I can do for one week," Chad said going toward the door and being stopped by the small crowd that was now there watching him and smiling. The crowd was all female and it was obvious they were enjoying seeing the new father made to do things a new father had never done before. "I wasn't raised around babies," Chad said to Christy seeing his wife painfully push herself up in the bed and reach out her arms for her crying baby.

"I need her," Christy whimpered for the baby and Chad knew, he somehow had to go and pick that baby up and not break the thing while getting it to his wife.

"All right," Chad went to the bassinet looking down at the baby starting to cry in earnest. And then he smiled a real smile of pure and simple joy as he pushed on that clear bassinet and it moved. "It's on wheels!" he cried out in a really loud voice seconds before he pushed the bassinet to his wife's bedside. "Here she is," he looked at his wife and he was relieved that Christy was able to bend over and pick up the baby.

"Where there's a will, there's a way," Christy attempted to put the baby to her breast and Chad backed up watching what was happening in front of him.

"And I have to get some fresh air," he said on a sigh and hurried past the crowd in the doorway that was now thinning out as Christy tried to feed her baby.

The room was quiet. The hardhearted nurse, the civilian nurse and the social worker were all watching Christy attempt to get the baby to latch on to her breast but it wasn't happening. The poor little baby didn't know what to do. Many attempts were made, all failed and Christy looked up at the three women holding her baby and asked them what she should do.

The civilian nurse brought in a breast shield to Christy but that didn't help. All three ladies in the room attempted to assist the poor little baby onto the breast and finally, more than an hour later, the baby was on and trying to suck, but the little thing kept slipping off and she cried the most heartrending cry Christy had ever heard.

"Oh baby mine," Christy cried brokenhearted for her little girl. "We'll fix this."

"We need the lactation specialist up here," the Lieutenant Colonel spoke in a serious voice and reached for the phone. Moments later Christy would learn the specialist had left for the weekend. She was on her own with only the nursing staff to help feed the baby.

"We can do this," Christy whispered into Amy's tiny ear. "You and me, we've got this together. We're a team now, all for one and one for all."

"I'm here," Chad said pulling a chair up close to the bed. "What do I do?" This was different than changing a dirty diaper, Chad thought. This was his family in trouble, his new baby needed him and he wasn't going to let his baby or his wife down. Together, he and Christy coaxed the baby onto her breast, each feeding took more than an hour to get the baby on and then to keep the baby on the breast.

"Feeding the baby this way is best," Christy spoke clearly when the nurses brought in a bottle of formula and Christy violently shook her head. "Together as a family, we can concur anything; this is a bump in the road only."

"She wants to do this too," Chad pointed to his new baby rooting around at his wife's breast. "Where there's a will,"

"there's a way," Christy finished his sentence for him.

Chapter Six

1 John 3:2-3: My little children let no man lead you astray; he that doeth righteousness is righteous…

Chad had left late in the night to go home for a shower and few hours of sleep. Christy looked at the baby in the bassinet and she knew, she had to get out of here. Her and the baby should be going home in the morning had this been a normal birth. But this hadn't been a normal birth.

The nurse came in at four in the morning to help get the baby onto Christy's breast, another long hour of working hard to help this tiny baby latch onto her mommy. "How do I get out of here?" Christy asked and the nurse frowned down at her. "I want to go home as soon as possible." She didn't tell the reason why. All the women on this floor shared the same shower and she was in a room with two other women. Christy was a private person, she wanted to work out this breast issue without a crowd and she wanted to be home in her own bathroom and her own bed.

"You had surgery," the nurse said giving Christy a sympathetic look before glancing at the other two beds in the room. One mother, nearest the window, had the TV on and the other mother's baby was crying his lungs out with the mother sleeping through the crying. "You have to walk and you have to pass gas first."

"I can do this," Christy spoke more to her newborn than to the nurse.

The baby finally fed at six in the morning and tucked back into her bassinet, Christy carefully pulled herself out of the bed ignoring the pain. "Walk and pass gas," she whispered looking back at the other two mothers in the room and hearing the TV blaring. "I gotta get out of here," she said and held onto the bed as she stood up reaching for her robe and pulling the robe on while slipping her feet into her slippers.

That first trip to the bathroom took all of her effort and energy. She kept thinking that from last Monday until the baby was delivered on Friday she had been battling contractions and fighting to get whatever little sleep she might get in this hospital. Once she finished in the bathroom, she moved to the door thinking that she had to escape and thinking too, that she was leaving her baby behind.

Holding onto the wall, Christy walked the long hallway of the maternity ward seeing every room had at least two mothers and two babies in the room. There was no chance that she was going to be alone in this hospital stay and Christy liked being alone, she needed to be alone. She wasn't like Chad, she didn't fit in anywhere and talking was an act for her, a show she had to put on in order to fit in and she hated that she didn't feel like she had fit in anywhere her whole life.

Christy thought of her past. She thought of the abuse and the suffering she'd gone through. And the blame, she added to herself as she clung to that wall and walked that long lonely hall in the dawn. Everyone blamed her for what went wrong in her relationship, but her primary care doctor knew. She closed her eyes remembering him giving her the yearly examine all young women must have.

"Who hurt you," his voice was strained and cold sounding when he asked her this question and even now, lost in the memory, Christy felt like she would fall apart. She hadn't answered the doctor, she hadn't had to answer the doctor. He knew it was the man that she was with. "Leave him," the doctor had said in a strong firm voice.

"You don't understand," Christy said in as firm a voice. "I'm safer with him than I am leaving him." And she had believed that at the time too.

Everyone thinks it's easy to leave an abusive relationship. Just walk out the door. And there were some people that didn't walk away without becoming even further harmed. She thought of the times her arm had been broken, spiral breaks the doctors had called them and all the doctors knew who had done that to her. It was the early nineteen nineties. In that time period doctors didn't report abuse by a spouse or significant other, they weren't required to by law; they were only required to report child abuse.

Christy thought now as she walked this hall seeing the sun coming up beyond the window that it had taken all of her courage to leave that man. He had strangled her in the car because she had to work and couldn't attend one of his family member's birthday parties. And too, she knew the relationship hadn't started out as violent. The man had been respectful and kind to her, they had dated for a long time and he had always treated her like a lady. By the time she realized something was wrong, she was trapped, and there was no way out.

They had been hanging a ceiling fan in the bedroom and she hadn't held it firm enough, he had slapped her down with the back of his hand. The force of his hand had been so hard on her face that her glasses had flown off. He was sorry, it was an accident, he had been frustrated over the fan and took it out on her, any number of excuses were given, all plausible. And weeks would pass with no hitting, sometimes as long as a month and he treated her well, he treated her like gold and he even made life fun with his joking and his laid back ways.

"If you'd just behave, I wouldn't have to hit you," the words were often said and the words were always believed. She couldn't make it on her own, he assured her. Her car was always breaking down; she needed him to fix her car. She wasn't reliable; she'd fail at everything that she tried to do. She needed his health insurance, if she left him, she'd have no insurance. On and on and on his reasons for her to stay became her reasons for her to stay. And too, she knew, as she thought her truth again, she was safer with him then without him. She just needed to please him.

And then something happened that made Christy know she had to find a way out of that toxic relationship. She must not tell anyone what was happening and had happened; she was ashamed, humiliated and degraded. She had to go. Christy knew, even if she died getting away from him, she was safer than she was with him.

She hadn't died; Christy thought as she made her way back into her room seeing her baby was still asleep and the sun was peeking in the window. She hadn't died, she thought on. Instead Christy had left him and he hadn't gone he had stayed and was in the house. He was watching her; he was outside of her work just sitting in the parking lot. Certain that she was going to wind up on the six o'clock news as a major story dead with a bullet in her head, Christy started staying late at work, going in at dawn instead of nine in the morning, she tried every way to avoid a routine and still he was outside of her home watching her and waiting for her. Until one day in early November he was gone. He had just disappeared and she would learn that he had married some woman he had known for a while and she was free, she was free at long last to start her life again and two years later she had met Chad and now she had this baby and looking down into the pale and pretty face of her newborn baby, Christy let the past go.

She couldn't change what others thought of her for leaving a man they viewed as wonderful, but she would always know what that man had done to her and that man, he knew what he had done.

She told him why she was leaving him. He knew just what he had done and for him what he had done was normal, but Christy knew, to ninety percent of the rest of the world, what he had done was degrade another human being.

"She's still not latching on with ease," one of the weekend nurses said in a gentle way to Christy as the new mother held her new baby. "They won't let you go until she latches on better than she is."

"We've got this," Chad looked around the empty room knowing the other two mothers that had been here in the night with Christy had easy births and were now gone home. But the birthing side of this hallway was full, soon this room would have more mothers and babies and Christy wasn't able to rest, Chad knew that. He knew his wife had survived a hurt in her past and he knew that he had to protect her and that he had to get her home safe and his baby as well.

"Show me what to do," he ordered Christy in his gentle way and together, his holding her breast and her holding the baby's face, they got their little girl on the breast and together they managed to keep her on the breast.

The baby was able to take Christy's breast five times that Saturday before Chad was forced to leave. He couldn't stay the night because Christy had another roommate. More determined than ever, Christy left her bed at three in the morning, walked the hall six times and it was a long hallway. She then begged the nurses for a shower which they allowed and she showered alone without any help beyond bothering a nurse for a washcloth and a towel.

"I'm getting you and me out of here in the morning," Christy whispered to her baby. Amy had been born at four in the afternoon and here it was only four in the morning on Saturday and this new mother was planning and plotting her escape as she went back into the hall with the baby in the bassinet and she pushed that bassinet up and down the hall three times hearing the nurses urge her on.

"A lot of babies have a latch on problem," the doctor spoke at six in the morning to Christy as the doctor made her rounds.

"Please, I have to go home now," Christy said sitting up in the bed. "Ask the night nurses, I'm walking well and she's doing fine," Christy nodded toward her baby. "With my husband's help, we're getting her on my breast. Please, I have to go home now," these last words were whispered almost frantically.

"I read your records," the doctor spoke slowly and looked at Christy sitting up in the bed. The doctors knew that Christy had damage that she wasn't speaking of. They also knew from their exam that the young mother had survived an assault on her body at some point in the past. Damage had been done that was permanent. "I think you can go home today," the doctor spoke in a kind and patient voice. "You're doing very well, healing nicely and we have a nurse that will come by your home daily and weigh the baby as well as make certain that the baby is latching on with little to no problems."

"I can go home," Christy whispered in relief. She could be with Amy and Chad and a support system and they could start becoming a family and that was what Christy wanted, someplace safe in the world with a family of her own. This baby would be raised in a peaceful and loving home. This baby would be shown the love of both parents, parents that would work together for the joy and good of this baby. There would be no cursing, there would be no yelling. There would be no foot stomped in her direction if she made a mistake. This home would be safe; Chad was making their home safe. She had a good husband. She had a man that would never strangle her or pinch her or do things that made her feel of less value than anyone else. Christy needed this new life and she was prepared to let the past go. She was prepared to not blame herself completely. She wasn't perfect, but what she had done was see herself safe. And now she had Amy and she would see Amy safe.

Something's the Matter with Amy

The baby cried the whole drive home from the base to their townhome only three miles away. The crying was an agony for the new parents as they couldn't comfort the little girl; she had to stay in her car seat, that was the law. Getting out of the car was something Christy did slowly with Chad's mother Cheryl taking the baby out of the car seat and into the house. Once inside, Christy looked up that staircase and thought it looked to be a million miles long and she had to walk up those stairs. Holding onto the rail, Chad behind her and Cheryl with the baby in front of her, she made her way up the stairs and to her room and within a few minutes, she was tucked into the bed and holding her baby.

That moment life became a challenge for the three Bac's known now as the three Musketeers in Christy's mind. The baby struggled with all her might to latch onto the mother's breast. Time and again Chad guided the baby on holding Christy's breast. The couple encouraged their baby to take hold with her little mouth and time and time again the baby didn't latch on.

The first twenty-four hours home, little Amy Bac only was able to feed two times and she cried hard and long in frustration as she wanted the food only her mother could give to her. And Christy noticed something was wrong with her as well. She was swollen up all over, her fingers were three times the size they had been, so were her ankles and her feet. The traveling nurse came by to check on them and found the baby had lost a pound and Christy's blood pressure was again a concern.

The peanut butter toast that Cheryl made for breakfast was rejected by the nurse, too much sodium. The chicken soup went the same route of rejection and Christy didn't mind, she wasn't up to eating anyway. Chad paced back and forth when the baby was asleep worrying and wondering what to do and by Tuesday, he was starting to become panicked. His mother had gone home to return to work and Christy's blood pressure was way too high. With the traveling nurse's advice, Chad took Christy to the doctor and was relieved that they treated her with medications, something was going right.

After an hour of leaving Christy sitting in the hospital pharmacy, Chad returned to his wife and with a natural ease, he took the baby from her and then held her hand pulling her down the hallway. Christy would become use to Chad pulling her behind him, she was a foot shorter than he was and slow, the only way to keep her up with him was to cling to her hand and pull her along behind him.

"Where are we going?" Christy felt like crying when she heard Amy start to cry.

"A specialist," he said and into an office they went near the pediatric center and within minutes they were sitting with a woman that was watching little Amy Bac struggle to take hold of her mother's breast.

"The good news is there's no deformities in her mouth keeping her from latching on," the specialist said after taking the baby from Christy and examining Amy from toes to ears. Within a moment, the pediatrician came in and weighed the baby seeing Amy was down two full pounds and watched as the baby tried to latch on.

"You can keep trying for a while longer or you can move to a breast pump and a bottle," the doctor said. "Some babies have this happen and we never know why. Amy's a healthy baby, she was nearly nine pounds at birth, and you have a few days to keep trying to get her to take the breast. I'll see you both again on Friday." With these words said, the doctor turned and left the room, her attitude seemed to be one of this being no big deal and they'd get past this problem soon enough. The lactation consultant felt the same way so with a confidence that didn't seem real, Chad and Christy went home hoping the blood pressure problem was now at an end.

On Wednesday morning, Christy walked Chad to the front door of their home, the baby held in her arms and she looked up into his dark eyes as he looked down at her and he told her that he was only a phone call away. Amy was still having problems latching onto Christy's breast, but the baby had been able to feed three times the day before and in the night once. They were moving forward with more gains than losses.

Life had to get back to normal. She had been home three days now, she was still swollen but not as swollen and there was no wheezing coming from her. There was no one to interfere with her day, Christy thought as she closed and locked the door behind Chad's leaving for the day. She was alone with her baby and she intended to do nothing more than work on helping her baby latch onto her breast. The quiet in the house was soothing and Christy made the bed with the baby held in one arm while she did so. She also cleaned the bathrooms with the baby in an over the shoulder sling before moving to the kitchen.

Little Amy Bac loved the sound of the vacuum cleaner from where the little baby was tucked safely into the sling draped around her mother. Christy took her time seeing the noise was soothing to the baby and vacuumed the stairs twice. Despite the surgery to get baby delivered and the blood pressure issue, Christy was feeling good, better than she dared to think she might feel though from time to time she felt this unreasonable urge to cry.

The major over Chad's squadron was known as Hollywood, Christy didn't know why the man was given this nickname, but he was a good and kind man and Christy felt comfortable with the man and his wife in seconds of their stopping by the house. They brought with them dinner of fried chicken and mashed potatoes, rolls and string beans. The baby may have trouble eating but her daddy had no trouble eating the food brought to them in kindness.

Chad turned on JAG after they were settled on the sofa, the three of them and Christy was tucked up beside her husband with the baby tucked up in her arms. Neither knew they'd be facing another long night and another long day of getting Amy onto the breast but both were determined not to fail. Amy wouldn't fail either. All for one and one for all.

The traveling nurse came in on Thursday late afternoon and Amy was down in weight to six pounds and nine ounces, almost a full three pound loss since birth. Together they got the baby latched on and the nurse stayed for two hours while Amy fed vigorously. The little girl sucked better than she had been and Christy felt that they had at last turned a corner only to be sick at heart in the night when the baby, even with daddy's guiding hand couldn't latch on and it was nearly time to leave for the appointment with the pediatrician before the baby did get latched on.

The doctor came into the room with the lactation specialist and they saw Amy sucking away with what appeared ease, but Chad and Christy knew this thing was hit or miss in getting Amy latched on. Thirty minutes of talking and the doctor assured the couple that they could keep trying to get the baby breast fed over the weekend pointing out that Amy was just nineteen inches long and almost seven pounds for a week old newborn wasn't a bad weight to be. An appointment was made just to weigh the baby for Tuesday morning and feeling like they might have a better weekend than the week they'd had, Chad took Christy home before he reported to work.

"You're a week old," Christy cooed these words to her baby as she washed the baby in the bathroom sink with warm water and baby soap. "And you got a good meal this afternoon too didn't you?" Amy didn't answer her mother in words, only those huge and expressive eyes looking up into Christy's eyes made this new mother know that her baby was happy and content.

"There you two are," Chad said as he came into the bathroom and put his finger into Amy's hand. "She's pretty," he spoke in a relaxed way a moment later as he followed Christy to the bed where his wife laid the infant down and put on a diaper before dressing the baby in a yellow nightgown.

Something's the Matter with Amy

"She did something odd today Chad," Christy left her husband sitting on the edge of the bed with the baby while she went to clean up the bathroom.

"What did she do that was odd?" Chad asked thinking that the baby only laid around and blinked or either pooped, burped or attempted to eat and those all seemed odd to him in the fact that he didn't do any of those things in the way Amy did.

"I had her lying on the floor on her blanket and her eyes went upward in an odd way," Christy came back into the room and reached for their new digital camera. "See," she showed him the photograph that she had taken. "Her eyes are stuck upward and to the side and her lips are blue."

"That is odd," Chad said taking the camera from his wife and looking closer at the photograph. Within five minutes he had the photo loaded onto his desktop computer and they were looking closely at the photos Christy had taken. "She's really blue around the mouth," he spoke in an assertive way and the couple both turned and stared at their baby. "She looks fine now," Chad spoke on in a worried tone and he saw his wife was frightened as well. "We'll watch her closely."

"And tell the doctor on Tuesday," Christy asked and Chad nodded his head in agreement. "Hopefully by then she'll be latching on to my breast without help."

"We can hope," Chad said before he stood and pulled on his shirt. "I'm going to Sonic, no cooking tonight. We all three need rest."

An hour would pass in the predawn night as Chad and Christy worked to get the baby onto Christy's breast. Several times Chad growled in a loud way and Christy pulled away from him fearing that he might hit her because she couldn't get the baby to stay on her breast. He would see his wife pulling away and regret his frightening her with his noise of frustration, but he couldn't stop himself as the situation was so hard on them all.

Saturday passed quietly, the baby slept and her parents slept when she did. The fail and success of breast feeding was a one minute win with a ten minute loss. Instead of it taking an hour to get Amy onto Christy's breast, it was taking only ten minutes and for that, Chad and his wife were grateful.

The baby, Amy, was an amazingly quiet little girl. She only cried when she was hungry. She loved lying on the floor beneath the television or under the front room window with the light coming in. Chad was growing more and more confident in holding her and most of his weekend he spent with the baby in his arms. He also noted that his wife was moving with ease around the house despite being cut open to get this huge baby out and he was impressed with her high pain tolerance.

By Sunday night it was only taking five minutes to get the baby latched onto the breast. Things were much easier and the calm in the house was comforting. Christy had a routine down of daily chores so that the house was always clean and she had the meals planned out for the week and thanks to Jodi, the grocery shopping was done.

She was calm, Christy thought as she leaned against the wall that led into the kitchen – dining area. She was calm and relaxed and happy and the pain from the c-section was bearable. Chad was lying on the sofa holding the baby and watching a movie with Dennis Quaid as a light rain had begun to fall outside. This was the life she had longed for. The safety, the security, the peace Chad had brought to her life and the baby, the baby made her feel whole and complete.

Amy had held her own in weight and Christy smiled up at her tall and handsome husband when she saw the number on the scale. They were going to survive this trial and they were going to win and the lactation specialist watched them as it only took two minutes to guide the baby to Christy's breast and the baby, once on the breast clung onto the breast until her meal was done.

"I'll see you on Friday for the two week well baby checkup," the specialist said as the pediatrician passed them by in the hallway and Chad stopped the doctor quickly explaining about how the baby had turned blue around the mouth and her eyes had appeared rolled upward and to the side.

"Babies do odd things all the time," the doctor spoke in a reassuring way and patted Chad on the shoulder. "She looks good, she looks real good. Keep up the good work."

Christy watched the doctor walk away and smiled at Chad relieved to know that what she'd seen and photographed of their daughter was normal. No worries, things were going in the right direction and that direction was going to be filled with joy and love, both of which Christy craved.

She didn't know what to do. Chad was at work and she was alone and Amy was laying on her bed jerking. The jerks were lightening fast and had she not stopped and knelt down beside the bed to look at her pretty little girl, she'd not have seen those jerks. But she had and now she was worried.

Pulling out the camcorder, Christy turned it on and videotaped two jerks. They were real, they were happening and though babies did odd things according to the doctor, Christy felt this was more than odd and she would report this to the doctor on Friday.

Two days later, Christy again had Amy on the bed and again rushed to the camcorder turning it on and videotaping Amy jerk. Then the baby pulled up her legs and her arms came inward, her head went to the side, her eyes rolled back and it appeared as though the baby was rigid and stiff. This wasn't normal. Christy was certain this wasn't normal, something was wrong with Amy.

The new mother closed her eyes and remembered her past. She remembered the accusation of her making a mountain out of a molehill. She was termed a worrywart and she was told time and again that she exaggerated things. She needed to calm down her abuser had insisted. He had told her how to think and what to feel, making certain that she knew whatever she might think and feel was wrong and that he was right.

She looked back at her baby and Amy was fine now. The little girl again smiled at her and Christy smiled back to her baby. They said infants don't smile but Christy and Chad knew that their daughter was an exception. Amy was smiling and she was smiling often and never did the infant have gas which everyone insisted was the reason for the baby to smile.

The pediatrician came into the room that Friday morning and examined the baby. She looked at the weight chart and she smiled, Amy was up to seven pounds and ten ounces. "It feels as though her fontanelle isn't as open as it should be," the doctor said this while feeling the top of Amy's head. "This is probably nothing but I want to see you back in two weeks. We'll watch this closely." After reassuring the parents that the baby was doing well and seeing that it was only taking a minute, two at the most to get the baby onto Christy's breast, the doctor was happy and told them so.

With great hesitation and feeling silly, Christy told the doctor about the jerking she'd seen Amy do. She also told the doctor of how the baby seemed to pull in and go stiff and for a moment. Christy saw the concern and care on the doctor's face and she felt less silly for having spoken up.

"Let me know if that happens again," the doctor said in a serious tone of voice before she walked the parents and their baby to the door. "It's probably nothing; babies do odd things and make odd noises, hang in there. You're both doing well, you've already jumped one hurdle that as a problem and solved it together as a team."

Feeling content and at peace, Chad and Christy left the base hospital hoping that in two weeks Amy would be latching on with no issues. But even as it was, the latch on problem was small now and no longer the nuisance in their lives that it had been at the start of their becoming new parents. They were relaxed and at ease with the baby and they went home holding hands with the baby making them both smile.

She's really pretty awesome," Chad said to his wife when they reached the house.

"Yes, and so are you," Christy said leaning into her strong and supportive husband. She was no longer alone.

Chapter Seven

Deuteronomy 31:8: "He will never leave you nor forsake you. Do not be afraid; do not be discouraged."

**Shalimar, Florida – outside Eglin Air Force Base
June 6, 2001**

She had that feeling of being all alone, and in that feeling she was afraid. Chad had left for work hours ago and she had completed her routine of chores and care for Amy around noon and she had laid down on the bed with the baby intending to take a nap, but instead she worried over her little girl.

Amy was doing that odd movement again. Her little legs were drawn upward and inward, her hands were fisted under her chin. Christy saw her eyes were again rolled up and to the side and the baby's mouth was blue. This wasn't right, Christy thought and wasting no time, slipped on shoes and grabbed the diaper bag intent on taking Amy to the hospital.

By the time Amy was in the car seat whatever had been happening to the baby had passed. Christy was assaulted by her past, the words from her past making her uncertain of what to do and afraid of what had just happened to her baby. She was an alarmist. She made things up. She wasn't believable; she clearly heard the voice from her past telling her these things as he had told her these things many many times.

She was a liar and liars lie well, he had insisted and it benefited him to say these words to her to keep her from telling others what he had done to her, what he was doing to her. And he made certain everyone around them knew that Christy was a liar so if she ever dared to open her mouth with his version of the truth he had forced onto her in abuse, no one would believe her.

She was alone again caught in that frightening world of wanting to speak up, but fearful to do so. "Don't believe a word she says," her abuser had insisted. "She stands on her soapbox shouting out for attention, just like her mother, always seeking attention." And Christy knew, her mother had died of the disease that her mother was supposedly seeking attention for.

She saw her baby was very still. Her baby was very pale and Christy took a deep breath knowing that babies did odd things and that was all well and good, but her baby had turned blue around the mouth and that was frightening enough for Christy to get into the car and go to the hospital emergency room just to have Amy checked out.

"If anything happened to her, I'd never forgive myself," Christy said as she pulled into the base emergency room parking lot and reached for her sleeping baby. Amy slept hard; almost too hard Christy noticed as the noise of the fighter jets flying overhead and very loud didn't disturb Amy.

The emergency room doctor came in behind the curtain and he examined a sleeping baby, a baby that made no move to awaken. Christy told the doctor what had happened and her voice was shaking, she couldn't stop the tears from falling and the doctor looked at her as though she were not normal and what he didn't know was that it was taking all of her courage to talk to him.

"Alarmist," she kept hearing her abuser say in that nasty tone of voice as she spoke on to the doctor, the abuser's voice echoing in her memory was overpowering and was making her cry.

"Babies do odd things," the doctor patted her on the shoulder. "Her vital signs are good, she looks good; her color is fine. I don't think it was anything to be concerned about." Feeling like a bigger fool by the doctor's words, Christy reached for Amy after signing a form that she understood her baby was fine and she left the hospital intent on never telling Chad what she had done. No one would know that she was an alarmist. No one would know that she was someone that would make a mountain out of a molehill.

Chad's father and Grandparents flew in for a few days to visit and meet the baby. His Grandmother spent time with Christy and they spoke of genealogy, something they both liked and had in common while Grandma Bac bonded with her great grandchild. The visit went by quickly and by the time the family left, Amy's latch on problem was a thing of the past.

Little Amy Bac was gaining weight and her smile now was real and her cooing for her parents had become precious. Not even four weeks old and she was cooing all the time, her huge eyes taking in everything around her.

Christy had a secret. Christy knew that Amy was doing the odd behaviors more and more. Soon Chad would notice as he was home on the weekends and she wanted him to notice. She didn't like being alone in this knowledge that something was the matter with their baby. She'd spoken up at Amy's appointment with the pediatrician of the odd movements and again, the doctor had assured Christy this was probably normal. Two more secret trips to the emergency room due to Amy turning blue around the mouth had Christy feeling stupid. The emergency room doctor had even taken a red sharpie marker and written on the front of Amy's file folder, 'nervous mother.'

"I'm leaving again," Chad spoke as he came into the house seeing Christy peek around the kitchen corner and meet his eyes.

"When?" she asked as she dried her hands on a towel and stopped to push Amy's swing as the batteries were winding down.

"My birthday," Chad said as he bent and kissed his wife before bending further to kiss his baby daughter.

"How long?" Christy asked as she watched him stand up straight.

"Two weeks, maybe three," Chad said putting his briefcase down on the sofa before taking the stairs up to their room. "I'll change and then we can eat," he called down not seeing his wife sit with a defeated look on her face as she more fell onto the sofa than sat on the sofa.

There would be no one to see the oddities of their daughter, Christy thought. Chad was leaving. She was a liar; the man in her past had said so. She was an alarmist and she made molehills into mountains. She looked at Amy and she saw the jerk and she knew, no matter what she was, no matter what anyone accused her of being, something was the matter with Amy.

The fever was high, too high and the baby was still, too still as Christy sat in the backseat of the car and Chad rushed Amy to the emergency room on base. Within an hour the baby was admitted, not yet six weeks old and a fever of one hundred six. "Spinal Meningitis," the doctor said. The same doctor that had written 'nervous mother' on Amy's file folder was now giving the mother a worried look.

Christy held her baby still while a spinal tap was done. Chad had left the room, he couldn't watch. The big, strong military man couldn't handle seeing his child in this condition and he stood out in the hall waiting and hoping that soon they would be home and a family again as he was leaving in less than two days time.

They were admitted to the hospital, the room was freezing cold. Chad went home and returned with warm clothes for Christy knowing that he was going to leave his wife and baby in the hospital and he was going far away from them. He saw their pediatrician come into the room as his wife pulled on a coat and he waited with hope that the doctor would soon tell them Amy was fine.

Christy had no such hopes similar to her husband. She was living with a secret, a fear that something was wrong with their daughter and no doctor would listen to her. She heard the pediatrician now, the concern in the woman's voice as she told them Amy needed a CAT scan of her stomach though she didn't say why and too afraid to ask, the couple never knew what Amy had and yet for three days every few hours a CAT scan was done of Amy's stomach looking at something known as free air.

Chad left and Christy was alone in the hospital. No one could visit if she did have a network of friends, which she didn't, because Amy was too ill. A week passed with the nurses being very supportive before Amy was well enough to go home and Christy was relieved. The whole hospital stay she'd seen none of the odd movements, no turning blue around the mouth. Those worries now seemed to be in the past just as the worries of the latch on problem as Amy was now feeding with gusto.

July passed slowly as Chad was gone and Christy was preparing for their move into a house on base. She was making curtains and packing their things a little at the time daily until almost all of their belongings other than what she and the baby needed was packed and ready for the movers to come. Christy knew the movers were coming on the twenty-fifth, Chad was due home a week later and he wouldn't return here to their townhouse to live, he would be coming onto the base and life was going to be good.

There was only one thing ruining Christy's perfect life. The jerks she was seeing Amy have. The baby hadn't turned blue around the mouth, but Amy's eyes had gone upward and become stuck several times. And these lightening fast jerks were happening still, mostly jerks in Amy's arms, legs and head.

Babies do odd things, she kept saying to herself as she'd brought her concerns to the pediatrician at every visit and at every visit her concerns were dismissed because Amy looked great. The baby cooed for the doctor and smiled. Amy completely charmed the whole medical staff with her smile and all of Amy's milestones were met early. The baby was perfect. Christy was an alarmist, Christy reminded herself. She made mountains out of molehills. She was a worrywart.

The night before the movers were due to come Christy took Amy and went onto the base to their new home where she hung curtains and put away breakables that she brought in her car and hung photographs on the walls and decorated Amy's nursery in the Winnie the Pooh decorations from the townhouse.

It was nearly ten in the evening when her cell phone rang and it was Chad. He had caught an earlier flight home and he was 40 minutes out in Atlanta. He wanted Christy to come to the airport and pick him up and he had no idea her head was shaking in a negative way and that she had said the word no, because he had hung up the phone.

Standing in their new home with dust on her clothes, wearing a button down the front plain blouse and a pair of shorts, Christy wasn't in any condition to go to the airport and pick up her husband that she hadn't seen in a month. She ran to the bathroom aware that she didn't even have a hairbrush here to do her hair with and her hair – yikes was all she could think upon seeing her reflection.

"I'll kill him for this," Christy said to her baby. "I've never in my life gone out in public with my hair a mess like this."

There was nothing else to do but lock up the house and take Amy to the airport, the baby fast asleep in her arms. But the baby wasn't fast asleep inside the airport, the baby was screaming her lungs out as it was nearly eleven at night and the baby was use to her bed by this time of night.

And Christy, she was surrounded by military wives that knew their husband's were coming home early and they were dressed in sundresses and their hair was done and cute little sandals on their feet. "Ugh," Christy fought not to cry as Chad came out of the terminal and reached for her not seeing that she was angry with him. Several of the wives had asked her why she wasn't dressed up and Christy told them, her husband had just called her forty minutes ago to inform her he was coming home. One of the wives said Chad needed to be murdered for that stunt. They were all going out to a late dinner at Denny's together and had babysitters for their children, they'd known all day their men were working their way home.

Christy allowed Chad to live and she calmed down on the drive home, though this was something that Chad would never forget and a valuable lesson that he had learned. Always give the wife a warning you're coming home so she can be dressed and ready to meet your plane. It is not cool for a wife to look like Christy had looked when she met his plane, Chad repeated to himself several times as Christy had nearly yelled this at him once in the car. And he had to smile; his wife had stood up for herself. His wife had let him know how she felt and for Chad, that was a good thing.

Living on the base was completely different than living off the base. The F-15 planes were loud and they flew over causing the windows to rattle and the front door to shake on its frame. Christy loved the noise and she liked living on the base. Chad was home earlier in the evenings and he could leave later in the mornings. Amy was lifting herself up and the baby was rolling over. Amy was babbling and making tons of noise and everything was good except for the jerks and Christy was forcing herself to believe that for Amy, those jerks were normal. The fact was, the jerks didn't bother Amy in the least.

The pediatrician had ordered a CAT scan of Amy's head as the fontanelle seemed to be closed too soon and within hours Chad and

Christy knew that Amy was being referred to a neurologist to see if she would need surgery. The night after they had received this news, Chad saw Amy doing the odd behavior. He had been sitting at the table and he had seen her legs draw inward, her arms pull inward and make a fist and her eyes roll upward. Within seconds, he and Christy had Amy in the car and were at the emergency room which was now only a half mile from their home.

The emergency room doctor, the same one that had seen Amy in the past came in shaking his head. Chad spoke loud, too loud maybe assuring the doctor that what he'd seen didn't seem odd, it was scary. The doctor said Amy looked fine now and shook his head. The couple left not even signing anything; they left with Christy in tears and Chad in shock.

"This has something to do with her fontanelle closing," Chad spoke as they left the building. "I'm calling that neurologist and getting us in as soon as possible." At that moment, outside the ambulance bay, the sirens went on and Christy looked up at her husband and away from her baby.

"Chad, whatever this is that happens to Amy, afterward she sleeps hard. She can't sleep through the vacuum cleaner running but look," Chad looked at their baby as she asked him too. The noise was so loud Christy was yelling at him and within a second he saw her walking toward the ambulance and their baby slept on.

"She can't sleep through the noise of the vacuum cleaner, but she can sleep through this noise," Chad noted.

Chad couldn't get them into the neurologist any earlier than October, a month away. In the meantime, Christy sat and watched her little Amy roll over and attempt to crawl at only three months of age. The baby had met all milestones, her development was advanced. And little Amy Bac jerked and her eyes would roll up and to the side.

Fear, the mother was in fear for her child and no one was believing this or was anyone taking this serious and for Christy, this was very serious. All of her attention was on her baby until the early morning of September eleventh.

Christy had gotten up, showered and dressed, and then the got the baby dressed for a routine checkup and immunizations at the hospital. Chad was going to meet them there when the phone rang and it was Cheryl, Chad's mother.

"Turn on the TV," Christy heard her mother-in-law scream into the phone and she did so wondering why. "MSNBC," her mother-in-law hung up as Christy put on the channel.

Thousands died that day in the World Trade Center as bad people flew planes into buildings where new mothers like Christy worked. This shouldn't have happened, Christy thought and she grieved the loss of innocent people that were only going to work today.

Chad met Christy for Amy's routine appointment, an appointment where everyone was watching the news channel and Amy's issues went unaddressed. And Christy was fine with that as she knew, she made molehills into mountains and in the real world a mountain had just been made of the World Trade Center and too many people weren't going home to their families tonight.

Amy had just finished feeding and being burped as Christy took a long drink of milk from her glass and looked down at her baby. Amy was blue, her eyes were stuck, she was drawn inward and stiff and for a second Christy thought to throw the milk in the baby's face to stop this behavior, but that was only a fleeting thought as she instead jumped up and grabbed her keys, her shirt unbuttoned, no purse, and ran to the car.

She didn't put Amy in the car seat. She didn't close the front door to the house. She didn't have her military identification. She had Amy and was driving fast to the emergency room. Amy was blue and stiff and this was real and Christy wasn't making a molehill into a mountain. Getting out of her car she saw the doctor that had written nervous mother in red on Amy's file folder coming out of the building and she knew, he would help her now. She ran to him fast, he had to see Amy, she was thinking in fear. Someone had to see this thing happening to Amy and that someone was this doctor that knew her and her baby. She reached the doctor handing Amy to him.

"Please," she begged of him, "please believe me. There's something the matter with my baby."

"I have an infant in full seizure!" the doctor yelled as he ran into the emergency room with Christy running behind him. And everything happened fast, too fast for Christy. A CAT scan was done, Amy was put under sedation and Christy had to sign a form stating that the sedation might hurt Amy. Nearly in a panic state, she signed the form then fell to her knees hugging the legs of the radiologist and begging him to not let anything happen to her baby.

Two hours later Chad was with her and they were going to Sacred Heart Hospital nearly an hour and a half away to join their baby. In the upstairs hall they were directed to a wing that was near the Pediatric Intensive Care Unit and ushered inside seeing Amy hooked up to a machine with wires all over her little head.

The doctor came into the room, he had been at a formal function and he was dressed in a tuxedo, a woman was with him. Chad and Christy would later learn that the woman was his assistant and handled many details for the doctor. He was a neurologist and he stood in front of the parents that were looking down at their baby and he asked Christy to describe what she'd seen.

With her voice shaking and anxious and even excited that at last someone was listening to her, Christy told of what she had seen and the neurologist had nodded his head stating that we were all entitled to one free seizure in our lifetime. Amy had just had hers. He went on to explain that Amy was hooked up to an EEG machine and they were seeing frontal lobe involvement. He had viewed the CAT scan and he was aware her anterior fontanelle had closed. In the morning he was having an MRI done. In the meantime, Amy was staying hooked up to the EEG and going into PICU.

Chad and Christy knew nothing of what was happening. They didn't even know what PICU meant and it was the nurse that explained Pediatric Intensive Care Unit to them and much more. The next morning Amy had to be put under sedation and intubated for the MRI and Chad stayed with her while Christy went outside in the garden and prayed and paced and prayed some more.

Two days later feeling that everything might be all right again, little four month old Amy Bac was discharged from the hospital with her parents knowing that the anterior fontanelle was indeed closed but it wouldn't be a problem for Amy and the baby probably wouldn't ever have a seizure again. The neurologist would do a follow up EEG in a month and see them then. Life was good and Christy felt like she had been a worrywart but she wasn't now. Everything was going to be fine now.

Winter – Eglin Air Force Base

Little Amy Bac was showing her personality and her little personality was one that was all smiles. She'd sit in her bouncy seat at her father's feet and she would smile up at him and glance over at her mommy and do the same thing. The child was all smiles and always cooing and making happy baby noises.

The follow up EEG in early November had been normal, the neurologist wanted to see the baby again in February. but otherwise, he was pleased and tickled that Amy was going to be all right. He'd told the parents that Amy was as cute as stink and the truth was. Amy was completely beautiful; everyone said so with her huge dark eyes that dominated her pretty face.

At Christmas time Chad and Christy had gone to be with Chad's mother Cheryl. Amy had been wonderful on the twelve hour drive to Cheryl's home and twelve hours drive back to Eglin after

Christmas. Everything was routine and Christy was dismissing the jerks Amy was making still as normal. There were no episodes of blue around the mouth and eyes upward or drawing in of the limbs. Amy was doing great and she was crawling at five months and before the appointment in February with the neurologist, Amy was pulling up on furniture and walking holding onto the furniture and she was only nine months old.

On Valentine's Day Christy woke with a crashing headache and in a rush to get ready for Amy's EEG. She had stayed up almost all night with Amy as Amy had to be sleep deprived for the EEG. Chad had woken at four in the morning and relieved Christy but two hours of sleep just hadn't been enough for Christy. They hurried into the car, Amy was certainly fussy, the baby wanted a nap but somehow on the nearly two hour drive in morning traffic to Pensacola, the couple had to keep their baby awake.

The music was blaring on the radio, the traffic was a nightmare, Amy was fussy and Chad was in the front seat alone as Christy struggled to keep Amy from going to sleep and the baby fought the mother to stay awake. "What are you doing?" Chad screamed when he looked in the rearview mirror and he saw Christy had Amy out of the car seat.

"She's going to sleep," Christy cried because Chad had yelled at her. "I was just going to reposition her." Chad had pulled off to the side of the road and yelled at his wife for not leaving Amy in her seat. When he got back onto the road, his wife was sobbing hysterically as was Amy and he felt terrible for overeating and causing his wife and his baby to cry. But at least this way, Amy crying as she was, the little girl stayed awake and she was in fact, very sleep deprived for the appointment.

"The EEG was abnormal," the neurologist said as he came into the room Chad and Christy were sitting in.

"Abnormal how?" Chad demanded to know and the doctor sat down across from them after patting Amy on the head, the little girl sitting in her mother's lap.

"She's epileptic guys," the neurologist said and he handed Chad a prescription. "We'll start off with Tegretol and see how that goes. I'll need to see Amy every three months and at the next appointment we'll do a follow up EEG in office."

Another sleep deprived EEG Christy thought and closed her eyes knowing that she had made Chad angry this morning. "So these times that Amy pulls her legs and arms in and her eyes roll up and her mouth turns blue and she's stiff," Christy saw the neurologist give her all of his attention as she asked this of him, "those are seizures?"

"Yes, they are," he said in a voice that held sorrow. "The good news is there's no sign of developmental delays. Amy's actually very advanced in all skills. She's cooing and I heard her saying both Dada and Mama earlier. She has a steady gait and she will be walking very soon. She's not even ten months old."

"She said Pooh first," Chad spoke up and the doctor smiled at him. "Her first word was Pooh."

"She looks great, all developmental milestones met, she's strong, she's even interacting with me and very good eye contact. Other than being an epileptic, Amy is doing great. And all over the world people are epileptic." The neurologist left the room and Chad, with the prescription in hand took his wife's hand and leaned against her.

"I'm sorry I yelled at you," he felt her hug his arm and Amy hugged his arm as well and he knew, all was forgiven. Amy was going to be just fine.

Chapter Eight

Romans 8:28: "And we know that in all things God works for the good of those who love him, who have been called according to his purpose."

Chad had to leave with the military again shortly after Valentine's day. This trip Christy knew where he was and she could talk to him on the phone. He was gone twenty-nine days and came home for three only to go out another twenty-nine days. When he returned at the end of April, Chad had a surprise for his wife and for his little Amy, a surprise that he was happy over and he had done for himself as well.

"I have a something for us," Chad said when Christy met him at the airport.

"I need you to see something," Christy said with a laugh and put Amy down on the floor in front of her husband. "While you were gone, look what our daughter learned to do." She watched Chad watching their daughter as Amy walked four steps to her Daddy before falling.

"Oh, I can fix this," Chad said when Christy told him Amy was only able to walk a few steps yet.

"Chad, she's not broken, she doesn't need fixing," Christy held Amy close while her husband went to retrieve his luggage.

"I'll have her running before dark," Chad spoke in a loud voice and several people turned to stare at him and he saw his wife laughing at him. "She has to run because I have us tickets to Disney World."

"You're kidding," Christy said as she rushed after him, with his long legs she often had to run after him to keep up with him, but then that running kept her thin.

"I'm serious," Chad reached the car and put his luggage in the trunk before reaching down and removing something from his briefcase. Within seconds Christy saw the tickets and she knew, while he was home on this short leave, they were going to Disney World. "Four days and five nights," she breathed while looking at the tickets and Chad reached down taking Amy from her arms and going to lock the baby in her car seat.

"So we need to pack. We'll be staying at the Day's Inn and Suites tomorrow night."

"I can't be packed that soon," Christy complained as Chad got into the car. "I need time to pack for little Amy."

"I'll help you," Christy laughed at her husband's offer and leaned back in her seat after putting on the seatbelt.

"You'll be busy teaching Amy how to run." Christy looked over at Chad and she knew, this man could do almost anything that he put his mind too. He was persistent and he had a drive that let her know often that she had to get out of his way.

They weren't home fifteen minutes before Chad had a pull toy by the string and he was walking with the toy behind him. He put his daughter on her feet and he pulled the toy and Christy watched as Amy toddled behind the toy trying to catch the thing. Amy would fall down; Chad would pick her up and put her on her feet again then take the pull toy by the string and start walking until Amy could take ten steps without falling, her little arms outstretched reaching for the toy.

He had done what he had said he would do, Christy saw. He had taught their daughter to run by using a toy and making a game out of what he was doing. By the end of the day two things had happened, the first thing being Chad was running pulling the pull toy behind him and the second thing that had happened that day was that Amy's Daddy called her by the nickname that he would often use for her throughout her life. Chad called Amy 'little one,' and she was little and always would be to him.

The trip to Disney World had been exciting and more than fun. Chad had a chance to bond with his daughter and he knew that he was missing out on her life as he was gone so much of the time. Christy had the camcorder running every day to capture all important and even unimportant moments of Amy's life for him to see and he was grateful, but seeing the videos just weren't the same as being with his child.

And then there was Christy, Chad thought as he watched his wife play in the park with their child and he knew that he was a blessed man to have a faithful wife. They had been together for more than two years now and they had yet to disagree on anything. They were a team, on the same page of the same book and in many ways they thought alike. And his wife, he had smiled watching her meet the Disney characters with Amy in her arms. Christy was changing. She wasn't as fearful as she had been. She was more confident and she was open with him sharing her thoughts and her feelings and he liked that she trusted him. He had wanted her trust.

"I'm going to Wright Patterson Air Force Base for two and a half months," Chad told Christy early in May.

"When?" she asked him and saw him coming toward her and pulling her into his arms.

"July," he answered while hugging her. "And I don't want to leave you and Amy here. I want my girls to come with me."

"Yes," Christy said in an excited voice. "I've never been to Ohio. And we'll drive through other states on the way up." She paused and looked at Amy banging a toy little people car on their coffee table. "Do you think Amy can manage a trip that far away and that long in the car?"

"Sure she can," Chad said with a smile. "Her last EEG was good, the Tegretol is working. And I have an idea that might help."

Chad never did anything without putting hours of thought into what he was doing. The engineer mentality, Christy would often say. Chad knew every route from his office to the house and he knew which one was shortest, even by a second, but Christy doubted Chad had a short-cut to the Air Force base in Ohio.

While Chad was working on his 'idea' for their fifteen hour trip north, Christy began packing and making certain everything for Amy was ready to go. The last week of June, the couple drove over to Pensacola and saw the neurologist and told him of the upcoming trip. Christy was hopeful the doctor would say Amy was fine to go and the doctor did, though he ordered some blood testing to be done before they left and he knew they wouldn't be home until the first of September.

Chad hurried them to the lab and had Amy's blood taken. She was always so easy to take blood from as she never cried or fussed, she just would watch with wide eyes filled with trust. Chad and Christy had come to know that Amy wasn't a fussy child, she was a loving child and they knew every single day just how blessed they were to have Amy as their little girl.

"I can't believe this," Christy fell into Chad laughing at what he had done. In the backseat of their car sat a thirteen inch television with a built in video cassette player and many of Amy's video cassettes that were Disney cartoon. Amy loved 'The Little Mermaid," she watched that over and over again and 'Sleeping Beauty." As far as Christy was concerned, this was a work of genius on Chad's part. The fifteen hour trip would pass with ease thanks to this television and Christy had taught Amy that when the movie ended, it

Something's the Matter with Amy

would rewind and pop out of the cassette player. All Amy had to do was pop the cassette back in to restart the movie.

"She'll be entertained," Chad said as they loaded the car with their luggage the night before and Christy saw the large packet of huggies diapers on the floor.

"Chad look," she stopped him in the doorway as they both looked and saw Amy pointing to the bag of diapers that had the cartoon character of Barney the dinosaur on them. Amy was talking to Barney, she was only thirteen months old and she was singing the Barney song. Within a matter of seconds she squealed out loud and her mother grabbed the camcorder and recorded as Amy ran to her room and seconds later came back with her stuffed Barney toy matching it to the Barney on the bag of disposable diapers before standing and singing again the Barney song.

"She's going to be as smart as me," Chad bragged and his wife agreed.

"Maybe even smarter," Christy laughed and hugged her husband knowing that all of Amy's high intellect would come from this man that was her husband, a man that she adored and loved.

The drive to Wright Patterson Air Force Base near Dayton, Ohio had been easy on Chad and Christy as Amy had sat in the car seat content with watching her Disney Princess cartoons. She loved Sleeping Beauty and by the end of the trip, both of Amy's parents knew the songs by heart. Christy took Amy from the car seat and sang the song to the little girl holding her close and Chad laughed at the play aware that until this moment he hadn't realized his wife could sing so beautifully.

They checked into their apartment like home before going to the Base Exchange for a few items and having dinner in the food court. Christy hadn't brought Amy's stroller as there wasn't room in the trunk so Chad bought a little umbrella stroller for their daughter and soon they were on their way, Amy hugging close a new toy Daddy had bought for her; a Blue's Clues Magenta.

Little Amy Bac had this way about her, whenever she saw pink she screamed to the top of her lungs. Both of her parents were certain that was her way of saying that she liked pink and over the past month almost everything they bought for Amy was pink including the new umbrella stroller.

"I'll be working every day, but I have Saturday off," Chad said once they were settled into their place. "The commissary is only a short walk away and with the stroller you can go daily and pick up food. The washer and dryers are just beyond our apartment in the building next door. You won't have any reason to go off base as everything is right here for you and Amy. But if you want to drive me to work and keep the car for the day, that's fine by me."

"No," Christy said as she picked Amy up into her arms and started walking to the bathroom to bathe the little girl. "I think I'll stay here with Amy and watch Disney and Noggin while you work. She and I can color and finger paint. I brought all of her art supplies."

"I'll not be where you can call me," Chad said and Christy understood. Where he was going he couldn't get interrupted.

"We'll be fine," she called out to him as she saw him laying his uniform on the bed.

"We're in a little city here," Chad said and he knew Christy would be fine. She kept to herself, she didn't have friends. She was social and fun to be around, but she kept a part of herself pulled in and he knew that was because of the abuser in her past. But time was healing her. She wasn't blaming herself now, at least not so much.

"Leaving is safer than staying," Chad said to himself knowing this was true. Until you've loved someone or been in an abusive relationship, you can't understand how they're trapped. They're afraid to leave, made to think they can't survive without the abuser and worse, if they leave the abuse may turn deadly.

Something's the Matter with Amy

"You need to leave and leave now," a woman in her sixties said to Christy and Christy pulled away from the woman that was standing too close and she hugged Amy close against her body.

"She doesn't have to go anywhere," a tall man in uniform joined Christy and the woman that was now pointing her finger in Christy's face.

"She can't control her little girl," the woman said and Christy held Amy tighter as she felt Amy jerking in her arms and making an odd squealing noise with the jerks. All Christy could think as the woman spoke, was what she'd been told by the doctor for all of Amy's life. All babies do odd things.

"This is the base commissary ma'am," the uniformed man spoke loud and clear. "As long as she has her military identification, she can shop here and the little girl isn't bothering you. Go away." As the man said this, Christy reached into her purse and pulled out her military dependent ID seeing the man glance at her ID and then meets her eyes.

The older woman had walked away, but kept looking at Amy as though Amy were bad and the truth was, Amy was only a one year old baby. "How long has your little girl had this tic disorder?" the man asked her and Christy backed away from him.

"She doesn't have a tic disorder," Christy spoke softly wondering who this man was and in that instant, the man introduced himself as one of the doctors on the base. "Amy has epilepsy," Christy explained.

"What medication is she taking?" the doctor asked and Christy again met his eyes.

"Tegretol."

"That's a good one," the doctor said and smiled at Amy taking a few moments to interact with the now fourteen month old child. "She can talk," he spoke as though he was impressed and Christy smiled the smile only a proud mother can give over joy in her child.

"She started walking when she was only ten months old," Christy beamed as she spoke of Amy and saw Amy looking at the man standing next to her.

"I can see she's a very bright baby," the doctor said and Christy's smile grew wide.

"She's like her Daddy that way," she spoke almost in a shy way and felt Amy lay against her shoulder.

"And her mother," the doctor spoke in a playful tone. "Talk to her doctor about that tic that she has. God bless her, she's a sweet child. I hate to hear of anyone struggling with epilepsy."

Christy watched the doctor leaving her before grabbing the few items she would need to make dinner tonight. Living in the temporary leave quarters was like an extended vacation and she was enjoying her time with Amy. The weather in Ohio was also proving to be much different than Florida. The days cooler and the nights were like fall in Florida.

On the weekends Chad took his small family to dairy farms where they drank fresh milk and had homemade ice cream. Amy loved looking at the cows and the horses and the chickens and running free and Chad loved watching Christy chase after Amy. The days were carefree, the days held no worries or concerns and when they weren't visiting the dairy farms, they were out in the antique stores and the old shops roaming the streets of towns that appeared to belong in another century.

The two months flew by and by the time they left Ohio in September the weather there was much as it was in Florida at Christmas time. The drive home was longer it seemed than the drive up here and they stopped and saw a balloon show in Tennessee, and in Kentucky the stopped and went to an antique car show. Both events Amy jerked and did her squealing noise which Christy now wondered was this a tic disorder or was this normal yet an odd thing that babies do. The mother didn't know which this was but she knew that once they reached home, she would talk to the neurologist and see what he had to say.

Both Chad and Christy loved Amy's neurologist. He made the appointments less like a doctor visit and more like a backyard BBQ. The parents were comfortable with him and they trusted him with Amy's care, after all, he had diagnosed Amy's problem, given her medication five months ago and the problem was no longer a problem.

Chad left the car with Amy in his arms and went to the mailbox knowing that he'd alerted the post office of their return date from Ohio. The mailbox was empty and he knew all their mail for the past two months wouldn't come until tomorrow. He came back to the car and reached for a bag before helping Christy by opening the front door, her arms loaded down with their luggage.

The house looked as it looked when they had left two months ago and Chad put Amy down on the floor to run and visit with toys the little girl had left behind while he went to push the button of the answering machine. The flashing red light told him there were messages to hear, which didn't surprise him and he expected those messages to all be from telemarketers.

"August eighth two thousand and two," the digital voice on the answering machine let Chad know when their first message was left and he saw Christy standing by the bed listening with him to the machine as Amy squealed and ran into the room with her big purple dinosaur Barney, a smile on the little girl's face.

"Mrs. Bac," a female voice came from the answering machine stating her name and that she was a nurse and she was calling from Amy's neurologist's office. "The blood tests that we had done on Amy at your last appointment indicate a problem that might be the cause of her epilepsy. We need you to call us as soon as possible, in fact, the moment that you get this message."

Christy stopped unpacking and with a worried frown she met Chad's eyes and saw him looking stunned. The message was more than a month old and worse, there were six more messages from that nurse. It was a Friday night and the neurologist's office was closed for the upcoming weekend.

"What do we do?" Christy asked in a near whisper and she saw Chad turn and pick up the phone quickly calling the neurologist's office. She was only hearing one side of the conversation and most of Chad's conversation was to grunt after he had first explained the voice messages on their home machine and then the fact that they were gone the last two months to a base up north and just now got that message.

"We have to wait until Monday morning," Chad turned to his wife to say and she watched him reach for the phone and dial another number and she knew that he was speaking to Hollywood, the major in charge of his squadron. Christy heard him as he explained the situation quickly and requested to be late on Monday.

"What do we do?" Christy asked again reaching to pick up Amy as the little girl had brought her mother her hairbrush and was attempting to brush her own hair.

Chad looked at Amy with the hairbrush and he stood still thinking for a long minute. "You know," he came and reached for his daughter taking the little girl from his wife's arms. "She's been fine on the Tegretol. We'll find out on Monday what's going on and it can't be serious, we'd have a sick child on our hands if this were serious." Even saying this to his wife, even presenting himself as calm, Chad knew that he was a nervous wreck and he wondered how they'd get through the weekend. What if Amy had some rare form of cancer that was hurting her? He bounced his baby in his arms very aware that besides cancer, he knew of nothing that could harm a child. All he could do was pray this wasn't cancer and that they'd be all right. Pray that his little one would be just fine.

Chapter Nine

Isaiah 43:1: "Don't fear, for I have redeemed you; I have called you by name; you are Mine."

Christy hardly slept Sunday night. She lay in her husband's arms listening to Amy in the room next to their room making noises. The squeal that came with the jerks was loud and Christy knew from the doctor in the commissary in Ohio that Amy might have a tic disorder. Maybe that was what the blood test found; Christy thought as she fought to go to sleep looking at the large red numbers on the digital clock on the bedside table and aware that it would soon be time to wake up. Maybe the blood test found something that would cause a tic and Amy wasn't epileptic at all. Maybe Amy just had something minor going on and they were over treating by giving Amy the Tegretol which was an antiepileptic medication.

The alarm blared and it was seven in the morning. Christy knew she'd slept only an hour but there was no way she was going back to sleep. "Chad," she shook him awake and saw him sit up on the edge of their bed before coming up behind him. "Let's get in the car and drive over to the neurologist's office in Pensacola. We can be there shortly after they open and they may not talk to us when we call. They may say they'll call back and not call back until next week. You know how doctors are." She felt her husband sitting still and she knew that he was considering what she was saying and she wanted him to get up, get dressed and go to Pensacola with her now.

"Let's call in an hour when the office opens," he said, his words disappointing his wife. "If they say they'll call back, we'll get in the car and go."

Christy heard Amy in the room next door to their room, the little girl rarely cried; in fact Amy was so good natured that she was easy to care for. "I'll get Amy fed while you dress," Christy left the bed and pulled on her clothes peeking around the corner and into Amy's room waving at her little daughter and hearing giggles coming from the child when she waved. "Mommy loves you," Christy said and disappeared around the corner only to peek back and see Amy burst into giggles. "Mommy loves you still," Christy spoke in a sweet baby pleasing voice before disappearing around the corner again. Each time that she disappeared Christy was doing something to ready for the day, be it pulling on her clothes or brushing her hair before peeking back around and saying Mommy loves you again to her giggling little Amy Bac.

Chad held the phone in his hand while he ate a bowl of cereal and told his wife that he hated being on hold. Amy was now at the coffee table banging on the table with a toy car and making that noise that Christy had come to view as a tic disorder. "Yes, this is Mr. Bac," Chad said into the phone and Christy came from the kitchen to take his cereal bowl from him to wash, praying that soon they'd learn there was nothing to worry about with their daughter, that whatever was wrong was minor.

"What did they say?" Christy asked as she heard Chad not speaking and he hung up the phone in a few seconds with only the words, "I understand," having been said by him in the conversation he was on that phone with the neurologist's office.

"They want us to come in now," Chad said as he saw his wife put his bowl in the sink and he went for his wallet and his keys and her purse. "They'll work us in this morning." He stopped and picked up the phone dialing another number as Christy reached for Amy and heard him talking into the phone saying that he wasn't going to be in today and that he had to take his little one over to the neurologist in Pensacola, that it was important.

"They had to have told you something Chad," Christy spoke in a pleading tone as she sat sideways in the car so that she could see both Chad and Amy.

"Only that we would be worked into an appointment and to come in now," Chad said looking over his shoulder at his baby in her car seat. "This drive is always long," Chad complained and he had an upset look on his face. "But right now it feels like it'll last forever."

Their stress level had reached it maximum in both parents as they searched the crowded parking garage at Sacred Heart Hospital for a parking space. Amy was also tired of sitting in her car seat and began to fuss, something the little girl rarely did making her parents more anxious than they already were. Chad finally found a place and Christy reached for Amy while he reached for the diaper bag and they nearly ran into the hospital relieved to get on the elevator without a wait.

The neurologist's office was crowded, standing room only and Chad looked at Christy standing still and nervous by the door while he signed them in. A minute later he came back to her and told her they had to go to another floor for testing, that the neurologist had ordered an echocardiogram to be done right away.

"Amy's so healthy," Christy said as they reached the floor and a nurse came out to them telling them they would be next, but the wait would be an hour. Amy was horribly fussy as it was well past the child's nap time and Christy, taking Amy's blanket and holding her child close began to rock Amy back and forth in her arms singing the theme song to Disney's Sleeping Beauty.

"We need her asleep when we do the test," the nurse said to Christy and Chad and they exchanged glances, both knowing that Amy was tired and it was her naptime.

"The little one will sleep through the test," Chad said in confidence as they waited for the nurse to call their name.

Christy hadn't known what to expect of the echocardiogram, but she realized quickly that it was a very non-invasive test and within thirty minutes the test was done. "The neurologist will have these results in an hour," the nurse said. "Why don't you go to lunch? There's a Wendy's in the lobby."

Taking Christy's hand Chad pulled her to the elevator seeing Amy was waking up from a good nap and the little girl smiled up at him. "She's fine," Chad predicted to ease his wife's worries. "Look at her smiling at me. That's all she does is smile Christy."

"I'm not really hungry," Christy said as Chad walked with her to the counter. "Get Amy a kids meal of nuggets and fries and she and I can share."

Within an hour they had Amy fed and the little girl had even enjoyed a chocolate frosty from Wendy's before they were ushered into the neurologist's office. This time the place was nearly empty of patients and their wait was short as it was later in the afternoon.

"The test was great," the doctor said this as he came into the room and sat down at a small desk built into the sidewall. "Amy's blood test showed that she's low in carnitine," he turned to face Chad and Christy on his rolling stool as he spoke and he stopped for a few seconds and patted Amy on the head. "Having low levels of carnitine can cause children to have a host of medical problems," the neurologist spoke on, "and one of those problems is epilepsy. It can also cause heart problems and more. I think the low levels was just a mistake, possibly due to the fact that Christy just discontinued with breast feeding. We're going to test Amy's blood again today and if everything's fine, we'll see you back in three months."

"That's it?" Chad asked in the most relieved tone of voice Christy had ever heard him use.

"Well," the neurologist looked at Amy smiling at him as she chewed on a toy her mother had handed to her. "Have you seen any more of those episodes of drawing inward and turning blue around the mouth?"

"No," Christy spoke in a confident way and looked quickly at her husband before looking back at the doctor. "Amy makes this squealing noise," she brought up the subject of her concern and saw the doctor roll closer to Amy. "She doesn't do it all the time. In fact, there's no pattern to the noise. It's a loud high pitched noise though."

"She's cute as stink," the neurologist said looking the baby in the eyes and making faces with Amy. "The noise is probably normal attention seeking baby." The doctor met Christy's eyes and smiled. "She's an only child; use to having Mommy all to herself. We'll keep an eye on this behavior, but it's probably a normal behavior for a normal child." The doctor took Amy from Christy's arms and carried her to the exam table going over her carefully and smiling when he was done. "She looks very healthy. This squealing noise might be a side effect to her Tegretol, but more likely it's just a behavior. Let's have her blood drawn and I'll see you in three months."

"We dodged a bullet," Chad said as they left the hospital after having gone to the lab and had Amy's blood drawn. Again the little girl was good as gold about the needle and even patted her daddy's back with an insight unusual for a child so young that her father didn't like her being stuck with the needle even if she were all right with having the procedure done.

"Thank you Jesus," Christy prayed as she buckled Amy into the car. "There are epileptics all over the world that are doing just fine with medications," Christy said as she closed the car door. "Amy will be just fine."

"Those epileptics all over the world doing just fine aren't fighter pilots nor are they in the United States Military," Chad said as he backed out of the parking space.

"Oh no," Christy said only now realizing what her husband had long known. Amy would not follow in her father's footsteps. Amy wouldn't be in Chad's military and Chad loved the military. His grandfather John Bac had retired from the Air Force as a Lieutenant Colonel after a long career that had spanned three wars and Chad had joined in the late eighties and had been a part of the first Gulf War and now here they were facing another war in Iraq and Afghanistan due to the events of September eleventh.

"It doesn't matter," Chad spoke on. "Amy's healthy and that's all I care about."

"Me too," Christy said looking back in the backseat at their daughter hugging her blanket and watching the television on the seat beside Amy. "She's fine, that's all that matters."

Every morning Christy was up and out early with Amy in her stroller walking the base. She walked at least four miles a day often seeing across the water the Mid-bay Bridge or the Destin Bridge or the Brooks Bridge as their house on base looked out over the Gulf of Mexico. Amy loved being outside and all throughout the base in the housing area were parks with swings and slides and monkey bars that Amy loved to play on and Christy loved to watch her little girl play on.

Life was good. The routine was good and Chad was home for a few more weeks. He had to leave again the first of November and it would be their first Thanksgiving apart from one another. This was a part of their lives, Christy would often tell herself as she prepared dinner and watched Amy playing nearby. The military kept Chad going and often he was going away from her and Amy.

Something's the Matter with Amy

The phone rang on a hot September morning a week after they'd seen the neurologist and Christy answered the phone with Amy squealing, the squeal Christy now knew was an attention seeking behavior and loving her baby, she gave Amy attention as she picked up the phone and picked up Amy too.

"Hello," she said in a laughing tone as Amy put a wet kiss on her cheek.

"Mrs. Bac," Christy knew the neurologist's voice and she stopped breathing when he spoke his name into the phone. "Amy's carnitine levels are still low. I don't think this is the cause of Amy being epileptic," he spoke in a slow and patient voice. "The gene testing came back and she only has one gene that would cause this condition, she would need two genes to have Carnitine deficiency. But because her levels are low, I want to start her on Carnitine right away."

"She'll be okay?" Christy asked in a very worried mother tone of voice.

"I believe this is just something we need to treat for right now. For whatever reason, she's low and we'll give her the supplement. We can't give her too much, she'll just urinate it out if we do. So we'll test every few months and monitor this condition just as we have the epilepsy. I really think this isn't important."

The neurologist's reassurance made Christy comfortable, and within the hour she'd gone to the pharmacy and picked up the bottle of liquid Carnitine with the pharmacist explaining it couldn't be given with a citrus juice and it must be given three times a day, every eight hours at the same time. They must not miss a dose and it must be given at the same time every day. He emphasized this to Christy and all she could do was nod her head as she understood she needed a routine for her little girl.

The Carnitine became the ruler of their home. Amy refused to take the medication, something that was very out of character for the little girl. The happy smile faded quickly three times a day, yet the Tegretol for her seizures was taken agreeably. Christy pleaded with her little girl to take the medication and Amy pinched her lips tightly closed after saying very clearly one word that couldn't be mistake and that one word was always, "no."

The parents were frustrated and to make matters worse, Chad had to leave and he was gone until the day before Halloween. For more than six weeks Christy prayed, pleaded, begged and cried for Amy to take the medication and this chore was never easy, nor was it getting easier. Amy had made up her mind that she wasn't taking that medication and Christy had made up her mind that Amy was taking that medication.

"This stupid liquid is ruining my relationship with my seventeen month old child," Christy said this to Chad pushing the bottle of Carnitine in his face as he returned home after six weeks gone.

"All right," Chad said looking at his wife and thinking he should listen to what she had to say rather than kiss her hello.

"Three times a day Amy and I battle to get this into her Chad. She's not even two years old and I'm having to pour this into her mouth and then hold my hand over her mouth to keep it in until she swallows. I lose half of the medication every month and the doctor is having to re-order another bottle."

"And you want me to," Chad asked this stopping short of saying everything he intended to say because Christy burst into tears. This wasn't the welcome home he had been expecting.

"Fix this Chad," Christy cried. "You fix everything, fix this." And she knew what she was saying was true. Chad was the fix it man and this was a major problem he had to focus his attention, his full attention on right now.

"Daddy," he heard Amy calling out to him from her crib as he pulled his wife into his arms.

"Let's go get our little one," he dropped his bag by the door and walked with Christy into Amy's room reaching for his child. "We'll figure this out today." He looked around Amy's room and then down into his wife's light eyes. "What happened in here?" He asked her and saw her frown and the worried look she often had on her face was more so on her face than it had been in months. "It looks like the Disney Princesses and Pooh came in here and exploded." He gestured to the twin bed under the window and then the walls.

"I got in on a yard sale," Christy smiled now knowing what he meant when he asked her what had happened in here. "The bedspread of the Disney Princesses was only three dollars and it looks brand new Chad and best of all, its pink. Chad, Amy told me she loves pink." She saw him bounce Amy in his arms while Amy pulled on his nose. "The posters of Winnie the Pooh and the Winnie the Pooh rug came from this base wide yard sale at the enlisted club the second Saturday in October. I only paid ten dollars for all of this."

"So we're going to yard sales now," Chad said as he carried Amy to his suitcase and pulled out a Care Bear. Every time he went away from his little girl, he was bringing home a Care Bear. "Pooh, Princesses, and Care Bears and pink is her favorite color," Chad said on a laugh as he watched his daughter hug the bear he'd given to her. "What's her favorite food?" he turned to his wife and saw Christy going toward his bag knowing she was going to unpack and do his laundry.

"Anything chocolate," Christy said to her husband knowing it was time to battle the Carnitine into Amy.

"Do we have anything chocolate in the house?" he asked his wife and saw her turn and frown up into his face before she left him and went into the kitchen.

"I was going to make a cake tonight with chocolate frosting," Christy reached into the cabinet for the Duncan Hines tub of ready-made cake frosting.

"And the Carnitine?" Chad reached for the tub of frosting seeing Christy pull down the liquid bottle of Carnitine.

"I know where you're going with this," Christy saw Chad put the frosting on a spoon and look at the Carnitine. Christy quickly dug a hole in the frosting on the spoon and poured in the Carnitine leaving Chad holding the spoon while she hurried to get Amy.

"Nummy good chocolate," Chad said to his little one as Christy held Amy and he put the spoon in the little girl's open mouth.

"Nummy," Amy said and Christy fell into Chad getting a hug from him.

"You fixed this," she cried and he nodded his head.

"Together Christy, you and I fixed this. All we have to do is stick together."

Halloween was fun for the couple because they had Amy. They dressed her up as Belle, the Princess from Disney's Beauty and the Beast and they went from house to house hearing her say 'Trick or Treat' in her sweet little voice. Christy used the camcorder and recorded Amy speaking in a sentence. Only seventeen months old and Amy was stringing together five to ten words at a time.

The camcorder was on a lot as Chad had been gone a lot and Christy was making a record of their daughter for him. Amy used a banana and made that banana into her pretend phone. Many times the little girl would pick up the cell phone and pretend to talk to Chad's mother clearly calling his mother 'Nonny,' though it was correctly pronounced as "Nana."

The weather had changed and Christy had Amy dressed up in pink sweaters and coats, hats and gloves, the little girl often crying out 'pink!' when Christy asked her what she wanted to wear for the day. Everything was pink and everything was good. The chocolate was going in with ease filled with Carnitine, there were no episodes of blue around the mouth or drawn in limbs. The jerks were often and the squeals but these Christy dismissed as not a concern, they were behaviors only.

Chad returned home the night of Thanksgiving and Christy met him at the airport. He had taken Amy from her arms and hugged the child close before hugging his wife close. "Has the cat got her tongue?" Chad asked his wife and Christy frowned after having been kissed by her husband and going to retrieve his luggage.

"What do you mean?" Christy asked and Chad held Amy out bouncing his child in front of him and saying, "speak," to her in his sergeant voice as though he were giving an order to the little girl.

Little Amy Bac was silent. Amy looked at her father and her father looked at her while Christy grabbed his luggage from the conveyor belt. Chad knew in this moment something was very wrong with Amy, and he turned to his wife reaching for her hand and in a demanding and harsh voice he spoke, "what the hell has happened to my child?"

Christy immediately backed away from her husband shaking her head. Nothing had happened to Amy, Amy was just fine, but seeing Chad's face, he was angry, and Chad was angry with her. "Nothing," Christy cried and blinked to keep the tears in her eyes from falling. "We saw the neurologist on Monday; he said everything is looking good. Her Carnitine levels are up to normal and she's not having any seizures."

"She's not talking and she's not smiling," Chad spoke in the tone of voice that was frightening to his wife and he didn't see her back up and away from him as he was looking down into Amy's very serious face. His child almost appeared to be looking through him and not at him.

"She's been quiet all day," Christy said still standing a good four feet from her husband and child. "It's been so cold out; I think she's coming down with a virus again. She just got over that hand foot and mouth virus that was going around the base." As she said this Christy knew, with the virus that she had just had, Amy had still been chatty and making her usual squealing noises. She looked at Amy and she saw the look on Amy's face that Chad was seeing. Something was wrong with their little girl and they both knew they needed to get home and get the little girl to bed.

"No fever," Christy called out to Chad as he finished unpacking and she took Amy's temperature. "Maybe she had a seizure in her sleep last night and she's sluggish today. You know after she'd have a seizure she'd sleep for hours and be quiet for the day."

"That's what happened," Chad said as he came around the corner seeing Christy holding Amy. "We've been invited down to my buddy's house for pie tomorrow, I need to cancel if she's sick." He touched Amy's cheek and smiled thinking that she would smile back for him, but his little one didn't smile. "Her eyes look almost empty," he said taking her from Christy and sitting down in the lazy boy chair rocking her.

"I'll get a doctor appointment with her primary for Monday," Christy said looking at Chad holding Amy and very aware that the night before Amy had been fine. She had videotape to prove that as well and without hesitation, she went to the television and turned it on putting in a videotape of Amy watching PB and J Otter on the Disney Channel late yesterday afternoon. Amy had been smiling with both arms raised dancing in a circle and singing the theme song to the show, 'noodle, use your noodle, noodle, do the noodle dance.'

"She was fine last night," Chad confirmed seeing Amy on television reaching for the camera his wife had been holding in the video. "What happened?" he spoke out loud and he saw Christy standing by the television and she was crying. "It's nothing you did baby," he said to her leaving the chair and coming to hug her. "We'll figure this out," he spoke with assurance. "We'll get an appointment for Monday and get her on some antibiotics and she'll be fine this time next week. If she starts running a fever before Monday, we'll go to the emergency room."

Chapter Ten

1 John 4:18: "Perfect Love Casts Out All Fear"

The next day Chad and Christy went to Chad's friend's home for pie and coffee. The house was full of children all playing and having fun and all near Amy's age, but Amy. Christy and Chad sat together and watched their child, little Amy Bac wasn't playing with the other children. She was sitting in a corner alone and just staring at nothing. When Christy called her name, Amy didn't even look up at her.

"Let's go home," Chad picked up Amy and reached for Christy's hand. "She's coming down sick."

On Saturday in the early afternoon Chad took their little dog Blackberry and went to the vet leaving a concerned Christy home with Amy. The couple had spent hours the day before sitting on the floor with Amy and attempting to get Amy to look at her Disney books or play with her train. They even made noises for Amy's toy cars and played with her talking Pooh and Barney. If they had expected Amy to interact with them, to play with them as the little girl often did, they were terribly disappointed and upset. Amy only sat on the floor with a blank look on her face not even responding to her name.

Chad was glad to leave and take the dog to the vet. He needed to think and he was worried. Amy was silent. Amy wasn't smiling. Amy wasn't playing with her toys. His little girl wasn't even watching television or looking out the window in the living room when he had left with the dog and Amy loved their dog. She would have been at the window beating on the window and screaming 'bye' to the top of her lungs to this dog he was taking to the vet and Chad knew that.

Then he thought of his wife. Christy was blaming herself for whatever was going on with Amy. She was anxious and he could sense that as well as see that in her. They both were waiting for a fever or some sign of illness to explain away what was happening with Amy, and he was certain when Christy said 'ear infection' that she was right on that as Amy appeared deaf to them.

He had to focus on the dog and the vet and parking the car, Chad went inside the base animal hospital knowing that he had to wait until Monday to take Amy to the hospital to see her doctor before they would know if this was an ear infection or a virus. He had to wait because Amy had no outer signs of illness. "Maybe she'll develop a fever," he spoke out loud to the dog thinking that Monday seemed a long time to wait when you're as worried as he and Christy were.

At first she didn't know what was happening. When she realized just what was happening, Christy screamed and ran to Amy. The little girl had been standing at the coffee table just staring at nothing, or it appeared the little girl was staring at nothing when Amy fell to the floor on her side. Christy saw Amy's arms draw inward and her hands were fisted under her chin. Next Amy's legs were pulled up and her eyes, Christy knew by Amy's eyes that the child was having a seizure.

"Help," Christy screamed to the empty room realizing that Chad was gone with the dog to the vet and she was alone. Amy vomited as Christy fought to keep the little girl on her side. Amy's

Something's the Matter with Amy

eyes rolled back in her head and now she was jerking and shaking all over, her head Christy was trying to hold still while Christy used her fingers to remove the vomit from Amy's mouth.

"Help!" she cried out seeing the front door was closed, no one would hear her and Chad had just left. "Oh God, I'm alone!" Christy screamed as the seizure went on and she didn't know what to do. No one had prepared her for this, in the past Amy had never done this shaking as she was now. In the past no seizure had been like this.

Amy was too pale, Christy saw and her lips were now blue turning almost purple. This was an emergency. She needed help, this little girl needed her mommy to help her. Leaving Amy on her side on the floor Christy jumped up and ran for the phone hitting 911 before going back down to Amy's side. "My child," she screamed into the phone and the operator that answered told her to calm down.

"Tell me what's going on ma'am," the cool toned operator ordered of her and Christy nodded her head holding Amy, the child positioned on her side and still violently shaking.

"My child," Christy cried, "she's epileptic. I think she's having a seizure."

"How long ma'am?" the operator asked and Christy looked at the clock judging that Chad had left about ten minutes ago. "Seven maybe eight minutes," she spoke into the phone crying hard when she did.

"Is your front door unlocked?" the operator asked and Christy shook her head instead of answering. "Ma'am, if the door isn't unlocked; get up and go unlock the door or my men are going to break your door down."

"I can't leave my baby," Christy whimpered into the phone.

"How old is she?" the operator's voice changed to casual, as though they were having lunch together talking of their children rather than Christy alone and holding her daughter, seeing Amy was now gray, her lips blue.

"She's eighteen months old and she's gray and her lips were blue," Christy screamed and the operator told her to tilt the child's head back and making certain there's nothing in Amy's mouth, then to give rescue breaths. As Christy had taken a CPR class she knew what to do and dropping the phone she gave Amy several breaths feeling Amy's body was still ridged.

A hard knock sounded at the front door and a voice calling out, "fire department," was all that would have made Christy leave Amy. She ran to the door and pulled it open thankful not to be alone before running back to her child. "We need oxygen in here," the fireman yelled beyond the door and Christy saw several men now bending over Amy.

"Do you have a rescue medication for her seizures ma'am?" a paramedic asked as he came into the house pulling a dark yellow stretcher.

"No," Christy said while standing near her child and wringing her hands.

"Put your shoes on ma'am," a fireman spoke from beside her and she wondered where he had come from. "You're going to the hospital." Christy ran and grabbed her bedroom slippers pushing her feet into them as the fireman handed her Chad's coat that was on the back of the dining chair.

"What medications does she take for her epilepsy," the Paramedic asked as they put Amy on the stretcher, her color wasn't gray now and her lips were a deep dark pink.

"Tegretol," Christy said running after the stretcher and soon she was being helped into the ambulance.

The paramedic was on a phone talking to someone and telling them their ETA was two minutes. At that moment it started again, Amy pulled inward with her limbs, her eyes rolled back and she began shaking all over again. The paramedic quickly rolled Amy to her side and Christy cried out in terror as the seizure took over their lives.

Amy was rushed on the stretcher into the emergency room. An IV was started right away and several doctors were standing over her as the seizure continued. Within a few minutes the emergency room doctor was talking to the neurologist and Christy had moved closer to hear the conversation when she saw Chad coming down the hallway.

"I was at the vet and the neighbor said you'd come here in an ambulance," he grabbed his wife and looked beyond the curtain at Amy very pale and very small in the bed.

"We're going to medivac her to the children's hospital. The neurologist will meet you there," the emergency room doctor said this as he shook Chad's hand. "Your little girl has had two grand mal seizures and the IV Valium doesn't seem to be helping. We've switched to Ativan in the IV now and she should be stable for the ride to Pensacola."

"Can I go with her?" Christy asked and the doctor nodded his head.

"You'll have to follow in your own car, sir," the doctor said to Chad and Chad looked down at his wife.

"You have to go home and pack a bag," Christy said and looked at her feet. "I need shoes Chad and warm clothes. Amy's diaper bag is hanging on a hook in her bedroom. I have it packed with a change of clothes already. Grab my toothbrush and toothpaste." She saw him nod his head before he went to his daughter and kissed Amy's forehead.

"I love you little one," he spoke in a tear filled voice. "Well," he turned to his wife as he spoke. "We know now why she's not been smiling and talking."

"I'm frightened," Christy broke into tears as the ambulance crew came back and asked them to move aside.

"She'll be all right," Chad hugged his wife. "Look at all of these people around her; they're taking good care of her."

"I hope so," Christy said as she hurried after the stretcher holding her precious and sweet child not seeing Chad had hurried in the opposite direction. He was going home to grab their things and to let Hollywood know he might not be at work Monday.

PICU at Sacred Heart Hospital was a good place to be. All of the nurses were kind and caring and showed nothing but compassion to Christy as they got Amy settled right away into a room. Before Chad arrived the neurologist came into the room and he explained that Amy might have built up a tolerance to the medication and the Tegretol needed to be increased. Amy lay in the bed hooked up to the IV and to the portable EEG machine and the neurologist stopped and looked at the machine. Before he left the room and Christy knew, Chad wasn't going to get to hear what the neurologist had said and she was going to have to tell him.

Christy hated relaying information. The truth was, Christy was haunted by her past in ways no one understood, not even Christy. She closed her eyes and sat down in the chair next to the bed Amy was in and went back in her mind to her past, a past that she couldn't change and a past that had created her.

She was a lair and liars lied well, her abuser had told her time and time again. She made molehills into mountains. He had told everyone not to believe a word that Christy said and she knew, if you asked one of her relatives what Christy was like, they would say simply, "she's a liar." It benefited her abuser to have her known as a liar, if she ever told on him, if she breathed a word of what he had done to her, no one would believe her. She was a liar.

But today, Christy looked at Amy, today had been no molehill she had created into a mountain. Today had been a huge mountain. Today she wasn't a liar, an ambulance team and firemen had seen what was happening to her daughter. Doctors and nurses and paramedics had seen. Today had been real and she wished today that she was that liar she was said to be by her abuser for all those years. And when Chad came in, she'd have to tell him what the neurologist said and she wouldn't be lying by telling him that Amy needed a higher dose of drugs, drugs they didn't want Amy to need.

Chad came into the hospital room and saw his wife crying and his little girl pale on the bed. He put down the bags that he had packed and went to Christy. "I saw the neurologist in the hallway," Chad spoke gently and felt his wife relax unaware that she hadn't wanted to tell him what the neurologist had said to her. "He said it's a breakthrough seizure and we'll increase the Tegretol and all will be well. No more worries and now we know why she's not been herself for the past couple of days. Our girl will be smiling again in no time flat."

"I was so scared," Christy said and they sat down in the chair together and she told him of Amy vomiting and of how their child had turned blue and gray and she had to breathe for Amy.

"I'm glad I wasn't there," Chad held his wife closer and let her cry, he felt like crying with her and he had learned something in these last few hours, something that he knew Christy was already aware of as she'd spoken to him of this fear. They were alone. They had no one. They were a typical military family far from home and they only had one another to rely on and Amy to take care of and often, too often, he feared, his wife was on her own. Chad was gone from the base to a place he couldn't tell his wife where he was and she was all alone with only Amy and Amy wasn't well.

The neurologist came into the room and looked at the EEG for a long time. Amy had awakened, but she was still not herself and her parents both expressed this concern to the doctor as he looked at that EEG strip that he held in his hands.

"Guys," he looked up at the couple and saw their worried faces and he looked at the little girl that he had defined as cute as stink and he tried to sound calm and supportive, though he was well aware the little girl now appeared sluggish. "She needs time to recover. She had several grand mal seizures and the medication wasn't rescuing her." He dropped the EEG strip and went to Amy looking her over and no longer speaking to Chad and Christy, he was speaking to himself. "I've not increased her medication," the neurologist spoke slowly and carefully. "The IV drugs she's gotten while here shouldn't have caused this." He kept examining the little girl and then shrugged his shoulders.

"I'm going to add on another antiepileptic medication," he said turning back to face Chad and Christy. "The pharmacy will have that new medication and also I'm sending you home with rectal Diastat in case she has another grand mal. Wait three minutes from the start of the seizure and then administer the Diastat and the seizure should stop within five minutes. If it hasn't stopped, you need to call 911 again. Don't hesitate Christy. If the seizure goes beyond five minutes, Amy needs more help than you can give." The neurologist shook Chad's hand, patted Christy on the shoulder and looked back at Amy one last time. I'll see you in four weeks; my office will call with the appointment time."

The couple thanked the neurologist and turned to their daughter hoping that soon their little smiling girl would be back to them smiling from ear to ear and life would be as it was.

Chad had listened to his wife crying in the night, he had awakened her and held her too many times and she wasn't getting better. Whatever the nightmares were, he had to find someone that could make them go away. After an hour of pleading with his wife to tell him what the nightmares were about he sat in stunned silence listening to her as she paced in front of his lazy boy chair, Amy asleep in his arms.

"I'm a liar Chad," she said to him. "What if I'm making Amy's epilepsy worse than it is? We're giving her all of these drugs." Chad knew his wife's fears. While he had been at work Amy had two more grand mal seizures and the Diastat hadn't helped, both times Amy had to go to the emergency room.

Something's the Matter with Amy

"You're not a liar," Chad said in a gentle way very aware of the abuse she had suffered. He had been living with her for nearly three years now. He could see by her behaviors that she was scared all the time. She didn't need to tell him what had happened to her, he was her husband, he was her intimate partner, he knew her well and he further knew Christy needed protecting because of her past. There were predators out there that were looking for someone to tear down, and his wife was that someone. He could compare Christy to the peck order with chickens; the stronger chickens in the pen pecked the weakest chicken to death.

"I make molehills into mountains," Chad heard his wife say as she came to a standstill in front of him.

"This," he lifted Amy up in his arms, "is a mountain. And I'm going to get us some help. Living with a child that's epileptic is hard and it's making you question yourself. I know you've had therapy in the past, but this is going to be someone for you. A support system for you and for me as we learn to handle all these seizures and be the parents of an epileptic child." Chad saw Christy relax and he was thankful that he knew what to do. Chad could figure out almost anything, and this had come easy to him. He had only had to make a phone call.

Chapter Eleven

Psalm 18:2: "The LORD is my rock, my fortress and my deliverer."

Two weeks before Christmas, Nancy came into their lives. Nancy had taught the baby class to new parents and she knew Chad as the class clown. She also knew that Christy was timid and frightened and easily intimidated. The relationship between Christy and Nancy was established that first day Nancy came to their home and the relationship was defined as Nancy being Christy's friend first.

"I'm the base social worker," Nancy said as she sat down beside Christy and reached for Amy holding the little girl on her lap. Nancy knew Amy and Christy well; the two had taken her parenting classes on base and were a part of the mothers group. Nancy found Christy to be very loving and patient of both Amy and Chad and Nancy knew Amy as the smiling child that called out in a sweet voice for Pooh bear and her Dad.

"You were there when Chad changed Amy's first diaper," Christy said to Nancy as they faced one another and talked.

"Yes, and I was there with the lactation consultant when you and Chad weren't getting Amy to latch on. I was also at the hospital the day she had two seizures and was medivaced to the

Children's hospital in Pensacola." Nancy leaned back and looked at Amy sitting still and silent on her lap. "On Halloween this little one wouldn't stop talking about trick or treating and eating candy."

"She doesn't talk so much now," Christy spoke in a quiet worried voice and Nancy put Amy down to play on the floor seeing the child lay down and become very still.

"Let's talk about you," Nancy turned and took Christy's hands. "Chad has told me some of your past."

"I'm a liar," Christy blurted out to Nancy. "I seek attention like my mother did and what if Amy's not an epileptic and I'm giving her these mind altering drugs."

"Any mother would feel this way," Nancy spoke in a calm and reasonable way to an upset mother, a mother that had a right to feel this way and needed all of Nancy's support. "It would be so much easier if this were something you were doing than what it really is." Nancy looked down at the child laying on the floor and being very very still. This was a child that had been smiling all the time. This was a child that was talking in five and ten words at a time. This was a child that was running at a year old. Nancy was afraid for little Amy Bac. Something was very wrong and that something had nothing to do with Christy and everything to do with epilepsy.

"Nancy stayed for four hours," Christy said to Chad when he came in from work. "Do you remember when she came to visit after the parenting class we took on Halloween and Amy ran to the door jumping up and down screaming out Daddy because you were home early from work?"

"I remember," Chad leaned down and kissed his wife.

"Nancy said Amy's quiet and she said I'm not making this up. She's going to come twice a week not to see me Chad," Christy reached down and picked up Amy. "She's coming to see Amy. She said if it is the medication causing Amy to be sluggish, we'll know soon enough."

"And I'm home for Christmas," Chad said as they sat down to dinner. "We're going to my mom's for the holiday. Let's take our minds off of this epilepsy and just get away."

"We have her medications," Christy said to her husband as she put Amy in the highchair. And maybe if this is something I'm doing, Christy thought, surrounded by Chad's family they'll see it's me and point that out and I can change whatever I'm doing that's causing this to happen to Amy.

She didn't know. Christy didn't understand that what she was feeling was normal and expected. When you don't have control of a situation, when you can't find a way to stop what's happening, you turn inward and blame yourself. With epilepsy and seizures there is no control. The seizures don't have a schedule, there is no warning to when they're going to start or when they're going to finish. The parents are helpless and they live in fear and that's where Christy was living now – in fear.

Haunted in the night that Amy might have a seizure and need her and she was asleep was causing this worried mother to not sleep well and to have nightmares. Haunted in the day that Amy would fall in a seizure and get hurt, and Amy already had fallen and suffered a black eye with Christy only feet away from the child when Amy fell was proving Christy's fears were valid.

When you're living in a world that's out of control, completely out of your control, then you find someone or something to blame. And for Christy, she blamed herself. With her past controlled by an abuser, with that abuser blaming her for his having to hit her, because she didn't behave correctly was making this situation with Amy's epilepsy even worse. Her past was making it easy for Christy to blame Christy.

She walked normally. She ran really well, Christy thought as she watched her daughter in the rest area along I-10 chase after their dog Blackberry in the grassy field near a river they had just driven across. Amy seemed to be in constant motion. The past few days had seen the little girl in constant motion. Even now the child was running in a circle instead of after the dog.

"Is this normal?" Christy knew this wasn't normal and she blamed the only thing that she could blame for the change in her daughter – the dramatic and obvious change was because of the seizure medication.

Chad ran his hands over his head before shaking his head looking at Amy and speaking to Christy in a frantic voice filled with frustration and concern. "What the hell happened?" he asked Christy and he didn't see the tears falling from her eyes. "This is insane. I've lost my daughter. Did you talk to the neurologist like I told you too?" these last words were very nearly yelled at Christy.

"Yes," she cried harder and saw Amy running still in a circle. "He said we'd address the medication at her next appointment."

"She's not spoken a word in weeks," Chad said as he reached for their dog, a dog that Amy was no longer chasing as Amy was running wild and in a circle.

"Her primary care doctor said she doesn't have anything to say right now,"

"Bull," Chad's one word interrupted whatever else his wife might have said. "Something's wrong and I've lost my daughter." Chad turned his angry glare on his wife not seeing her back away from him and he didn't see her fear. He was too torn up over what had happened to Amy in the past eight weeks and no one was taking this seriously.

But soon, far too soon, someone would be taking Amy's situation seriously and Christy would walk away broken. The holiday was a disaster. Everyone in the family could see within minutes that something was wrong with Chad and Christy's child and many hastened to point out what they saw as wrong. Amy wouldn't leave the light switch alone and on and off the lights were turned all day long unless Christy moved Amy away and Christy was always moving Amy away.

They had seen the family in September and now there were questions aimed at Christy that she couldn't answer. "Amy was fine the last time I saw her," and Christy agreed that was true. "She was talking endlessly when I was visiting," again Christy agreed this was true. "What do the doctors say?" this was asked in a demanding way.

"She has nothing to say right now," Christy answered honestly and still more questions came from the family, questions Christy couldn't answer and sadly, Amy was lost in a world that Chad, Christy or none of this family could enter. Something had happened to this little girl and that something happened in a seizure.

Chad packed his family up the day after Christmas and headed home with his wife crying the whole way home. And he knew, his wife was blaming herself. Sadly, their appointment with the neurologist wasn't until mid January and an appointment with the primary care doctor was the usual and Chad spoke up to that doctor in complete frustration.

"If she has nothing to say, fine," Chad's tone was belligerent as he faced the doctor. "But look at her; she's not in our world. My wife can't get her to interact or play. And you don't understand, my wife and Amy are a team. I'm gone a lot and it's just the two of them. Amy has always clung to Christy and now," he pointed to his child standing in a corner spinning, "Christy is alone, that child's not here."

And still the primary insisted that Amy was fine and would interact and speak when she was ready to do so. He pointed out that Amy was only nineteen months old. The little girl had talked well in the past, it was reasonable to assume that she'd talk well in the future and as soon as the antiepileptic medication was sorted out, Amy would be smiling again.

"You better be right," Chad roared at the doctor before reaching and picking Amy up into his arms. "Idiot," he said within hearing distance of the doctor and he did so with intent.

"Chad," Christy looked back at the doctor knowing that the man had care of their child and her tone was one that let Chad know she was upset with his having called the doctor an idiot.

"I'm sorry," he put his arm around his wife and handed Amy to her. "I gotta get to work," he kissed her quick and watched his wife go off in the direction of the pharmacy. He knew where she was going, the escalators. Amy loved to ride up and down the hospital escalators and every day Christy would walk here and ride those escalators with her child, something that Amy use to look forward too.

"I've written a letter of my concerns to Amy's neurologist," Nancy said to Christy the morning before their appointment with the neurologist in Pensacola. "I mailed it last week so he should have seen it by now and I want you to have a copy."

Christy took the letter from Nancy and read of Nancy's concerns. The blank stares, the faraway looks Amy often had. She also wrote how Amy's lips would have a bluish tint to them in these episodes. Nancy reported in the formal letter that only a social worker could write that Amy no longer ran to the door excited to see Daddy, she no longer played with her cars and trains at the table. That the child had changed again right before Christmas and was now in constant motion and appeared deaf.

Reading this letter made Christy relax and settle down. She had been torn up for days over the Christmas visit and Nancy gave her a quick hug. "Listen to me," Nancy said this as she looked at Amy. "She's not well. I don't know what she has, but she's not well and it's not your fault. You need to learn how to fight now Christy. You need to learn how to fight for Amy. And you need to fight for yourself. You can't answer the families question now nor could you at Christmas and it's unreasonable of them to question you. If they can't be supportive of this child and her parents, then they need to back off."

"But what if this is the medication?"

"This isn't the medication," Nancy spoke in a certain way and when Christy saw the neurologist enter the room an hour later she knew, this wasn't the medication.

"The far off looks and staring are very likely seizure activity," the neurologist said to Christy with Chad sitting beside his wife. "I want another sleep deprived EEG done next month and I want to increase the Tegretol. If this continues, I'm probably going to change the medications. But first, let's give the Tegretol a chance."

Amy slept through the entire appointment so the neurologist didn't get to see the changes in her. He didn't get to see the constant motion or the running in a circle. Chad and Christy both told him and he nodded his head in understand and then told them what they had already suspected. "That behavior is probably the medication. Let's do that EEG in a few weeks."

"Tegretol in a large amount can cause that," one of Chad's troops said to Christy and she frowned up at the man wishing that he wasn't standing with the sun to his back. "Chad's all worried over Amy and all that's wrong with her is the Tegretol."

Christy had been out on a walk with Amy, she hadn't meant to run into this man. From the first time that she had met him, she hadn't like him. He reminded her of the abuser in her past, he didn't look like the man, but he acted like him. Self important, Christy thought and right now she didn't like the way that he was talking to her. He wasn't a doctor, he wasn't even a nurse.

"I have to go home," Christy said and turned the stroller with Amy in it around and away from this man.

"You need to stop drugging this child and she'll talk and smile and be like she was before," the man called after her and Christy picked up her pace running home. "Stop drugging the kid!"

"Hey you," Chad said as she came in the garage door. "What's wrong," he saw that she was crying and he went to her.

"Nothing, just the sun in my eyes," Christy made excuse and lifted Amy up out of the stroller.

"Let's go out to Chinese," he said taking Amy from her. "Go grab your purse."

"Chad," she spoke his name as they were getting in the car. "Your buddy said Amy isn't talking because of the Tegretol." When she said this she saw Chad go stiff in the car beside her.

"Yeah," Chad looked at her quickly and then back at Amy. "He was studying once to be a nurse. He's a jerk, ignore him."

"Okay," Christy said also looking back at Amy. This buddy of her husband's did know something of medicine. More than she knew, Christy thought looking at her little girl that had changed so drastically and was now lost in one of those stares.

The Tegretol had been increased. Pinching her lips together Christy remembered the neurologist's nurse had called to discuss the frequency of staring spells and the nurse had said the neurologist probably would have us wean off of Tegretol and onto another medication. With this in mind, Christy knew, she was going to start weaning Amy off of Tegretol now, three weeks before their next appointment and hopefully by then Amy would be smiling again and all would be right. Everything for Amy would be back to the way that it was before the Tegratol was increased.

Christy couldn't go into the neurologist's office and sit in the outer room and wait with Amy. The truth was Christy couldn't go anyplace and wait with Amy. Even going to the base hospital to ride the escalators had stopped being something Christy could do with Amy and now she watched as her little girl ran up and down the hall outside of the neurologist's office making that loud squealing noise.

"Excuse me," a doctor in a white coat came up to Christy and touched her shoulder. "Are you seeing the neurologist?" he pointed to the door that led to the neurologist's office.

"Yes," Christy said and she saw Chad stick his head out beyond the door.

"They're ready for us," Chad said nodding toward the doctor that was standing with his wife.

"Make certain that the neurologist knows about this," the doctor said before he walked away.

"How's it going guys?" the neurologist asked as he came into the room more than thirty minutes later and all he saw was Amy asleep in Christy's arms. The little girl had worn herself out running in the hallway and now the neurologist wasn't going to get to see how active Amy had become. Christy looked at Chad and thought she'd let him do the talking this time, but he said nothing and she knew, he was waiting for the neurologist to tell them the results of the sleep deprived EEG.

"The EEG was what I expected," the neurologist said looking at Amy's file and not her parents. "Tell me how things are going," he pulled his stool up and faced Christy.

"I did something wrong," Christy said this not looking at her husband, but from the corner of her eye she could see him looking at her with a shocked expression on his face. "My husband's co-worker told me that the reason Amy isn't talking is because of the Tegretol. He said that's why she's like she is and I knew you were going to start weaning her off of the medication and weaning her onto the Topomax alone so I started weaning her off the Tegretol and she's only on a fraction of the dosage and she's still not talking again and she's not smiling."

"That jerk told you the medication was making Amy not talk?" Chad asked in an angry voice before the neurologist could speak.

"The night we went to Chinese, he stopped me on my walk with Amy and he told me that and then you said he was studying to be a nurse and I wanted Amy to talk and smile again,"

"Good grief," Chad shouted. "The man is a jerk, not a medical professional!"

"Calm down folks," the neurologist said seeing Christy was now crying and the veins in Chad's neck were sticking out and the father of his patient was red in the face. "I was going to wean Amy off of the Tegretol anyway. Though Christy," he faced the mother and saw her looking up at him. "I want you to be assured; the Tegretol has nothing to do with Amy's not talking and smiling. Don't listen to anyone else about Amy's medications or epilepsy but me. I'm the one that has the test results and I'm Amy's doctor. That man doesn't know what he's talking about and seizures can kill a person. We need seizure control first and foremost for Amy." The neurologist then tuned to Chad and saw the father of Amy was calming down.

"This epilepsy has been hard on Christy and I," Chad said and the neurologist nodded his head in understanding.

"When a mother is facing this kind of situation, she'll grasp at any and every answer that might help her child," the neurologist said in a compassion filled voice. "It's understandable that frightened parents will do anything to see their child well again. And I'm not saying this isn't going to get better again. What I'm saying is let doctors be doctors."

"The primary care doctor told us that Amy just doesn't want to talk," Chad said looking at his wife nodding her head and holding his hand.

"That's not a reasonable diagnosis for a little girl that was talking up a storm and is now silent," the neurologist said while shaking his head. "I heard that Eglin is going to have a Pediatric Developmental doctor coming in this spring. That's the right doctor for Amy. I'll see if I can get you in to him when he arrives. In the meantime, we're going to wean all the way off the Tegretol and go up on the Topomax."

"I'm sorry," Christy said to her husband and he hugged her knowing that she was desperate to have Amy back as Amy had been only a few short months ago.

"I know, she was so much fun and now it's as though we've lost our little girl." Chad leaned into his wife as the neurologist stood up and patted him on the shoulder.

"Sometimes it takes time to figure these things out," he went to the door after handing them the new prescriptions. "I'll see you back again in April."

The Tegretol was soon a thing of the past and there was no change in Amy. No talking and she still appeared deaf and ran in circles. Christy spent the day recording her on the video camera as Chad was gone again and she accepted the seizures as they were happening. Amy would fall to the floor rigid and stiff and her eyes rolled back in her head. Sometimes Amy would shake, other times she would just clinch her jaw and turn blue around the mouth. Several times the Diastat failed when the seizure went on more than three minutes and the ambulance came and took them to the emergency room. And every time the Diastat failed, Christy would cry and the neurologist would order an increase in the medication. This was becoming way of life, a way of life that no mother would want.

Nancy was Christy's saving grace at this time. The social worker was coming to the house three times a week with Chad gone and the social worker saw one of the seizures and like Christy, she was scared to death. They were frightening. The seizures took complete control and the seizures lasted as long as they wanted. It seemed no one could do anything more than ride them out, be it in the hospital or at home.

Chad returned home after being gone more than a month and he saw right away the change in his little girl. Not only was she not talking, but it was as though she were lost deep inside of herself, far worse than when Amy was on the Tegretol. She spun in a circle all the time; she was pinching her cheeks and biting herself. Christy's arms were covered in bite marks and the coffee table, Chad couldn't believe the condition of their coffee table. That article of furniture had been chewed up. Even Amy's blanket had been chewed on.

"If she's not spinning," Christy said to Chad as they watched Amy spin, "then she's standing on her head or she's running back and forth screaming. But wait, she's started doing something new." And it only took an hour before Chad saw his daughter running the water in the sink and splashing. "She does that night and day. I'm having her sleep in our bed with the door locked."

"We see the neurologist in five days," Chad said watching Amy as she ran past him. "She's as beautiful as ever," he spoke of his much loved child.

"And she's one hundred percent non-verbal," Christy said as Amy ran past her squealing to the top of her lungs.

"When did she start eating the coffee table?" Chad asked looking at what was left of the piece of furniture.

"Last week," Christy answered as Amy ran up to her and pushed on her hard.

"I'll take it out to the trash," Chad picked up the table thinking they didn't need something like this in the house for his daughter to chew on. This table might make her sick.

"I've been working on something," Christy said to him as she reached and picked up Amy, the little girl slapping Christy in the head and screaming loud as she did so. "It's in front of the car," she pointed and Chad went to the table that was painted a sky blue, a fire engine red and bright green.

"What is this?" he carried the table into the house passing Amy and Christy. "Stop beating on your Mama," he said to his little girl seeing Christy trying to avoid the blows from her daughter.

"Last week she snatched my earrings out," she said as she put Amy down on the sofa and went to the colorful table Chad had brought into the house as he looked at the tear marks in her ears where Amy had yanked out her earrings.

"Yikes," he said seeing the dried blood. "That must have really hurt."

"Only for a few hours," Christy said to him as she went to her knees. "Amy," she called the little girl's name uncertain if she might get a response from the child. "Look what Mommy has," and she held up Thomas the Train. "The table," Christy pointed to the table she had built, "is for Amy's train set."

"Cool," Chad fell to the floor on his knees and the parents put the train set together having more fun than Amy and aware the little girl was watching them, though Amy made no move to come and help.

"Wait," Christy said to Chad as he went to stand up after the trains and track were all in place, the wooden track he'd seen, had been chewed on.

"No way," Chad screamed as in less than one minute Amy had torn the track up and scattered the train on the floor.

"Wait," Christy said as Chad sat on the floor wondering what his little one was going to do next and thinking his little one had become a little monster.

Amy looked at the tracks and the trains, a look on her face that was blank and yet, the look wasn't blank. Within a few minutes the track was pieced together and the train set was just as Chad and Christy had made it only a few minutes ago and before Amy had destroyed the thing.

"That's impressive," Chad said and Christy stood up going to their bedroom.

"Watch this," she said and went to the dining table removing the plant in a vase she had there in the center and called out to her daughter seeing Amy sort of looking her way. "Amy," she spoke the child's name loud and clear as though Amy were deaf. "Look what Mommy has," she said again in the same way. "Come here and help Mommy."

Christy took a two hundred and fifty piece adult puzzle and dumped it into the center of the dining table. She saw Amy, not even two years old, climb up onto a chair and look at the lid of the puzzle before Christy put the lid of the puzzle on the kitchen counter.

"This will take a couple of hours," Christy said and went to Chad's suitcase intent on getting the laundry on.

"What will take a couple of hours?" Chad asked as he watched Amy with the puzzle pieces.

"Before she'll have the puzzle together," Christy answered and Chad laughed thinking that she was making a joke.

"Yeah, right," he said and watched as she emptied his things into the washing machine. "That's a two hundred and fifty piece puzzle baby. Amy's only a toddler. She can't put that together."

"Chad, things have changed," Christy said in a very serious voice. "Amy's part monkey, see her on the table. She climbs everything. You'll see, she can even climb into the windowsills. She's closed off and she's quiet and it's really sad, but she's also able to do amazing things. Wait, you'll see." Chad followed Christy back into the kitchen and saw her open the oven door and check on the chicken she had baking for dinner. "And we see the neurologist soon, I want you to bear witness when I tell the doctor all that Amy's doing."

"She's hitting and pinching and biting herself," Chad said looking down at his wife. "And anyone can see that she's hitting and biting you. I just took our coffee table that looked like leftovers of our daughter's dinner out to the trash; you don't need a witness Christy. Something has happened to our child and whatever it is, it's still happening."

"I'll show you more this weekend," Christy said to him more than two hours later as Chad stood at the dining table and looked at the puzzle put together. "And I only showed her the lid for the count of twenty Chad. This," Christy pointed to the completed puzzle, "this is amazing. She can write her name, Chad. She can write her own name and she's still a baby."

At five in the morning Chad woke up to find his daughter sitting in the windowsill more than four feet off the ground and his baby wasn't two feet off the ground. "How in the world?" he asked this as Christy reached for Amy and pulled the child in her arms putting Amy in the playpen and turning on the television with the Little Mermaid on again. Christy knew this movie by heart.

"I don't know how in the world she does these things," Christy said to her husband as she crawled back under the covers. "I never know what to expect next."

Over the course of the day Chad watched his daughter climb onto the top of her playhouse, she didn't go inside to play, Amy played on the roof. Christy sat down at the piano and played the song Greensleeves, he watched as Amy followed Christy's fingers and played the song with only a few mistakes. And he ran and snatched his little girl from off of the top of her chest of drawers as she was standing up and he was certain that she was going to fall.

"You weren't kidding when you said she was a monkey," Chad said to his wife as he sat with his chin in his fist and bent forward watching his little girl tear up the train set and then piece it back together. "That's not how you play with the Thomas, Amy!" he yelled at her as though yelling at her was going to get her attention. Instead Amy tore the train set up again and rebuilt the thing.

"That's how she plays with the train set," Christy said feeling that she wasn't alone in the wonder of what her baby could do. And for her, no matter what, Amy would always be her baby. "Chad," she sat down across from him and watched Amy. "I know she doesn't talk and she doesn't respond like she use too, but she's very neat. I love her. She's amazing." Christy reached on the table for a Disney World brochure and opened it up to the map before handing it to Amy. "Watch," she said to her husband as Amy sat down and seemed to be studying the map. "It's like she understands more than we do. It's like she sees more than we do."

"She is different," Chad said in an agreeable tone.

"I painted the back porch with blackboard paint while you were gone and I got chalk. I've not disturbed her drawings Chad." Christy stood up and Chad followed her looking at the floor of his back porch. "See," Christy pointed and Chad stepped forward seeing what his wife was showing him and amazed.

"Amy Lynn isn't even two years old," he said in awe as he looked back at his child.

"And you know what she's drawn," Christy looked back at Amy as well.

"That's Blackberry," Chad pointed to the dog Amy had drawn. "And the bear looks like Tenderheart Care Bear."

"And she wrote her name," Christy said seeing her husband bend down and touch the A and then the M written in chalk on their back porch.

"She can't talk," Chad said looking up at his wife, "but she can write."

On Sunday Christy spent the day showing Chad how Amy loved watching Winnie the Pooh, the cartoon series from the eighties. They watched ten episodes and Amy stood in front of the television, she never moved away from the television not even to sit down. After the shows were over and before dinner, Christy took Amy outside and Chad watched as his wife chased after their child riding her Big Wheels. She was an amazing little girl, Chad thought, full of energy and he ran to help Christy when he saw Amy get off of her Big Wheels and start to climb the mailbox.

"I told you she was a monkey," Christy laughed as Chad put Amy back on her Big Wheels and they chased the little girl home.

Chapter Twelve

John 14:25: Peace I leave you, my peace I give unto you; Let not your heart be troubled, neither let it be afraid

Chad Bac had a problem and he wasn't happy over the problem that he had. He honestly felt nothing could get worse in this moment until he came into the house and saw his wife's red and swollen eyes and her near hysterical crying. She knew, and he knew that she knew by the way she was looking at him. His only female co-worker had a big mouth, Chad thought as he pulled his hysterical wife into his arms feeling her head shaking against his chest.

"It's not true Chad and you know it's not true," she cried harder and Chad nodded his head.

"I told you that idiot was a jerk," Chad said to her as he sat down to remove his boots and he saw Amy was pinching her cheeks and his little girl's face was bruised up already from having done that in the night.

"No no baby," Christy spoke in a soothing way reaching down for Amy only to have the little girl slap her hard in the head. "I think this is her way of talking," Christy said as she attempted to avoid another blow to the head.

"I could talk that way to that jerk," Chad said putting his boots beside the table and stretching out in the chair.

"Tell me what he said Chad," Christy's voice was filled with her pleading and Chad closed his eyes missing Amy slap Christy hard in the side of the head, but aware of what had just happened as his wife cried out and he heard the noise of Christy being hit. There was nothing he could do to keep them safe from Amy's biting and hitting and pinching. He was powerless and he and Christy agreed, this wasn't Amy trying to ruin their day; this was an illness they needed to have diagnosed and properly treated.

"That jerk," Chad spoke in a frustrated voice, "told me he knew what was wrong with Amy." Chad reached for his little girl hoping to distract her and help Christy have a pain free moment.

"What did he say Chad? And be honest," Christy asked knowing this was important. In the neighborhood on this base no one would speak to her. Everyone was treating her like she was trash or worse and she knew the jerk was very popular on this base and in this area.

"He called me to his desk and he said he knew what was wrong with Amy," Chad tried rocking Amy, but she slapped him hard in the head and he put her down going to her train table and messing up the track and the trains hoping that his little girl would give him five minutes to talk to his wife by focusing on fixing this table back as it was. "He turned his computer screen around to a site on Munchausen's by proxy." Chad saw his wife breathing hard and he knew the insult this was to her as a mother and more so as a mother of a child that was in a lot of trouble.

"And everyone up and down this street knows that of me too," Christy started crying and Chad felt like crying with her.

"As we're trying to find out why Amy's changed and blaming ourselves and questioning what we did and what we're doing," Chad said to his wife as he sat down in front of her. "There are idiots out there pointing a finger at us and worse, at you when you're trying your very best to help Amy." Christy covered her face and cried harder. "Damn," Chad swore. "Why can't people see we're in hell right now?"

"Our child is in trouble and no doctor we've seen has any idea what's going on. Instead of offering support or being kind and understanding, people have to throw stones at us like we're not busted up enough," Christy cried these words and saw Chad nodding his head.

"And you're the one the stones are aimed at and you love our little girl most of all." Chad saw the train table had been set right and Amy came over, raised her arm and slapped her mother hard in the top of the head. "Good grief," he said and went to mess up the train table again while Christy pulled Amy onto her lap and kissed the little girl from her cheeks to her nose.

"Laugh for me baby mine," she pleaded of Amy and instead turned her head so that her face wouldn't take a direct hit from the arm Amy had swung at her. "She's not doing this to ruin my day," Christy said in a certain voice to her husband. "Think about it Chad. If you were unable to speak wouldn't you be frustrated and lash out at others?"

"I'd write what I wanted," Chad answered in a reasonable tone of voice. "But the truth is, if I couldn't read and write and talk," he looked at Amy get up and run to the sofa where she stood on her head, "I'd be mad as fire."

"And that's Amy," Christy said seeing Amy standing on her head with her legs held up high. "She's mad all over because no one can hear her. Her words are trapped inside of her. And when we saw the primary care doctor today, he said to use Melatonin to help her sleep at night."

"We've been using that for over two months and we've not slept a night yet," Chad said as he stood to go change his clothes for dinner. He and Christy knew the truth of their lives. Amy would fight going to sleep, she would scream to stay awake and it would be after one in the morning with Christy rocking and singing for hours before Amy finally went to sleep and then Amy was back up before five in the morning. And no naps in the daytime. "They'll blame the Topomax," Chad said to Christy and she nodded her head in agreement. Maybe the Topomax was to blame.

No one knew what they were living with and this situation. Biting, hitting, pinching, in constant motion, climbing on everything, swinging from the shower curtain, standing on her head and more. Just getting Amy from the front door of the house to their car was dangerous. The cars were going too fast down this road and there was no hope because no doctor they had seen had a solution. No doctor really saw the problem, Chad thought as he heard Christy screaming and he rushed into the kitchen to see that Amy had sunk her teeth into Christy's thigh.

Nancy wrote another letter to the neurologist, a detailed letter of Amy's behaviors. Chad had gone to his commanding officer and reported the accusation made by the jerk he worked with. Several other troops in the office also reported the incident and Chad and Christy along with Nancy, who had also reported the incident and explained how devastating this accusation was to an innocent mother learned that the jerk was soon getting out of the Air Force and they wouldn't be subjected to him again.

Anxious and nervous, Chad and Christy went into the neurologist's office and then waited their turn. This time Amy was awake and she was being as she had been much of the time these last few months. Christy had a secret, a secret she was keeping from Chad and she kept breathing hard and fast hoping that what she had learned and what she knew wouldn't be true.

The neurologist came into the room and sat down on the stool looking at Amy and not the little girl's parents. He frowned as he reached back and turned the lights off, Amy stood where she was with her back to him swinging a poster back and forth against the wall. He clapped his hand and made a booing noise and still Amy didn't turn to face him, she just kept swinging that poster back and forth on the wall. The neurologist turned the lights on and off, he made more noise and still no reaction. By the time he turned to face Chad and Christy, Christy was crying hard, tears covered her face.

"We have a problem guys," he said in a sorrow filled voice. He hadn't said 'Amy has a problem,' and he hadn't said to them that 'they' had a problem. He had included himself and for that, Christy knew that he was a good doctor. "She's autistic," he looked back at Amy as he said this. She wasn't even two years old yet and he was diagnosing autism and from the look he was giving to the child's parents, he felt certain they knew he was stating an obvious fact. "Here," he said and handed Christy a prescription from his prescription pad.

Christy looked down at the prescription and read what he had written, "Amy Bac has autism."

"Listen to me," the neurologist rolled on his rolling stool to the mother that was crying hysterically. "This is not your fault," he insisted. "You haven't done anything wrong."

"I need to tell you what happened," Chad said and he told of the jerk and Munchausen's by proxy and of the neighborhood having heard the horrible rumor.

"I have had Amy as my patient since she was three months old," the neurologist said to the parents of the little girl that still stood in front of the poster swinging it on the wall. "Her EEGs are not normal. They are indicative of this."

"Is this why?" Christy pulled the book from her purse and opened it up. "What to expect the toddler years," she showed Chad. "It has a paragraph on Carnitine deficiency and it says a child with that can have autism."

"I don't know if the low Carnitine in Amy is the reason for her autism and her epilepsy," the neurologist said in a patient voice. "Amy's Carnitine numbers are normal on the supplement so I think they aren't related. The military has a multidisciplinary clinic over

Something's the Matter with Amy

at Keesler Air Force Base. I'm going to refer Amy there right away. She's really too young to be diagnosed as autistic and I've read the social worker's letter showing hyperactivity and I don't want to prescribe Ritilan at this time either. I do want to add Tenex twice daily and you can keep using the Melatonin."

Christy reached for Amy and they followed the neurologist out of his office and he watched Amy in her mother's arms as Amy punched Christy in the head. He would write in his notes praising the parents for their patience and their love of Amy. They would have benefited hearing that from him, but much later they would know the truth of what he thought of them by obtaining all of his records on their child. On day they would know what he thought of them as Amy's parents and that would bring them comfort.

Chad was gone again and Christy was dealing with Amy's behaviors as best as she could. The little girl was talking again, the only thing was, Amy was talking in a language that only Amy understood. Chad insisted that his little one sound Chinese and Christy felt it was baby talk, either way, Amy was trying to communicate and that made Christy hopeful.

The warm summer mornings were spent on the back porch with Amy playing with her shape sorter or puzzles and the little girl did something that caused Christy to spend hours recording the little girl. Amy talked in her language to someone or something that Christy couldn't see. This was real, the child was interacting with something invisible and though it was odd, it was also as though little Amy Bac had a friend of her very own.

When Chad was home they took another four day trip to Disney World and even there Amy hit and pinched and bit herself and her mother. Christy's attitude was one of taking Amy out into the world no matter what. Amy would learn how to cope if they exposed her to things as though she didn't have autism and Amy was learning to cope as Christy was learning to cope with Amy's meltdowns.

The power went out during a storm in June and Chad wasn't home. Christy packed up Amy and went to the local Walmart knowing that there would be air conditioning there and she could get some shopping done. Amy did not like automatic doors, the little girl was terrified of those doors and Christy had to beg, plead and coax her daughter into the store. She hadn't realized in her lifetime how many places that she went that had automatic doors until she had Amy and now it seemed everywhere they went there were those doors.

"Well," a young woman in her twenties stood over Christy as she attempted to get Amy to calm down while sitting on the floor at the entranceway of Walmart and spoke of Amy. "If that child isn't the national pro abortion poster child, I don't know who is."

"Pro-abortion," Christy whispered to herself and realized this woman was saying that her precious Amy could be the poster child for abortion.

"Retard," the woman said and walked past Amy and Christy.

"I hope that woman doesn't have a child," a man in a wheelchair said.

"Amy's a sweet girl," Christy spoke up. "She's just afraid of automatic doors."

"I don't like them myself," the man said in a firm voice as Christy stood with Amy in her arms and reached for a cart doing what she had planned to do. Some hateful person's bad attitude wouldn't stop her and Amy from living. "I'm blessed to have you baby mine," Christy said to her Amy as the little girl sat in the cart. "God made no mistake in trusting you to me. We go together like corn and lima beans. We're succotash." Amy spoke in the language that only Amy understood and Christy hugged her child close. Life was good because Amy was in her life. The world might see Amy as autistic, but Christy saw Amy as her beautiful daughter.

The last two weeks of August Chad and Christy went back to Wright Patterson Air Force Base. Christy needed a break from all of Amy's therapies. The little girl was in speech, occupational and applied behavioral therapy twice a week. This had become Christy's career, driving to therapy and Amy wanted to stay home and play with her shape sorter and watch Winnie the Pooh. But for now, they were driving north with Amy watching a thirteen inch television with a ten hour tape her mother had made of Winnie the Pooh.

"I wish you could stay the whole two months I need to be here," Chad said when they checked into temporary leave quarters and Christy noted that the world seemed uneven. "Are you all right?" Chad asked and she nodded her head certain that she wasn't all right, but she didn't want to tell Chad that.

"I have to keep Amy on her routine of therapies," Christy said as she unpacked and settled Amy into their temporary place. "A two week break and then we're going back to it. All of the therapists are seeing how smart Amy is. She has normal intelligence. If we can just get her talking the speech therapist is certain that she'll stop hitting and biting."

"I'm all for that," Chad said as he lifted his wife's hands and saw scars that would be there for life of his daughter's teeth where they'd bitten into the back of Christy's hands. "Poor girl," he said speaking of both Amy and his wife.

She never complained, Chad thought as he watched Christy brushing Amy's teeth later that night as they got ready for bed. Amy grabbed the toothbrush and poked his wife in the eye and Christy never cried out or complained. He had seen Amy pulling her hair, biting her, even running into Christy with her head and knocking Christy down to the floor. And in everything he had seen, in everything that he had known in these past hard months of losing the child they had, Christy never complained. And some idiot that had no idea what was happening in their house blamed this angel that he was married too.

"I love you," he said to her as he came to bed and saw Amy was tucked up between them. "You're a good mother."

"You're a good Daddy," Christy said laying on the pillow beside him and looking at him as he turned on his side and faced her with Amy staring at nothing and still for the second.

"I suck compared to you," Chad spoke honestly and he knew this was the truth. "I've left too much of her care to you."

"When you're home you're at every doctor appointment, Chad. You know what's going on with her because you watch the videos and read my diary." Christy kissed his hand and he ruffled her hair before turning out the lights.

"One day Amy will read those diaries you keep and we'll laugh at the hard times we've had and be thankful for the good times to come." In the darkness Amy cuddled up into her mother's arms, they had been sleeping this way since the tenex had first started being given to Amy. "And it's nice to get some sleep for a change," Chad joked, the last words spoke before they all went to sleep.

Something wasn't right with Christy's world. She had known something was uneven in her stance the whole two weeks in Wright Patterson but now driving home to Eglin she knew there was something very wrong with her world. She had to change Amy's diaper in Kentucky and get a drink and she almost fell, she had fallen several times in the past weeks but dismissed it as being tired. Now, with Amy on tenex, she was sleeping and yet she was still falling.

Chad called her when she entered Alabama and she told him she had to get back to flat land, she was dizzy in these hills. But getting back into Florida didn't help; in fact the dizzy was ruling her life. She managed to get Amy into the house after fifteen hours on the road and it was well after midnight before they got to sleep.

Something woke her up at six in the morning and she sat up fast in the bed seeing that Amy was gone. Her heart stopped for a second when she saw the gate knocked down that she had in front of her door to keep Amy confined to her room in the night in case the little girl woke up. "Oh God," she prayed in fear as she went out and in relief she saw the front door and the sliding door both closed, Amy was still in the house. And then she saw felt the wind blowing and she knew, the carport door was open. She had a child proof cap over the knob and that cap was half on the floor, the other half outside the door.

"Amy!" she screamed as she ran out onto the carport and saw the water across the street and no sign of Amy. Her little girl loved water! These words echoed in her brain as Christy ran in her nightgown and barefooted across the street and into the water screaming for her child. A neighbor saw her and thinking she was insane, that neighbor had called the base security police.

The officer pulled her out of the water not understanding a word she said. She was hysterical and she knew that she was hysterical and her husband was far away and couldn't talk for her. She had to calm down and make known what had happened. "My two and half year old daughter," she spoke this and the officer knew what she was going to say and he pushed the button on his radio.

"We have a missing two and half year old girl," he said seeing the mother go back into the water. "She might be in bear creek or in the bay."

Several of the neighbors knew that Amy wasn't well, and many of those neighbors had heard the rumor of Christy having Munchausen's by proxy. Right now, none of that mattered to them, they all banned together and went searching for the little missing girl.

"Christy!" Nancy called out her name waving frantically to her as the security police officer helped her to her house.

"She's gone Nancy," Christy was crying too hard to talk. "I lost her." She took Nancy's hand and showed Nancy the child proof cap that had been over the doorknob and the one still over the front door. She didn't know the security officers had followed her into the house and were also taking photos and making notes of the gate in front of her bedroom door crashed down.

"I'm so sorry," Nancy hugged her. Christy had taken every precaution and still Amy had gotten out of the house. And sadly the statistic showed that autistic children drowned because they had no fear of water.

"We've got her," an officer ran into the house and Christy rushed to the front door pulling off the safety cap and snatching the door open. Expecting to see someone coming out of the river across the street with the dead body of her child, she screamed when she saw Amy, the little daughter that she adored was hugging her blanket and walking down the sidewalk seemingly oblivious to everyone around her. The child walked up the driveway and into the house and sat down in front of the television staring at the blank screen.

"I knew your little girl was deaf or something," a Marine that lived across the street spoke to Christy as though it were completely natural to be speaking to someone in a soaking wet nightgown at her front door surrounded by security police and the base social worker. "I saw her leaving the house at four this morning when I was going to work and I approached her but she never even looked at me. So all this time I've been following her." The Marine looked at the man in charge of the security police and spoke to him. "She tried to go into the six lanes of traffic on Eglin Parkway, she walked eleven blocks and never even looked at me when I yelled, 'hey kid,' and I yelled that a lot. I stood in front of her to keep her out of the road and she finally came back here."

Christy had heard enough. She ran to her little girl and picked her up cuddling her close and crying hard not caring what anyone thought. Amy was the way Amy was and Christy was thankful the little girl was her daughter. All she wanted in this life was her little daughter and her husband Chad.

"Thank you God, thank you," she kept saying over and over again. All that mattered was that Amy had come home.

Chad was still in Wright Patterson when the snow was falling. Christy had gone through three grand mal seizures with Amy; all three the, little girl had required rescue breaths and a trip to the hospital with an IV of Ativan. The Diastat never worked and Christy was upset, frightened and frustrated.

Christy was also dealing with her own issue of dizzy spells and falling, but she had no time to focus on herself. There were therapies for Amy and back to the neurologist where he decided to wean her off of the Topomax and onto Depakote. They had already tried Keppra and Lamictal and neither had stood alone, so now they were on the Depakote sprinkles and they would see where that would lead them in this battle with the seizures.

Chad came home for Christmas and they didn't go to be with any of the family. As a couple they felt it was best not to take a long trip on roads where there were very long stretches of nothing. With Amy's seizures so uncontrolled and the Diastat not working, home was the safest place to be. And too, they were dealing with Amy's behaviors and therapy wasn't getting the little girl to talk yet though she was saying one or two words they understood by now.

Chapter Thirteen

John 14:27: "Peace is what I leave with you; it is my own peace that I give you. I do not give it as the world does. Do not be worried and upset; do not be afraid."

In early January they were notified that they were accepted to be studied at the multi-disciplinary clinic at Keesler Air Force Base. They had to be there at seven in the morning so Chad had decided to drive to Biloxi, Mississippi the day before and get a hotel room. There was a problem when they arrived, the hotel didn't have their reservation and with the gambling that went on in Gulf Port, there were no rooms available. Chad tried temporary quarters on the base and at nearly midnight they had a place to stay worrying because it was so late and they had to be at the hospital at six in the morning and neither Chad nor Christy knew what to expect the next morning.

The day was long and hard for Amy and for her parents. They had seen the Chief Neurologist that was stationed here at Keesler over at their base, Eglin Air Force Base, two months before and he had been more than kind of their little girl. Today Amy ran down the hallway screaming her head off as she often did and the neurologist ran after her and picked her up giving her a hug and smiling at her parents. This neurologist was a wonderfully kind man that

Something's the Matter with Amy

seemed to care a great deal for his patients. Christy was glad to be here and she hoped that there would be help for Amy, that Amy would start talking again.

The neurologist had seen Christy fall and he took an interest in the way that she walked hearing her laugh that she walked like a drunk. Within an hour of being with him, he told Christy to call him when she was diagnosed as he felt this might be connected Amy.

The geneticist came in with the neurologist and sat down with Christy hearing of her balance and dizzy issues. He then pulled out paper and pen and started making a chart of Christy's family tree. Christy was suffering from balance issues with an abnormal gait and stance was clumsy, falling often. Her mother Sara had died young of multiple sclerosis and and now Amy was having troubles with seizures. Asked if her mother was epileptic Christy confirmed that yes, her mother Sara had indeed been an epileptic.

A pattern was established and Christy didn't know that until right now. "My mother's uncle was a neurologist," Christy said thinking of Jack and how he was elderly now and retired. "He lives on Dolphin Island. He can give me more information about my mother and her family if you think it's important to helping Amy."

"I think it will help," Doctor Michael, the geneticist said to Christy and saw her write down his information to send him her family history after she met with her Uncle Jack.

"Is Amy autistic?" Christy came right out and asked the neurologist and the man refused to say that Amy was autistic.

"What came first for this child?" the neurologist asked of Chad and Christy and they saw the geneticist listening to what they'd say intently.

"The latch on problem," Chad said and the neurologist shook his head.

"Lots of babies have that problem Chad," he spoke patiently with the geneticist standing next to him, the geneticist was nodding his head. "A common problem is latching on shortly after birth and Amy conquered that problem within a few weeks."

"The anterior fontanelle closing prematurely," Christy said holding Amy in her arms when she said this.

"Another common issue we see in children and the MRI and CAT scan showed that wasn't going to hinder Amy in anyway and it certainly didn't. Amy met all early milestones in advance." The neurologist looked at the geneticist.

"The epilepsy," the geneticist spoke slowly and carefully. "The autism followed the epilepsy much later. Amy's been dealing with grand mal and partial complex seizures since infancy."

"Amy's Carnitine level was low," Christy hurried to say and the geneticist agreed with her.

"Often right after mothers finish breast feeding their baby the Carnitine will test low. Amy's levels are normal now and have been for months. The genetic testing shows that she has only one of the genes that cause Carnitine deficiency; she needs two, so she can't have that disease. We need to look for something else. We need to know if your mother had multiple sclerosis." The Geneticist had looked at Amy's toes, he had looked at the whorls in her hair and he had measured every inch of her and he had ordered several tests to be run and all tests would come back normal.

Three months later, Christy spoke again to the Keesler Air Force Base Neurologist and she pinned him down on the autism issue. All the doctors at home were saying autism but this doctor refused to do so.

"The autism diagnosis opens doors to therapies and services," the Keesler Neurologist said patiently. "Amy has delays and peaks and valleys. She has behaviors we expect to see in autism but Amy pretend plays. In my office she picked up a banana and turned it into a phone. She's a very social little girl with fantastic eye contact. She only presents with behaviors. I honestly feel there's something else happening with Amy and we need time to figure out what that something is."

Christy had to accept what this doctor was saying and his whole team at the clinic. Not one of them would confirm a diagnosis of autism; in fact, they all were steadfastly against diagnosing Amy with autism. They would NOT be the last doctors that saw Amy and questioned the autism diagnosis.

Chad left again after they're return from Keesler and Christy was alone with Amy. The seizures were not well controlled and several more trips to the emergency room via ambulance were needed with IV medication to stop the seizures. Amy was also medivaced to Sacred Heart in Pensacola in one of those seizures that was prolonged, only this time Chad was gone and Christy was there alone with no one to even bring her a change of clothes.

The neurologist came into the room after another EEG had been done and he increased the Depakote. He asked Christy if this was all that she was seeing in Amy, these convulsive seizures, and Christy said that it was. He then spent an hour talking with Christy and explaining to her that one in every four autistic children were epileptics and Amy fit that criteria, there was nothing he could do; the little girl was autistic and she was epileptic.

Jodi, Christy's long time friend drove over to Sacred Heart and brought Christy and Amy home on the day that Amy was released from PICU. Christy didn't know what to do, and she cried in Jodi's car half of the trip back to the base. Jodi was supportive and called all doctors clown for not being able to figure out one little girl. Jodi had also seen the normal development in Amy, the little girl was walking and talking early, this regression and these seizures were awful and Jodi was vocal in stating that what was happening to little Amy Bac as far as Jodi could see, just was not normal. This was scary.

In late May, Chad finally came home. Christy picked him up from the airport and the couple hurried home happy to be together after months apart. Amy had changed while her father was gone. The little girl was calmer, she was quiet and she spent hours at her train table and playing with the V-smile system her father had given to her for Christmas.

"She's amazing Chad," Christy said as he watched Amy playing the V-smile Winnie the Pooh count on you game. She was able to recognize all of the numbers and all of the letters and she was able to put in her own name. Amy was only three years old yet she knew her numbers and how to spell her own name. "I bought her a leapster book system," Christy showed it to her husband and Amy ran and took the book from her mother. "You use the pen to read the book, watch her, she can do it all by herself and Chad, that's the one for six year olds and up. Amy's already mastered the one for pre-school."

"If only she could talk," and Chad knew that more than a year had passed with Amy not talking except in her own language.

"I want to go out jogging," Christy said and hurried to pull on her jogging shorts and t-shirt. "Will you be all right alone with Amy?"

"I'm her Daddy," Chad said as he set up the Nintendo sixty-four game and Christy watched her little daughter reach for the control. Amy might not talk, but she could do everything else well. The little girl was a gamer and her daddy loved that she was.

Christy ran nearly four miles getting the tension out of her body and she ran the base housing area. It was almost dark by the time she returned home and she saw Chad holding Amy in his arms and Amy looked pale and weak. "We were playing games, everything was good," Chad said as he watched his wife go into the bathroom.

"She's tired," Christy reached for Amy. "I'm killing two birds with one stone. She's taking a shower with me." Christy put Amy in the bathtub and closed the door taking off her shirt while turning on the water. Amy looked up at her and Christy saw the blue tinge around Amy's mouth. "911," Christy called out to Chad and reached for Amy as her husband rushed into the bathroom and took Amy from Christy seeing his wife reaching for her shirt.

"She died," Chad held his daughter out as she was now blue in his arms and he didn't see Christy drop her shirt and grabbed Amy.

"Call 911 now," she screamed at her husband as her child vomited and she laid Amy on the floor finger sweeping the child's mouth so that Amy wouldn't choke. "911," Christy screamed again as she began giving Amy rescue breaths.

Chad had frozen. He had never seen a seizure this bad. He now knew what his wife had been dealing with all the times that he had been gone. He couldn't move nor did he know his wife had pushed past him and was running for the phone to call for help.

Christy cried into the phone for help before she breathed for Amy again seeing Amy was a deathly pale in color. She looked at Chad and she saw him frozen and she wondered how her big, strong, commanding, bossy husband could just stand there as he was. She also realized that all the times she had been alone in these seizures with Amy that and she'd needed Chad here and now he was here, but he wasn't here.

The paramedic pushed past Chad and reached for Amy. Christy was unaware that she was barefooted and only in her shorts and bra as a fireman put his coat on her and they all rushed out to the ambulance. Another medivac trip to the Children's Hospital with Chad bringing his wife clothes and shoes and a tooth brush and upset over his behavior, but Christy understood. These seizures Amy had were terrifying beyond words.

Chad was home for over a month and Christy was able to take a day and go over to Dolphin Island and meet with her Uncle Jack. The older gentleman welcomed her warmly and she was thankful he had taken the time to meet with her. Before the day was done Christy would learn that her family heritage might play a key role into diagnosing Amy. Not only had Christy's mother had signs of MS, but her Grandmother, Sara's mother had also not been well and was unsteady on her feet. Christy had always known her Grandmother died of cancer, but she hadn't known that her grandmother was suspected of having MS.

Uncle Jack further revealed a cousin named Christine that died at age sixteen and had been unwell since the age of seven with loss of skills and ability. There was also another cousin Eugene that had been diagnosed with autism and he died at age nineteen. Later Christy would learn her Grandmother Merrill's father had been wheelchair bound toward the end of his life as had his sister, the Aunt her mother was named for, also confined to a wheelchair and her Great grandfather's mother died of a wasting disease at the age of forty-one as did her brother Charles.

The family history might play a role and Christy wondered, was Amy like Christy's mother? She hoped not because her mother had died. Christy nearly panicked on the drive home until she realized all that Amy had in common with her mother Sara was that they were both epileptic. And they were both born on the same day in May.

Chad left in early June before Christy's birthday and Amy had another seizure that the Diastat failed to control. The ambulance came and again they went to the emergency room where an IV was placed with Ativan and that stopped the seizure. Within the hour Amy's new primary care physician entered the room and holding Amy's file she turned and faced Christy.

"Amy has been in this emergency room and often taken to the children's hospital many times now Mrs. Bac," Christy stood by Amy's bed knowing this to be true and wishing the doctors would figure out what was going on with Amy and get the right medication on board to fix this problem. The truth was, they'd tried several drugs now, one of those drugs should be working. "Can't you manage these episodes at home?" the doctor asked her and Christy frowned in confusion as she saw Amy sleeping hard in the hospital bed.

"I thought if the seizure went on for more than five minutes or she choked on her own vomit that I was to call 911," Christy spoke in a hesitant voice feeling that she had done something wrong. Oh no, she thought to herself, she had been doing this wrong and she now knew she wasn't supposed to bother the doctors every time Amy had a seizure like this that wouldn't stop.

"Tell your neurologist when Amy has these events and stop coming to the emergency room," the doctor spoke from the curtain doorway. "Since this seizure lasted so long, we're going to do a CAT scan. But you need to get a diary and keep a record of these seizures and tell the neurologist and stop running back and forth to the emergency room."

"I will," Christy said and when the doctor left the room she broke down and cried. Amy was still asleep, Chad was gone, these 'episodes' as the doctor called them were terrifying her and no one could or would explain why no medication was stopping them and now she learned she was supposed to stay home and manage them alone and they weren't manageable.

Christy lived in a panic state as Amy continued to drop to the floor, pull inward and clench her jaw, become rigid and stiff only to shake apart and lose all bodily fluids. She couldn't call 911, the doctor had said for her to handle these at home, but the Diastat never worked and the seizures went on well beyond five minutes. After the fourth 'episode' Christy called the neurologist and got an emergency appointment. Chad was flying in the night before and she knew that she wouldn't be alone.

As usual the neurologist's office was packed but the neurologist had a new partner and that was who they were seeing today. The man came into the room with a spinning light up toy and turned off the lights watching Amy in the darkness reach for his toy and he laughed when she did. Within five minutes the man jumped up from his stool and ran out of the room. Christy and Chad were shocked, they'd never known a doctor to do that before and he had taken the toy with him which caused Amy to cry as she liked the toy.

The new neurologist returned and he had Amy's EEG report from their last visit and he had a video cassette along with a booklet he handed to Christy. "You need to learn all about the different seizure types, Mrs. Bac," he said in a serious voice. "You're only seeing the grand mal also known as tonic clonic. Amy just had a seizure with my light up toy; it's called a partial complex. Watch this video and you'll know what to look for." As he said this Amy's eyes shot up to the top and to the side and she lost tone. "This is a seizure," he said and he wrote out a new prescription increasing the Depakote.

"The primary care pediatrician told me not to go to the hospital anymore and to keep a diary and tell you," Christy said as the neurologist was moving toward the door.

"Excuse me," he said in an angry voice turning back to look at Christy.

"She said to handle the 'episodes' at home and I'm trying too, honestly I am,"

"Stop," he held up a hand and sat back down on the stool. "Seizures can kill people," he spoke on in a harsh and hard way not seeing Christy was pulling away and standing now behind her husband. He was frightening her and Chad knew this. Christy was afraid a lot of the time because of her past. "If Amy has a seizure that lasts more than three minutes, you are to administer the Diastat rectally and call 911. I don't care what that doctor said to you. Your daughter is at risk of death in a seizure. And get a new primary care doctor for your child immediately."

"No other doctor has told us that Amy's at risk for death," Chad said holding his wife by his side.

"I'm telling you the truth Mr. Bac," the new neurologist said. "Amy's brain isn't all right; we can see that on the EEGs we've done. She's never had a long term EEG and that should be considered." He stood again and moved toward the door saying that he wanted to see them back in two months and advising them again to find a new primary care pediatrician for Amy, preferably one that knew epilepsy.

Chad and Christy stopped at the front desk on their way out and asked to be seen from now on by the old neurologist. He wasn't as frightening or as alarming about the seizures as he seemed to think Amy's seizures weren't that bad. The couple didn't want their only child's seizures to be that bad.

Within the month a new doctor would arrive at Eglin Air Force Base. A doctor that was known as a Pediatric Developmentalist, and this doctor spent time with Amy. He spent time with the parents. And he saw things that concerned him and he spoke to the neurologist directly over what he was seeing. Chorea and nystagmus, but Chad and Christy didn't know this. They were never told of these things. They believed Amy was autistic, that one in every four children with autism have seizures. This new doctor, this developmental doctor, he saw more in Amy than autism and he was concerned.

Miracles happen every day or so the saying goes. Little three year old Amy Bac was given a miracle. The little girl woke up one morning a year and seven months after she had stopped talking and while her mother was fixing breakfast she was watching The New Adventures of Winnie the Pooh on the television when Christy heard Amy saying, "Pooh," or trying to say the word Pooh.

Breakfast forgotten Christy grabbed the camcorder from the counter and put in a new blank tape and started to film. "Who do you like best?" Christy asked Amy, her voice loud and clear on the camera recording her child making an amazing recovery.

"Winnie Pooh, yes," Amy said with a smile and Christy followed the child around handing Amy her Dora doll.

"Who is that Amy?" Christy asked and Amy attempted to say Dora, all of this being captured on film. The windows in the living room were dull with the morning sunshine as the house faced west. All day long Christy filmed Amy's recovery from non-verbal to talking and laughing and telling the names of all of her stuffed toy and her wooden trains and the small child even pulled out her leapster book and not using the pen to touch the book and have the book read to her, Amy read the words herself pointing to the words with her finger.

The bright afternoon sun was flooding into the living room windows as the day was ending. The day was ending with Little Amy Bac talking perfectly to her mother, even telling her mother that she loved the color pink and noodles for dinner.

Two days later Chad came home and he walked into the house with Christy holding the camcorder and Amy standing by the desk that held their desktop computer. "Amy," Christy said her darling child's name and saw Chad put down his suitcase. "Watch this Chad," she said and he looked at Amy looking at him. "Daddy's home Amy, I told you he'd go and get you some ice cream when he got here. What do you say to Daddy?"

"Ice cream Daddy," Amy said and ran to Chad saying the word ice cream over and over again.

"My God," Chad said as he put Amy down and his little one ran to the piano counting out loud the care bears he'd brought home to her after each trip away. Chad heard his daughter count to fifteen and a bear fell and she said, "sorry," as clearly as she had said ice cream. "How did you do this?" he asked as he reached down and picked up his little girl. Amy was now three years and seven months old and she had been silent for a long time. She wasn't silent anymore. Overnight Amy Bac became a real girl and she talked a lot, in fact, she talked all the time and she talked well and her parents recorded her talking. She had recovered. Their daughter had recovered from autism.

The speech therapist released Amy one month later; there was no reason to continue coming as Amy was never quiet. The occupational therapist said that with words Amy wasn't combative and released her as well. Then came the applied behavioral specialist, she released Amy also and Amy was in school four hours a day so she was getting all the support and guidance that she needed.

The main handicap that Amy had at this time was her hyperactivity. Little Amy Bac never stood still. The little girl ran everywhere she went and she had to touch everything she saw. And the seizures, since the increase of Depakote, the seizures weren't as many, but they still happened and they were always frightening when they did. But life had become more 'normal' for the family with the control of the seizures with both Christy and Chad learned to run to keep up with their little girl.

By the age of five Christy had found a way to deal in a positive way with the hyperactivity. She had Amy enrolled in the bowling team and the swim team. By late summer Amy was on the soccer team and the baseball team. Christy felt that keeping Amy focused on sports was key to teaching Amy how to control her hyper behavior and too, Amy loved everything that she was doing with her mother.

They ran 3k and 5k runs. With Daddy when he was home, every Memorial Day and Labor Day they ran in the base gate to gate run. Christy found a stable that offered horseback riding and took Amy out to the horses twice a month. Christy took Amy to the beach and they would fly kites. Every day in some way, Christy was searching to burn up Amy's hyper energy and Amy was thrilled with all the fun and games. While Chad was gone, Christy was rarely home as she was often outdoors chasing after her child and loving her life in the fresh air even in the summertime.

The training wheels came off of Amy's bike the day she turned five years old and Christy jogged beside the bike that Amy rode. Amy wore a pink helmet on her head and was easy and often seen by their neighbors and friends on the base. Christy knew all the neighbors because of Amy, her daughter never met a stranger and

Amy had to speak to everyone. The neighbors across the street and down one house had met Christy and Amy in a very unique way, a way that made Amy well known to these new neighbors.

Chad had been gone for two weeks and a new chair had arrived for Amy that the pediatric developmental doctor had ordered. The chair was known as a rifton chair and the doctor had assured Christy that she could put Amy in this chair and there was no way that Amy could get out. With Chad gone so much of the time, Christy was now able to put Amy in this lockdown chair and take a shower, a luxury that before Christy had taken for granted, but now she was more than thankful for.

Amy was securely locked down in the chair outside of the bathroom as Christy stepped into the nice hot shower and began shampooing her hair. Alarms had been placed on each door in case Amy was ever to attempt to leave the house again. As Christy shampooed her hair, one of those door alarms went off.

"What in the world?" Christy spoke these words as she stepped out of the shower and reached for her towel. "Oh no!" she screamed. Her child, her beautiful Amy had somehow escaped that rifton chair! With no thought to her state of dress, or undress, Christy ran out the door seeing Amy running down the street after a family walking their dog. Little Amy Bac never met a dog that she didn't love and Christy started running barefooted and wrapped in a bath towel after her daughter, the shampoo still in her hair.

The family walking the dog were the new neighbors across the street and one house down. Both were nurses at the base hospital now and both understood ADHD. Within a few minutes they helped Christy grab up Amy and force the little girl home, Christy fighting to keep the towel closed and very aware of the shampoo in her hair, shampoo that she would wash out in the kitchen sink while holding tightly with one hand to Amy's hand.

Later, when Christy met with the Pediatric Developmental Doctor he asked how the chair had worked out for Amy and Christy told him of Amy's escape of that chair. The doctor tickled Amy and called her 'Houdini.' The ADHD was all the focus now. The autism seemed to have become a thing of the past; Amy's behaviors were few and far between. Amy's speech was near normal and she was doing very well in school. The Depakote had brought about seizure control and the little girl was happy with her life.

Christy left the doctor's office and went to the hospital escalators with Amy and together they rode the escalators, Amy laughing and enjoying the motion and Christy grateful that all she had to worry about was Amy's ADHD. Life was good. And every time Christy passed a mirror she was grateful for Amy's constant motion as Christy was thin and in shape. Forty-seven years old and Christy was in the best shape of her whole life and that was because she was always on the run trying to keep up with Amy.

Christy's dizzy spells continued and were becoming more than a nuisance for her. With Chad gone so much of the time, and even when he was home, he was gone long hours leaving Christy as the primary care for their child, there was just little time for Christy to focus on herself. By the time Amy entered the school on the base for kindergarten, Christy knew it was time to try and figure out her own health concerns as she had become clumsy and unsteady.

Christy failed the tilt table test and the Romberg test and the doctor referred her to the University of Alabama where Christy was diagnosed with Meniere's disease. There was no clear cut treatment for this, Christy had to live with the symptoms and carry on being a wife and the mother of an ADHD child. Her focus became her child and her husband and she attempted to push aside her own health issues and her walking like a drunk and falling and dizzy. There was nothing anyone could do and her little girl depended on her and Chad needed her to take care of their home while he worked protecting their country.

Life went on, happy and safe and secure, the problems were managed and Christy was learning to cope with her illness. There were vacations taken to Disney World. Hours were spent playing video games, Amy loved her hand held Nintendo system and by the end of the year she had more than twenty games. She had mastered Star Wars Legos with ease and went on to Indiana Jones Legos. As each game came out geared for everyone, Amy played and in short time mastered the game. PlayStation was easy for the little girl and she'd spend hours standing in front of the television with the Wii system on. There seemed to be nothing that Amy couldn't do when it came to video games.

Amy was also doing well in school. She could do single number addition and subtraction and she was learning to read. Every night Christy and Amy would lie in bed together and Christy would read to her child. The mother wasn't reading children's books to Amy, she was reading books that were for older children and Amy sat and was attentive enjoying the stories and often relaying them to her mother the next day so that they could finish the story. The Box Car Children series of books was loved by Amy but her all time favorite story was, 'The Doll in the Garden,' and Christy read that one over and over and over again to her daughter, the story quickly becoming Christy's favorite as well.

Chapter Fourteen

2 Timothy 1:7: "For God has not given us a spirit of fear, but of power and of love and of a sound mind."

When little Amy Bac turned the age of six Christy and Chad went to a routine appointment with the neurologist. Amy had been happy in the backseat on the ride over from Eglin to Pensacola as she was wearing her puppy pants and shirt and the little girl adored that outfit, it was Amy's favorite thing to wear. The top had a black poodle embroidered on the front and the pants had that same poodle embroidered all over, the outfit was adorable and Amy was often seen wearing these clothes.

The neurologist was upbeat, Amy's last EEG had shown some spike waves that were indicative of seizures, but she had no obvious seizures recorded. He felt it was safe to decrease the Depakote and the parents were thrilled. This was their dream, to have their daughter weaned off all medication and no longer epileptic.

"I'm glad you've told us this," Christy had spoken in a teasing manner while Chad put his arm around her and they were watching Amy read a Dr. Seuss story out loud. "I left the house this morning and forgot the Diastat. I feel better about being out on interstate ten and the bear creek road in the country for our trip home."

"Yes," Chad agreed looking at the neurologist with a happy smile. "We have no cell phone signal most of the drive back to the base."

The couple left with Amy, the little girl holding her mother's hand and her father's hand happy to be between her parents. Everything was going to be good, Chad thought as he buckled Amy into the car. The ADHD would be controlled by medication, the autistic behaviors were behind them; Amy was doing very well in school and had many friends. The little girl was the star of the baseball and the soccer team and she was now on the swim team swimming faster and better than children twice her size.

Little Amy Bac sat in the backseat of her Daddy's car and she worried. She had that feeling again in her tummy, a feeling she couldn't get mommy to understand and Amy didn't like this feeling, it frightened her. She saw that cloud, that cloud was her best friend and he was standing outside the window of the moving car. What was her friend cloud doing here, Amy wondered as she touched her tummy wishing that frightening feeling would go away.

Christy was putting on a CD in the car CD player when she heard a noise. The family was more than halfway home in the country on a quiet rode that ran from interstate ten to the base. "Are you okay baby?" she turned and asked her little Amy and she saw the child waving out the window.

"Mama, look, its boy and girl cloud, my friends," Amy said and Christy frowned. Amy had these two invisible friends that she often spoke of and to. Amy referred to these friends that only Amy could see as boy and girl cloud. And every time Amy did speak of them and to them a seizure followed.

"Oh God," Christy cried out as Amy vomited, the child's eyes rolled up, to the right side and back as Christy undid her seatbelt and climbed over the seat quickly doing a finger sweep of Amy's mouth to remove the vomit. "She's turning blue!" Christy cried out in panic as Chad accelerated the car and within seconds they were driving eighty miles an hour toward the base as Christy pulled Amy into her arms and began rescue breaths.

Since 9/11 the base had been locked down. In order to get onto the base you had to stop and show your identification to the gate guards. Today Chad did not slow down. The father was in a hurry to get to the emergency room. Amy, his child, was in full seizure and she had been for more than ten minutes, his wife doing rescue breaths on the little girl as Amy's body jerked beyond any human's control.

"Oh God Chad," Christy screamed as her husband pulled into the ambulance bay. "She's still in seizure!"

The base Security Police had followed them into the ambulance bay and Chad exited the car with his hands raised in the air screaming for help. A team ran out of the emergency room and this team knew the family well, they knew Amy was an epileptic. "Stand down," the doctor called out as he opened the backdoor of the car and reached in for Amy pulling the little girl into his arms. Amazingly it was the same doctor that had written nervous mother on Amy's chart when Amy had been a baby.

Christy stood outside the room where the team worked on Amy putting in an IV line and cutting off Amy's much loved puppy outfit. Chad had gone with the Security Police and moved the car, but he was only gone a few moments, an officer moved the car for him and brought him the keys as Amy continued on in the seizure.

"What do we usually use to get this to stop?" the doctor that had referred to Christy as a nervous mother all those years ago asked the parents. Chad and Christy could only look at one another in confusion before Chad finally looked at the doctor with frustration and fear obvious and etched onto his face.

"We don't have a medical degree," Chad said in frustration. "You guys use something there," and he pointed to the IV line.

Two hours passed with Amy trapped in the seizure. A CT scan was done and an ambulance loaded the little girl up and took her back to Pensacola and Sacred Heart Hospital where she stayed for four days. The neurologist increased the Depakote while the family was admitted to the hospital and after an EEG the neurologist put the child on Clonazepam. Little Amy Bac was now on three anti-seizure medications.

By the summer of 2007 Amy was able to sit at the piano with Christy and watch as Christy played music by Bach and Beethoven and when Christy was done playing the complicated piece on the piano, she would move down on the stool and watch her daughter play the same piece without following the sheet music or even looking at the sheet music. Amy was gifted in this way and the little girl rarely made any mistakes. No matter what song Christy played, Amy repeated her mother's finger movements over those piano keys.

During services on Easter Sunday in 2008 Amy had stood in front of the church and sang the song "Were You there When the Sun Refused to Shine." The child sang the song alone and she sang the song without fault. Everyone in the congregation was impressed and Amy was very proud of herself taking several bows before she was encouraged to sing the song again.

At the end of church services, the Reverend came and knelt down before the little girl and gave her a smile as he spoke to her. "Amy, do you know what Easter is all about? Do you know what Easter means?" Christy stood stiff hearing the Reverend asking Amy this question and the mother held her breath certain that Amy would tell of dyeing eggs or the Easter Bunny or of the candy she had eaten from her Easter basket this morning before church.

"Yes, I know," Amy said smiling at the Reverend before looking up at her mother for a brief moment. "Today, Jesus died so that I can be a really bad girl and still go to heaven."

The question was answered in the way a six year old child would answer this question and Christy burst out laughing seeing

Something's the Matter with Amy

Chad was smiling nearby as the Reverend nodded his head and said that basically, Amy was correct.

"I learned that from my Mama," Amy said and Christy blushed shaking her head hard when the Reverend looked at her.

"That's not what I taught her," Christy stammered and heard Chad laughing before he pulled his wife into his arms.

"Amy's answer to my question was fine," the Reverend said and taking Amy's hand, the family left the church going to an on base Easter egg hunt.

Little Amy Bac knew something was wrong with her and she didn't want her mommy and her daddy to be scared and she knew, her mommy and her daddy were already scared. The bad thing was happening to her often. Her head would feel bad and her tummy had that funny feeling Amy didn't like and she would see her friends, boy and girl cloud. And then suddenly she would wake up with mommy looking down at her, mommy always looked scared and sometimes mommy was crying. Sometimes she'd wake up in the hospital and the doctor would look scared too. Little Amy Bac knew something was wrong with her and little Amy Bac was scared.

At school something different was happening to Amy and Amy often bit her lip and worried over what was happening. She was afraid and she knew that she was bad. But because Jesus died on the cross for her, so Amy knew that if she died from these bad things that were happening to her, she would still get to go to heaven. When she heard her mommy talking to the teacher one day about one of those bad things happening to her, Amy wanted to cry because the teacher said it was Amy's fault and mommy stopped talking to the teacher. Her mommy had tears in her eyes. On the drive home, Amy saw her mommy was crying and Amy cried too.

"I'm sorry," Amy said over and over again as she cried and her mother hugged her close.

"No baby, this isn't your fault," Christy spoke in a confident voice. "I don't know what this is, but I'm getting you into the developmental doctor right away."

Christy made the call on the drive home to the doctor's office and the appointment was for seven thirty the next morning. The developmental doctor came into the room and looked at Amy lying still on the table and he glanced quickly at her mother seeing the concern on Christy's face.

"We're quiet today," the developmental doctor said looking down at Amy and seeing the child hid her face against her arm.

"I'm bad," Amy blurted out and started to cry, her face still hidden by her arm.

"She's making these noises," Christy said wanting to burst into tears with her little girl and the doctor gave the mother his undivided attention while patting the child on the back. "She's honking like a horn. Sometimes barking like a dog. And she's unable to stop herself. Honestly, she's not doing this for attention, but the teacher insists that she is and she's disrupting the classroom in this attention seeking behavior."

"Amy," the developmental doctor looked down at the little girl and saw her crying still.

"I'm bad. I'm really really bad." Amy hid her face against her arm again and continued to cry.

"Tourettes syndrome," the developmental doctor said to Christy while patting Amy's shoulder. "One in every four autistic children have this happen to them."

"And one in every four autistic children have seizures," Christy spoke these words in frustration. "Everything is blamed on the autism, yet Amy has empathy and compassion and makes friends with everyone now. She has good eye contact and she's on grade level."

"She still meets the criteria for PDP," the doctor said and wrote a script that he handed Christy. "This medication should help."

"And another drug to take," Christy stood up and helped Amy down from the table before going to the door not thanking the doctor and completely unaware that her little daughter had another worry.

"Its cause I have epilepsy," Amy spoke of her other problem to her mommy as she rode the escalator with her mother. She didn't tell her mother what more was happening to her, Amy kept quiet because she didn't want mommy more afraid for her than mommy already was. And as they rode the escalator, Amy saw her mommy's face wet with tears.

The weather was very hot and Amy's teacher felt a party at school would help her classroom children be happier on the playground. Christy came to help with the party and Amy was jumping up and down in joy as her mommy blew up the three ring pool. The children were going to play in the water while on the playground after lunch.

Amy hurried out of the classroom dressed in her pink bathing suit; her mother hurried after her and was laughing. Amy liked it when her mother laughed and she turned and ran back to Christy giving Christy a hug and looking up at her mommy with a smile. "I love you mommy," the child said and was glad when her mother hugged her back.

"Bet I love you more," Christy said and took hold of her daughter's hand and ran to the pool she had blown up that was now full of cool water.

"I'm sorry about the tic disorder," the teacher said to Christy and Amy's mother nodded her head wishing that Amy didn't have all of these problems.

"It seems like it is just one thing after another," Christy sighed and met the teacher's eyes not seeing Amy had stopped splashing in the pool and was now sitting still in the water. "Everything is blamed on autism or the seizure medication."

"We need to talk," the teacher held Christy's eyes and had gave Christy a look of sorrow. "Amy's not progressing in her school work Christy. She's leveled off. She can add double digit numbers and subtract single digit numbers but she's been able to do that since the end of last year when I first had her in my classroom. She hasn't progressed in reading either. She was advanced but now she's right where she was at the start of the year. And Christy, her hyperactivity isn't as big an issue. Amy's become still. I think it's best to put her on special standards before she goes into the third grade."

"No," Christy gasped as she turned around and Christy saw Amy sitting in the pool of water being too still. "What is that?" Christy forgot what she was protesting as she saw her daughter's hands. "Amy's developed a tremor."

"I've noticed that as well," the teacher said as they moved closer to Amy sitting in the pool of water and not splashing around. "I think it's the medication.

"No again," Christy said more to herself than the teacher. "She's still," Christy wanted to cry in frustration. Had the Clonazepam done this to Amy? If so, then Christy knew things were not good. Amy had several breakthrough seizures in the past month and the neurologist had again increased the Depakote and he said if this continued, he would increase the Clonazepam as well.

At home over dinner Christy fell apart on her husband. Amy had gone to sleep early and Christy, instead of eating paced the floor and fretted until Chad couldn't eat. "She's developed a tic disorder, now a tremor. She's not hyperactive anymore and she's sleeping. Chad, Amy's never slept much and now she's in bed and it's not even late yet."

"I've noticed," Chad spoke in as concerned a voice as his wife. "When do we see the neurologist again?"

"Tuesday and I want you to take off work and come with me." Christy sat down and covered her face with her hands. "This is the Clonazepam."

"Then we'll come off of the Clonazepam," Chad put his arm around his wife. "We'll fix this Christy; we just need to tweak her medication."

"That's all these doctors do Chad," they just tweak the medication, go up, add on and the seizures still happen and OCD and ADHD and tic disorder. What is next?"

The neurologist ordered another MRI at their appointment that Tuesday. He also told Chad and Christy that he felt the Clonazepam was not to blame. He increased the Depakote again seeking better seizure control and the family went home feeling like nothing had really changed. Amy was falling behind now in school, she was having seizures and tics and this tremor.

"Old people have tremors," Christy said to her husband as they went inside their house. "Not little kids."

"What's a tremor, mommy?" Amy asked and her mother bent down and took her hands.

"A tremor is what your hands are doing Amy," Christy spoke gently and saw the worry touch her little girl's face.

"I didn't want you to know mommy," Amy said putting her finger over her mouth. "Sh sh, that was my secret." And Amy knew, her hands shaking wasn't a secret from Mommy and Daddy anymore.

Christy had asked what next would happen to them of her husband. What happened next had nothing to do with Amy's health and everything to do with Christy's fragile emotional state over all that was happening to her child.

First Christy had been in the hands of an abuser, a man that had told her that she was to blame for everything bad that happened. A man that had hit her and hurt her for years and she'd had no safe means of escape. The man had total control over her life.

A restraining order was just a piece of paper, Christy knew that. There was no physical restraint offered of the man that was in control of her life and no protection would be afforded her should her abuser do more than he had in the past to her.

The second reason Christy was so fragile was because of the allegation made by the troop that worked in her husband's squadron of Munchausen's by proxy. The man had been dealt with harshly and the man had suffered loss in his military rise, but nothing that happened to the man took away the hurt that allegation had caused Christy.

Chad didn't know, no one knew, Christy was blaming herself for all of Amy's problems. Christy was questioning herself over everything she did as Amy's mother. The giving medications to her child, the seizures, the tic, it was all something Christy felt she was making into a mountain, when what this was to the doctors was a molehill.

Christy didn't understand Amy's epilepsy because she knew, many children have epilepsy, they take a pill and that's the end of that, the seizures are controlled, the child is okay. Why wasn't this the case for her child? She didn't understand and she was frightened as any loving mother would have been.

Chad had made a new rank and they were being afforded a large house on base. Christy had packed everything in boxes, cleaned the house they had been living in and was ready to move. She had gone to the housing office to pick up the keys and as usual, the office was crowded and she sat down to wait her turn as she could wait her turn because Amy was in school.

That morning Christy had learned from the principle that a mother had come to the principal's office and requested that Amy be put out of the base school because Amy was violent. The principle had been shocked over this mother's request and alerted Christy that the base school could support Amy and Amy was in the right place.

While she sat trying to read a ladies home journal Christy wondered why anyone would take such an interest in Amy. And why in the world would anyone call Amy violent? "Excuse me," she heard a woman say and Christy looked up to see the woman going to the front of the line in the housing office. "I'm here to stop a violent retard from moving into our neighborhood."

Christy recognized the woman; her son was in Amy's classroom.

"Where is this violent retard moving?" the woman behind the desk asked and Christy slumped down low in her chair, she didn't want this woman to see her and come sit down and talk to her. Saying the word retard as this woman just had was wrong and Christy vowed never to go near this woman again. And then she heard the address the woman was giving to the housing office receptionist and Christy looked down at her new address.

"Oh no," she breathed in a gasp. The violent retard this woman was speaking of was her little girl Amy. "Amy's not retarded," Christy whispered and stood from her chair looking for a backdoor out of this place.

"Excuse me ma'am, you can't be back here," a man spoke to her and Christy peeked out to the receptionist's desk and heard another woman was now at the desk also giving her new address to the receptionist and referring to Amy as a retard. "Good heavens," the man almost swore. "It's politically incorrect to use that word." He pushed on Christy while going toward the receptionist desk and Christy pushed back.

"You don't understand sir," she whispered urgently, "the child they're talking about is my child."

The man stood still only for a second. He grabbed Christy's arm and pulled her with him to an office and closed the door reaching for the papers she held. "No one tells anyone where they can and can't live. Not on my base." He handed Christy the keys to her new house. "Ignore that ignorance. They will be dealt with."

Christy was crying too hard to thank the man for his assistance or his kindness. He walked her to a backdoor of the building and then out to her car. She sobbed herself nearly blind on the drive home before she took pictures and dishes and curtains to the new home. She would spend the day hanging pictures and curtains until Amy arrived on the bus.

Within a few minutes of getting to her new house, Christy saw the two women from the housing office that had referred to Amy as a violent retard. They were standing in the yard of her new home staring at the house. Across the street in a golf cart was the man that had given Christy the keys and told her no one told anyone where they'd live on his base.

Quietly, Christy put everything she'd brought to the new house back into her car and went to her old home preparing to unpack. She wasn't moving into that house. Amy wouldn't be safe there and she now knew who had tried to have Amy removed from the base school.

"Parents of children on the spectrum," Christy cried as she unloaded her car. "Parents like me that should understand my life calling Amy that ugly name."

"Ma'am," the man on the golf cart called out to her and Christy stopped with her arms full of things and looked at him. "You need to come with me."

"My child will be home from the bus within the hour," Christy called out to him before she turned to go inside.

"Then bring your child to the housing office in an hour," he ordered her and Christy shook her head hard.

"My child is not violent, nor is she a retard," Christy burst into tears. "She's epileptic with some problems due to her epilepsy. That's all."

"Don't cry," the man spoke in a tender voice. "We'll figure this out. I'll see you in an hour."

Something's the Matter with Amy

Christy put Amy in her car and they went to the base housing office. Little Amy Bac knew that her mommy was upset and crying and she was afraid. She ran to her Daddy when she saw him pull up on his motorcycle outside a building that Amy had never been to before and her Daddy lifted her into his arms holding her tight before he reached for her mommy.

"What a mess," Chad said to his wife as he held her crying in his arms.

"How do you know what happened?" Christy pleaded with her husband to tell her.

"My commander called me into his office for a meeting. My buddy was there, the commander said to him that he couldn't believe what my buddy's wife had done. I know everything; even that Amy was called a horrible name." Chad held the door open for his wife and the man from the housing office shook his hand.

"You folks get back in your car and follow me," the man ordered and Chad turned around with Amy still held close in his arms.

"This little one isn't violent," Chad said more to Amy in a playful voice than to Christy. "She's part monkey, but she's not violent."

"I want a hotdog," Amy said and pulled on her daddy's nose as he locked her in the seatbelt.

"We'll get you a hotdog later, little one," Chad kissed her cheek before getting in the car with his wife.

"This is your new home," the housing director said to Chad and Christy as they left their car with Amy running ahead of them.

"Um," Chad reached the door and held it open for Amy while looking at the man from the golf cart. "Sir, my rank can't support this place." He looked out the window of the house and lost his breath. He could see the Mid-bay bridge and the Destin bridge from the window. The whole Gulf of Mexico was in his backyard. "This is a six million dollar view."

"This is your house Sergeant Bac and we're very sorry for what happened to your wife today. And your little girl is adorable." Chad and Christy turned around seeing the housing director holding their daughter and Amy pulling on the man's nose as she often pulled on Chad's nose.

"She's part monkey is what she really is," Chad took his daughter from the man and held her in his arms as they walked through the house that was three thousand square feet. "We're gonna get lost in here," he teased his wife. "The house we've been living in is only nine hundred square feet."

"We really don't need this big place," Christy said to the housing director and he looked into her eyes before reaching for her hand.

"Anyone else would have been screaming at those two women this morning for what they referred to your child as being. But you reacted as a true lady." The housing director looked up at Chad holding Amy in his arms. "Your rank will support this place. You're good parents and your daughter is precious."

"My mommy and daddy are my best friends ever," Amy said and hugged Chad around the neck bursting into a fit of giggles as her father hugged her right back and growled at her as though he were an old bear causing the little girl to laugh. Amy loved her mommy and daddy best of all and the child told them so often.

Chapter Fifteen

1 John 4:18: "There is no fear in love. But perfect love drives out fear, because fear has to do with punishment. The one who fears is not made perfect in love."

Within a month the family had moved into their new home on the base. Christy worked hard putting the above ground pool up in the backyard for her and Amy to enjoy when summer came. Chad was home for a while and they were enjoying their lives, and in the winter months they again went to stay for ten days in Disney World.

Christy was coping with the Meniere's disease as best as she could and had increased her physical activity now jogging four miles a day hoping to regain her balance. She had no time to complain of her own situation because in comparison to Amy, her balance and coordination issues were minor.

The seizures were happening often only now Christy and Chad had been educated by the developmental doctor as to what Amy's seizures were. Amy always had grand mal seizures. She would drop to the ground, become ridged and stiff, often pull her limbs inward, vomit and urinate and sometimes lose bowel control before the jerking began. Those were the seizures that Amy's parents knew and understood.

In the developmental doctor's office with him in the room Amy did what Christy and Chad felt was a behavioral problem. Amy completely ignored them. She stared across the room and stuck her tongue in and out of her mouth, her pupils dilated, though the parents never recognized this until the doctor pointed it out to them that day.

"Her EEGs show partial complex seizures," the developmental doctor said to the parents. "This is a partial complex seizure."

"She's just staring and ignoring us," Chad insisted and the doctor nodded his head in understanding.

"Amy's having a seizure," the doctor said with compassion in his voice. A call to the neurologist and the medications were again increased.

"We can't win for losing," Chad said as he geared up for work. His motorcycle was already running and he was yelling to be heard over his bike while Christy got Amy ready for school early in the morning of a cool day. "The seizures Amy's having now don't look like seizures. She looks like she's lost."

"She looks like she did when she was diagnosed with autism," Christy said buttoning up Amy's sweater.

"I don't feel good mommy," Amy whined and Christy touched the child's forehead.

"Seizure means fever," Chad said in a worried tone of voice and met his wife's eyes.

"I'm keeping her home from school," Christy reached to remove Amy's sweater and Chad mounted his bike.

"I'll call you when I get to my office," he lowered the visor on his helmet. "Love you little one," he called out to his daughter and saw his wife lift her hand in a wave before he backed out of their driveway.

"I feel funny Mommy," Amy said as they went into the house and Christy saw Amy sit down on the floor.

"Do you see boy and girl cloud?" Christy asked knowing now that these invisible friends were an aura that came upon Amy before a seizure assaulted the child.

"No mommy, they're not here right now," Amy spoke slowly and Christy could see the child didn't feel well.

"I'll get you something to drink baby mine," Christy went into the kitchen to the fridge glancing back in time to see Amy fall forward and lay still on the floor. "Baby!" she screamed out and ran to Amy pushing the little girl over. "Amy, oh Amy!"

Little Amy Bac didn't move. She wasn't ridged or stiff. She was breathing though her lips weren't blue but she was turning gray all over. Christy ran for the Diastat and waited for the jerking, the shaking, for something, any sign that would let her know this was a seizure. "Amy," Christy screamed the child's name and got no response. "Oh God," Christy spoke in prayer before she jumped up and grabbed her phone hitting 911, Amy's lips were turning blue.

In the past year there had been easily two dozen ambulance rides to the hospital due to seizures, surely this was another seizure. Christy remembered one time not long ago when she attempted to get Amy to the emergency room on her own. Amy had shaken the whole backseat of the car forcing Christy off the road to hold Amy still. The garbage men saw the situation then and called 911.

Now Christy was all alone. She was alone and Amy wasn't shaking. Amy was still and her lips were blue and Christy started breathing for her little girl. This isn't a seizure; Christy thought and then frowned as she breathed on for her daughter. This was a new type of seizure; she thought and jumped up when the paramedic came into the house.

"My child is epileptic," she saw him put the oxygen mask over Amy's face, another paramedic was kneeling beside Amy with the paddles out and a noise was sounding. "Wait!" Christy screamed out as the man touched Amy with those paddles. "She's epileptic."

"She's not in sinus rhythm," the one paramedic said to another as the noise sounded again and Amy's whole body jerked with the paddles.

"What are you doing!?" Christy screamed and tried to reach her daughter, a fireman held her back. "She's epileptic. She's just turned seven years old three days ago and she's epileptic, dear God in heaven, don't use those on her!" She fought to be free of the hold the fireman had on her as the paramedics picked Amy up and put her on the stretcher and hurried from the house.

"Her heart fluttered," one man said as they shoved Christy into the ambulance and she threw her face in her hands crying.

"She's epileptic, she's epileptic," Christy cried again and again as they went to the hospital.

"Ma'am," the paramedic helped Christy out of the ambulance, "this isn't epilepsy. Something else is happening to your daughter."

"No, no," Christy said this as though saying no would make everything all right.

"Her husband's with JAWS 36th squadron," she heard a security police officer call out as they took Amy into a curtained room and two doctors ran past Christy, they closed the curtains and a nurse pulled her back and away.

"Their doing everything they can," the nurse said and Christy shook her head.

"She's epileptic, she's got high functioning autism and she's epileptic," Christy was sobbing these words when she felt someone grab her and she turned and it was her husband. "Chad, oh Chad!" she fell against him and he grabbed a hold of her tighter than he had ever held her in his life.

"What's going on?" Chad demanded to know and no one answered him. "I was in my office when Security Police came in and got me."

"Amy had some sort of an odd seizure," Christy cried while clinging to her husband.

"This isn't a seizure," the doctor said as he came out from behind the curtain. "Her fever is 106 and her heart is beating way too fast. Her heart fluttered, the cardiologist is on his way down now."

An hour passed as Christy and Chad sat by their daughter's bed each at Amy's side holding her hands. The cardiologist had come and gone and he blamed the fever. The emergency room doctor came in two hours later, all blood tests were back and Amy had no signs of bacteria or virus, she has some slight increase in an enzyme and he'd called the pediatrician.

The developmental doctor was gone, deployed and the doctor that took his place didn't know Amy at all beyond what was written of autism and ADHD. He said this had to be a virus and it would run its course and he saw no need to follow up. The parents were stunned. Amy was still not awake, her fever was still up over 106 and that was it, no worries, she was fine.

"We expect things like this in autistic children," the doctor spoke to Chad.

"Well, maybe you expect things like this, but we damn sure don't," Chad said in a hard and upset tone of voice. "This isn't normal."

"I don't know what happened to your daughter today," the emergency room doctor came in behind the curtain after the pediatrician had left. "But I've seen Amy many times in non convulsive seizures and what happened today wasn't normal." As the emergency room doctor was saying this, Amy sat up in the bed and looked at her Daddy.

"Can we go home now?" she asked and Chad looked from Amy to the doctor as Christy hugged her child and kissed Amy's face.

"I want to keep her for a few more hours," the emergency room doctor said to the worried parents. "We'll see where we are in a bit."

Nine hours after Amy first dropped to the floor and went gray then blue and she had the paddles put her heart in normal rhythm, the little girl sat up in the hospital bed with no fever and a normal heartbeat and the emergency room doctor released her. The child walked out of the hospital with her parents following her and her talking about how fat the clouds were in the sky like in Care-a-Lot, her Care Bear movie. The child was even singing the carealot song. Everything was normal in little Amy Bac's world.

Life went on for Amy and her parents. Amy took out the trash daily and she washed the dishes while her mother cooked dinner. At the age of five Amy had become a picky eater but no one thought much of this as all children become picky over some things. For Amy, the problem became a major concern for her parents as the neurologist saw Amy as overweight and not hurting for food, yet the parents could only get the little girl to eat hotdogs and drink apple juice.

The neurologist told them not to give Amy those foods and Amy would eat what they put in front of her eventually. Sound advice, so Chad and Christy did this, together as a team though at times they both felt like they were ganging up on their child. If they stood together as a solid front, Amy would see she couldn't exist on hotdogs and apple juice and soon she'd be back to eating as she always had been, the foods Christy prepared for mealtime.

At the time of the food issue there also became an issue over sleep. Melatonin was discontinued and the Depakote and Clonazepam were blamed though Amy had been on those two medications for nearly two years. The developmental doctor that knew Amy well was deployed still and the parents, Chad and Christy felt stuck with the new pediatrician.

"I'm very concerned," Christy said in her timid way and the doctor looked at her with a look she would describe as disgust.

"Mrs. Bac," he spoke in an impatient tone of voice. "First you come in here complaining for years because Amy's ADHD and now, she's finally settled down and you come in here complaining still. We just can't please you."

If Chad were here, Christy thought, her husband would argue with this doctor. But Chad wasn't here, Christy was alone and she was nothing like her husband. Feeling awful, she took her daughter from the room thankful that the developmental doctor had ordered a Convaid stroller for Amy to keep Amy safe when Christy shopped as her little girl liked to touch everything and run wild. Now the chair was holding Amy as Amy slept all the time.

Thirty one days, Christy thought as she and Chad became more and more frantic. Thirty one days their child had slept. The pediatrician refused a referral to the neurologist. He said there was nothing to concern themselves over. Amy lost seventeen pounds in that month and they were frantic. The child would wake up and suck on her sippy cup for a few minutes, but other than that, Amy slept. And every day Christy went to the doctor's office to show him that her child wasn't waking up.

"This isn't normal!" Christy yelled at Chad as he called the head of the pediatric team and finally a referral for the neurologist was in his hands.

"I can't get an appointment with neurology for a month!" Chad had screamed into the phone and not at Christy. He knew his wife couldn't bear being yelled at. A few minutes later he hung up and turned to Christy. "We're being seen tomorrow."

"Thank you Jesus," she prayed and held Amy in her arms. Someone that knew Amy would at last help the child. A doctor would help Amy.

Chad left the neurologist's office feeling confused and upset. More than an hour he and Christy had sat listening to this doctor say that one in every four autistic children had sleep disorders and eating disorders. "And one in every four autistic children have tic disorders, and OCD and ADHD and epilepsy," Chad had shot back at the neurologist in frustration. "And let's not forget whatever that was with her heart a few months back."

"Let's do a swallow study," the neurologist said and Christy could only cry all the way out to the car with Chad using words he shouldn't be using in front of Amy.

"This is stupid," Chad slammed his car door shut. "The seizures and you being a nervous mother, the autism, the tic, the insanity of Amy never sleeping and being in constant motion and now sleeping all the time and the doctors act like it's our fault!"

Christy cried harder at his words.

"No one cares to figure out what my little one has," Chad slapped the steering wheel and cursed long and loud before reaching for his crying wife. "First it's all on the autism and then all on the drugs to stop the seizures. And we need some help."

"I just want Amy well," Christy cried as Chad started the car.

"As her parents that's all we want," Chad backed out of the parking lot and started down the street. "Is Amy awake?" he asked and Christy looked in the backseat at her little girl.

"Yes, sort of, she's sucking on the sippy cup."

"We're going to Toys R Us," he said and turned the car around. "We give her everything," Chad said. "We go to Disney World often and give her everything. We deny her nothing."

"We live as though every single day is her last," Christy spoke in a firm voice knowing that Chad knew what she knew. Any day, with whatever Amy had, might be Amy's last.

Chad took Amy in for the swallow study and it showed mild dysplasia. The neurologist felt that was the reason for Amy's feeding difficulties and for the change in Amy's speech pattern which he referred to as dysarthria. Christy and Chad had been shocked after Amy woke from sleeping for more than a month with a stutter, though the stutter wasn't bad and later on, the neurologist would assure the parents that one in every four autistic children develop a stutter.

The little girl that Chad and his wife Christy adored had changed. She was quiet. She took two naps a day and slept twelve hours at night. By the time she was eight years old she couldn't play on the baseball team or the swim team any longer. They stayed in soccer because that had been Amy's favorite sport but Amy never left the bench. The little girl overheated easy, she had trouble sweating and she was weak. They were using the stroller to go everywhere they went as Amy tired out after only thirty to forty steps.

"The developmental doctor is back from deployment," Christy told Chad as her husband was preparing for deployment to Afghanistan.

"When's our appointment?" Chad asked and Christy told him the next morning.

With great hope and nervous fear Chad and Christy went into the doctor's office with Amy in her stroller. Things were different now; this doctor met them with wide eyed concern. When he had left Amy had been twenty-eight pounds heavier. She had been running all over his office and now she was with him sitting very still and very quiet. Her shoe size hadn't changed in a year. She'd not grown at all while this developmental doctor was gone. She'd lost a lot of weight and he wondered why no one was worried because he was very worried for Amy.

He said words that Chad and Christy had never heard; myoclonus, chorea, nystagmus and he wrote the words in the records. Christy broke down in tears while Chad told this doctor about Amy's fingers jerking and her shoulders jerking and the doctor saw those things happening that day in his office. A call between him and the neurologist and a test was ordered for another MRI. This doctor also ordered a VCUG test of Amy's kidneys and bladder as she was having chronic UTIs. He ordered a gastric emptying study and another swallow study. He was concerned and he told them he was concerned. Finally, someone was as frightened as Amy's parents.

The MRI was normal, the VCUG test was not and a kidney ultrasound was ordered. They found that Amy's bladder wasn't emptying, but the urine wasn't backing up into her kidneys yet. If the UTIs continued, Amy would need to see a specialist and Christy would need to learn to use the catheter. The swallow study showed not just a swallowing issue but GERD and the gastric emptying study revealed slow emptying of the stomach. The g-tube was discussed for a moment but the team decided feeding therapy was best.

Twice a week Christy was with Amy in feeding therapy and speech therapy. They were back where they'd been when Amy was little and stopped talking. The doctors seemed to Chad and Christy, to blame the seizure medication, so the couple decided as Chad was getting ready to deploy for a year and five months, that they had no choice but to accept what they were being told.

"I'm not strong enough for this," Christy said as she lay in her husband's arms. "Amy's seizures, life in general; Chad. I'm not strong like you are."

"You'll do fine," Chad insisted as he held his wife close. "And I'll be on Skype every night talking to my girls."

"Tell them you can't go," Christy said knowing this wasn't possible.

"You'll do fine," Chad rolled over and looked down into his wife's eyes. "I'll be home in five months for three weeks. We'll move into Shades of Green and enjoy Disney every day all three weeks."

"You're crazy," she laughed while looking up at him and they both turned and looked at Amy sleeping soundly in their bed. They slept with Amy in their bed every night. The child was too prone to seizures and they had the Diastat ready at all times. "I love her Chad," Christy said softly as her husband kissed Amy's cheek and she saw that he was nearly crying.

"I love her too," Chad asserted. "She's our only child and everything we do is for her. She's our way of life. And hopefully, when I get home, she'll have taken a turn and these damn seizures will be controlled and our lives can be good again."

"The doctors haven't found the right seizure medication yet," Christy said when her husband looked to her again.

"That's partly our fault. We didn't know these odd behaviors Amy was showing were seizures. They should educate parents," Chad said knowing now that an ambulatory EEG had been done and the neurologist had told them last week that Amy was having atonic or drop seizures. Myoclonic was the dominant seizure and the neurologist had tested for an SCN1A gene feeling certain that Amy had Dravet syndrome. The test had come in negative, no answer as to why this was happening to little Amy Bac was found….yet, no answer was found yet, Chad thought.

"Maybe we've not found the right doctor," Christy said as her husband stood up from the bed and reached a hand out to her for her to stand up.

"It's our fault Christy," he said once she was on her feet and they were getting dressed for the day. "We didn't know all of these other seizure types to report to the doctor and we've been seeing these behaviors for years. Let's give our medical team here time to figure this out."

"I messed up again," Christy said going to her daughter and kissing Amy lovingly on the cheek. "I didn't want to be influenced by what I read so I never looked up seizures on the internet."

"We didn't know and now we do know," Chad pushed his wife out of the room in front of him. "Let the little one sleep while we finish packing for me. She's just really tired."

"I don't know what child your teacher had last year," Amy's new teacher spoke to Christy in a firm voice as though Christy were one of her students, "but that child," the teacher pointed into the classroom toward Amy, "cannot do what the teacher last year wrote in the cumulative folder Amy could do."

"I don't understand," Christy said and the teacher turned and faced her.

"Amy's in the wrong classroom. We cannot support her in a normal classroom environment. She's struggling to read and write and she has memory issues. Maybe it's the antiepileptic medications, I don't know what it might be, but Amy's moving today into another classroom that's self contained and for special needs children."

This was not good, Christy knew as she left the school and turned to see that Amy was now on the playground sitting on a swing and not swinging. Her wild child that ran everywhere was gone. "It's the drugs," Christy thought and made an appointment to see the neurologist right away.

Within two days the neurologist had Amy in the neuropsychologist's office across the hall and Amy was being tested. Christy was able to watch the testing and she was horrified that Amy heard a story only three sentences long and couldn't tell what the story was about. This was a child that loved her mother reading her the book 'the doll in the garden.'

"Something's happened," Christy cried to Chad on the phone that night and he assured her everything would be all right. That was all Chad could do, he was far from home, from his wife and his child and he couldn't be any help.

Christy was like Amy, she was struggling to eat though her problem was emotional and concern for her child. She lost thirty pounds and was too thin and Amy was just as thin. Mother and daughter clung to one another as Daddy was gone and they were all each other had.

Christy took Amy out on her bike and before they even left the driveway Amy fell off the bike and cracked her helmet. A new helmet bought and training wheels, Christy made the bike rideable again for her child, but Amy couldn't go far even with the training wheels on and the bike, she fatigued after only a few yards and the bike was put away never ridden again by Amy.

Christy woke up on a Sunday morning in July of 2009 and passed Amy's bedroom door. The little girl was standing in front of the television and the television was off. "Hey baby, whatcha doing?" she called into the room and Amy looked up at her mother.

"Who are you?" the little girl asked and Christy laughed at the game she thought Amy meant to play with her.

"Mom yesterday," Christy said in a teasing tone, "Mom today and gonna be Mom tomorrow." She snapped her fingers at Amy and left the room to go get breakfast ready.

Christy came back with a bowl of oatmeal and some apple juice for Amy and she saw the little girl still standing in front of the television. "Who are you again?" Amy asked and Christy frowned seconds before she felt the uncontrollable urge to panic. She ran to the dining room and put down the tray of food reaching for the camcorder and her phone going back to Amy's bedroom and turning the camcorder on.

The phone rang and it was Chad. Frantic Christy told her husband that something had happened to Amy and she turned on the camcorder filming her child as she spoke to her husband. "No, something is different Chad. Amy has changed," Christy cried into the phone as she asked Amy how old the little girl was and Amy stuttered worse than she ever had in her life

"I think I don't know," the child answered her mother's question.

"Chad, something's the matter with Amy," Christy cried and she knew, for a long time now something had been the matter with Amy and no one would help them, no one would help Amy. The medical team blamed everything on the autism and Amy wasn't like any other autistic child. Christy and Chad had joined support groups for autism. They learned everything they could about autism and they were certain, whatever was happening to Amy, was not autism.

Early the next morning Christy was in her car and going to the neurologist's office to meet with the nurse. Amy had suffered a seizure that night and her eye wouldn't blink and close and her smile was only half way on her face. She had the little girl in the front seat beside her; something Christy never did as twelve and under in the State of Florida had to sit in the back seat. But right now there was only Christy and Amy, they had a missing Musketeer in Chad and Christy was frantic that she guard and protect Amy and if the little one had a seizure in the backseat Christy wouldn't know. So Amy was in the front seat and the child would stay in the front seat until Daddy came home.

The nurse came into the room and saw Amy's eye stuck open and the child's half smile and she had Amy squeeze her hand and explained that Amy had weakness was due to Todd's paralysis and things would get better soon.

"We expect this with our Lennox Gastaut patients," the nurse said casually and Christy frowned fiercely.

"What is that?" the mother asked as she held her child on her lap.

"A seizure syndrome," the nurse answered. "Amy's diagnosis. She's been epileptic most of her life, the seizures are often impossible to control, she has a slow and spike wave on some of her EEGs. Clinically that's Amy's diagnosis."

"No, I've never heard this," Christy said knowing that they had been coming here for years with Amy, knowing that Amy had been in and out of the hospital all of her life with seizures, might this really be the answer they were looking for? All this time they had been diagnosed?

"We're doing a trial on a drug called Clobazam," the nurse said and Christy sat numb and in shock and wondering if what she was hearing was true. "If the trial hasn't closed, I think Amy would be perfect for the study."

The neurologist had never even hinted about this Lennox Gastaut to Christy and she didn't believe this diagnosis now. She had the nurse write down the name of this seizure syndrome and she left. She carried Amy out not even stopping to pay on her way out and went home intent on getting on the internet. As it was, Christy's only connection to the internet was a caring site that she journal on for Chad to read. She made the trip to the base in a shorter time as no traffic was out and she went into the house with a sleeping Amy cradled in her arms and she turned on the computer and looked up the Lennox Gastaut.

"Oh God," she prayed as she read. Amy had regressed. Amy was losing skills at school. Amy was on a large dose of seizure medications. Amy had been diagnosed autistic, ADHD and now she couldn't ride her bike, she couldn't run without getting tired and sitting down. She was no longer able to play soccer, baseball and be on the swim team. All Amy was doing now, was bowling.

This LGS – Lennox Gastaut Syndrome sounded correct and Christy held her Amy close and hugged her child and cried waiting on Chad to call so that she could tell him what the nurse had said and Chad, his first words were the nurse had the wrong file; the nurse had made a mistake. Amy didn't have this and Christy hung up thinking Chad was right, a mistake had been made.

Chapter Sixteen

Psalm 94:19: "When anxiety was great within me, your consolation brought joy to my soul."

The neuropsychologist's office called and Christy went into the appointment taking Amy with her as Pensacola was more than an hour away from the base and if Amy had a seizure at school; well Christy wasn't comfortable with being that far away from her fragile child. The doctor sat down with Christy, Amy sitting at a table across the hall playing with her my little pony toys as the mother listened to what the doctor said of his testing.

Amy's IQ had been tested at age six; the child was eight years old now. In that time Amy's IQ had dropped twenty-four points and he had tested her using two different scales and both held the same results. Christy knew this wasn't good and she listened as he explained that what he was seeing in Amy's intellectual decline was consistent with Amy's diagnosis of LGS.

This neuropsychologist was confirming to Christy what the nurse had said and still she couldn't believe what she was hearing. She took the copy of his report and a copy of the testing he had done on Amy for herself and for the school. She then took Amy's hand and went across the hall making an appointment to see the neurologist. In one week, that doctor would confirm that with the akinetic seizures seen on the EEG that Amy did fit the clinical criteria for LGS. And yet, still Christy held on to hope this wouldn't be Amy's diagnosis, unaware that she was in denial as any mother would be.

She sat in the car on the drive home from the neurologist's appointment with Amy beside her. This wasn't the end of the world. Children with LGS rarely died. She and Chad would love Amy no matter what. Amy was their world. And soon Chad would be home on leave and they would be together again and they could put this worry behind them.

Chad came home for three weeks and the family went to Disney World. Amy had changed. She was slow in her walk, she slept more than she had been and she appeared easily confused. Her being a chatterbox was also no longer the case. Amy was speaking as though it were taking all her effort and energy to speak and she was only eating hotdogs cut up as they would be for a baby in tiny pieces and Doritos in small bites and those she wasn't eating much of. She was tired. Their little girl was tired and the neurologist assured them it was not the seizure medications. No doctor knew why Amy was tired and Christy and Chad felt all alone, as though they were on a deserted island with their child and only they cared that Amy was far from okay.

After they returned home from their stay in Disney World, Chad met with the developmental doctor one on one and when Chad left all the papers had been filed to bring him home on compassionate orders as his daughter had a degenerative disease and might be changed even more than she already had been by the seizures.

The paperwork hadn't been filed in time and Christy took her husband to the airport knowing that he was going into a new position overseas and he would be gone more than a year. He had already been gone five months and she would be alone with Amy very unwell.

"I'll probably get turned around somewhere in route," Chad said to his wife as he hugged her and Amy goodbye.

Christy sobbed hysterically holding Amy close as she watched Chad leaving them and she had no idea when he'd be back. She had Amy, Christy thought. She wasn't alone, she had Amy and that's all that mattered right now. Keeping Amy well and keeping Amy safe. Daddy would be home soon.

Chad was stopped in Charlotte, North Carolina where he called home and explained to Christy that they had pulled a base in South Carolina but the base didn't think they could support Amy so he was being routed to Washington, DC where he'd stay until they decided what base to send the family too. Both Chad and Christy hoped it was somewhere near a University hospital. They needed a University hospital. No, Christy thought, Amy needed a University hospital.

Two weeks later Chad would be on his way home from Washington, DC. He was staying at Eglin and they knew, they weren't going to get a second opinion for their child, and they wanted another doctor to go over Amy's medical history. They needed another doctor open minded to look at their child and help Amy because they just weren't trusting of the LGS diagnosis.

Five months after Chad returned, he and Christy decided to stay where they were and feeling confident that Amy didn't have LGS, Chad and Christy bought a home in the country. They were trying to live as normal a life as possible spending long weekends in Orlando and playing in the Disney parks. They had also hired an advocate to help with Amy's feeding disorder. The little girl wasn't growing and she wasn't eating and the therapist was getting nowhere in helping Amy eat.

The Friday before Mother's Day, Christy met with the advocate and made plans for the advocate to follow through with the developmental doctor about what to do for Amy's inability to eat more than a handful of foods and Christy was hopeful that soon a solution would be found in that problem.

That same Friday Amy developed another UTI, the child suffered from these often and it was frustrating for Christy as they no longer gave Amy's tub baths, they kept her clean and dry and Amy had gone into pull-ups because she leaked sometimes. Nothing was working. The UTIs were frequent and the developmental doctor spoke to the parents again about the VCUG test showing that Amy wasn't emptying her bladder and this was to blame.

By Sunday morning Amy's fever was 103 and she was dehydrated. A trip to the emergency room and fluids given, Amy's fever came down and she was sent home. On Tuesday Amy was back in the emergency room, her fever again over 102 and again she was found to be dehydrated. This had been a problem for months now, Amy was often dehydrated and she hadn't grown in three years. Amy was still wearing the same shoe size that she had been wearing at age six.

On Thursday the little girl was back in the emergency room having a seizure and they spent the day also getting fluids. Christy told the doctors what she knew; every time Amy had a fever, the little girl had a seizure. The fever down they went home and Christy could only hope that this infection would pass.

On Mother's day morning Christy woke and found Amy wasn't in the bed. The little girl was on the potty and she was crying as she had to go to the bathroom and couldn't. Amy had started suffering chronic constipation the year before and that situation had become worse as the months passed. Another gastric study showed slower motility and the doctor again said, "we see this in children like Amy with autism."

"Don't push baby," Christy said as she came into the bathroom concerned over hemorrhoids as those had also become a problem. She lifted Amy up, the child was now the smallest one in her classroom and she was in a classroom for handicapped and globally delayed children.

The blood was everywhere and Christy knew this wasn't right. Wrapping Amy up in a quilt she hurried down the stairs forgetting that today was Mother's day. "Chad," she screamed her husband's name as she laid Amy on the front seat of the car and ran to the driver's side. "I'm going to the emergency room now!"

Her husband stood with a fork in his hand in the garage doorway, she'd left him eating breakfast.

Christy drove to the emergency room and picked Amy up in her arms hurrying inside. The man at the desk saw the blood and told Christy to go clean up the child. "What?" she had asked him in a voice that she knew made her sound stupid and he pointed for her to leave. Not knowing what else to do, being a victim for most of her life, Christy left holding Amy close in her arms and wondering where she should go now and aware that she had left Chad at home. She went into the bathroom with Amy securely held and she stood there feeling too afraid to move.

"Am I gonna die mommy?" Little Amy Bac asked her mother and Christy shook her head leaving the bathroom and going back into the emergency room area where she stood screaming her head off one word and everyone in the downstairs area of the hospital heard this horrified and frightened mother screaming.

"HELP!" over and over she screamed and a doctor grabbed Amy from her, a nurse pushed her into a room and within five minutes Christy, with Amy was in an ambulance, were being medivaced to the Children's hospital in Pensacola.

Amy had malnourished. Amy's rectum had prolapsed and she was malnourished. The advocate they had hired came to the hospital with all of Amy's medical records that Mother's Day afternoon showing how the family had been fighting for months over Amy's weight loss and failure to grow. The advocate showed that three times a week Christy was taking Amy to feeding therapy and she

showed of the GERD testing and the gastric emptying study. The team at the children's hospital decided that the g-tube needed to be placed. But the neurologist and the developmental doctor said no.

And while Amy was in PICU with her rectum prolapsed, the poor little girl developed c-diff.

"She can't catch a break," Chad swore as he paced the room.

"I've gone over her records and your right Mr. Bac, this little girl hasn't caught a break," the surgeon said to the parents. "The g-tube will elevate the feeding disorder. The VNS is going in within two months from now to help with the seizures. Right now let's concentrate on the prolapsed rectum and on the c-diff. Amy needs to get well before I put in the g-tube.

The GI doctor came in and he told the family upfront that he felt feeding therapy needed to continue and Christy knew that she would never give up trying to get her child to eat. The GI left satisfied and Christy held on to the hope that the G-tube was premature. Chad held no such hope. Since Amy had gone to sleep that month two years ago his child had come awake changed and he didn't care if the doctors said it was an eating disorder due to autism, he knew his child wasn't getting nourished and the tests in this hospital proved that to be the case.

Christy kept remembering the year and seven months that Amy didn't speak. She kept in the front of her mind how in one day Amy had made a complete recovery from the silent world the little girl lived in. Amy had come back and she had come back strong talking better than ever. What had happened before would happen again. Amy would come back and make another recovery. The little girl just needed time and her mother decided to cling to that hope.

Christy had joined an online support group for LGS a few weeks before Amy's rectum prolapsed and in that group; she had met a mother that was certain that Amy didn't have LGS making Christy feel comfortable that Amy wasn't going to get any worse. This mother was saying what Christy needed to hear, what

Christy wanted to be true and the mother's words allowed Christy to believe that with the right medication, her daughter Amy would have seizure control.

The plans had already been made through the military to send Amy to Portsmouth, Virginia to have the vagal nerve stimulator placed and for Chad and Christy to speak with the neurologist there in Portsmouth about the LGS diagnosis. Christy had been speaking with the mother online about LGS and that mother kept insisting that Amy didn't have that diagnosis. Christy brought this up with the developmental doctor and he encouraged her to cut any tie with this woman that lived in North Carolina and was very popular both on the internet and in the LGS community. The developmental doctor stated clearly that it was no concern of some internet popular woman that didn't know Amy to state that Amy didn't have a diagnosis that highly educated doctors said that Amy did have. He was also worried because he knew Christy was in denial and he further knew that like almost every mother, Christy was blaming herself because nothing she was doing for Amy was helping Amy get better.

"This woman in North Carolina wants to meet and have lunch with us on our way up to Virginia," Christy confided to the developmental doctor as he met with Amy to clear the little girl for travel.

"No, Christy," he spoke firmly to her. "You don't want Amy to have LGS, and maybe she doesn't," he looked down at the little girl and he wrote his concerns, he felt Amy had some sort of a metabolic disorder. "But the fact is Amy has seizures and they're not well controlled. She's regressed a lot in the past two years. She was in the 95th percentile for growth and now she's in the 40th percentile. Something is the matter with Amy and no internet popular woman in North Carolina is going to diagnosis this child with what you want to hear. Stay away from that woman; she sounds like she has her own agenda."

Something's the Matter with Amy

"I won't go near her," Christy promised and with the all clear to go to Virginia, she and Chad started their trip heading north-east.

"That woman is calling again," Christy said to her husband speaking of the North Carolina mother that was popular in the LGS group and on the internet.

"She's inserted herself into our lives," Chad said in a harsh voice. "She calls at one in the morning and at eleven in the evening. I know you've told her not to call that late because we go to bed early. But this is awful. She's calling all hours of the day and night. Do not answer that phone."

Christy didn't tell her husband of her talk with the doctor, instead she told him that the woman wanted to meet for lunch and that she didn't want to meet the woman. He agreed and they drove through North Carolina intent on getting to the base in Virginia. They both needed to see this neurologist. They had seen he had every record and test done on their daughter and they were almost sick over what he might say. Had they found that right doctor that would tell them this wasn't because of autism?

Settled into their hotel room, Chad and Christy took Amy out to IHOP. The little girl loved scrambled eggs and so they knew that she would eat something. The surgery was coming up and they wanted her as strong as possible for that surgery. They had some time to kill and they went to Busch Gardens and then to Williamsburg, neither answering their phones and they had no laptops with them so they never got online. They made the most of their family time together before the surgery.

They finally met the neurologist at the hospital and he sat down looking at the nervous parents and he held up the file and assured them that their daughter had a seizure syndrome. "She's been epileptic all of her life. I know she had years of normal development with autistic features, but your daughter never had true autism. This is some form of a progressive disorder or disease." He looked at

Amy and Chad and Christy saw him frowning when he did. "How long has your daughter had chorea?"

"That just started about a year ago," Christy said as the doctor looked into Amy's eyes with some funny thing on his eye.

"She has nystagmus as well," He reached and helped Amy to her feet. "Can you walk for me sweetheart?" he asked Amy and she ran around the room. He opened the door and he saw her walking down the hallway and he said, "Well, that's good. She has a normal gait and station." He sat back down and Christy saw him looking at the MRI reports. "This is hopeful," he said and looked back up at the family. "The MRIs are normal. That makes me more confident that this is a seizure syndrome. The VNS should help."

Christy broke down and she told this neurologist of the popular internet woman online saying this wasn't LGS, that Amy was only mildly mentally retarded and Christy wanted the popular internet woman to be right. The doctor was kind and he was patient asking what medical school the popular internet woman went too and Chad told the doctor the woman was uneducated.

"Grasping at straws," the doctor spoke kindly to Christy. "Amy has a diagnosis of LGS right now. She fits the criteria for a seizure syndrome. Let's hope that's all this is." He patted Christy's shoulder, shook Chad's hand and let Amy hug him. "I want to make this clear to you both," the doctor turned from the door and held up Amy's file. "Amy's lost a lot of skills and abilities in the past two years, is that due to the seizures? I don't know. What I can tell you is that this is not autism and this is not caused by medication. God bless her and she's a beautiful little girl."

The North Carolina woman that was popular on the internet called as Chad was driving off the base and Christy spoke to the woman hoping this was the last time. She didn't need this woman in her life. She was too afraid for her child and her child had to be her focus and concern.

"The neurologist diagnosed LGS. I can't talk now. Goodbye." Thinking that would be the end of this popular internet woman, Christy and Chad moved forward with Amy's surgery and the VNS was placed. When going home two weeks later, Chad decided to take I-95 and avoid Charlotte and the Winston Salem area where that popular internet woman told Christy that she lived.

"We have to be careful of getting online," Chad said as they came home and Christy agreed never dreaming in a million years how dangerous it was to have the caring site, a site established when Chad was deployed as a way for Christy to journal to him and a way for him to read, with ease all that was happening back home. And too, many videos of Amy were posted on youtube, posted there so that a father deployed far away, could see his little girl growing up in those videos.

Amy had a seizure two days after they returned home from Virginia and together Chad and Christy took the child to their neurologist and he turned on the VNS. Praying and hoping the thing would cure their child they went home and within hours they learned that Amy could no longer be supported in the local school. The school system was putting Amy in the school for the globally developmentally delayed and handicapped children.

"There's been a mistake," Christy said in tears. "My child can read."

"She isn't even on a first grade level, Mrs. Bac," the school psychologist spoke in a patient voice to the upset mother. "I know from her cumulative folder that Amy once could read and was doing well in math, but by the second grade everything began failing for her. She's struggling to talk; the stutter and slurring are slowing her speech way down. In this school we can target Amy's weak areas and hopefully help with her feeding disorder."

"I don't want this," Christy said to Chad as they left the school each holding one of Amy's hands.

"We've got a full plate," Chad said looking at his wife. "Amy's got too much going on. That lady is right; our child is going backwards Christy. If our little one keeps up this pace of sliding backward, she's going to be an infant in a few years."

"Don't say that Chad," Christy couldn't cry, Amy was with them and Amy was listening.

"It's time to push the neurologist for more testing," Chad said and he pulled out his cell phone and in the parking lot of Amy's new school he made an appointment for not just the neurologist, but to go back and meet with the geneticist at Keesler Air Force Base.

Christy went home that Friday afternoon and Amy was asleep on the sofa when she turned on her computer and saw this popular internet woman in North Carolina had posted on Amy's caring site in the guestbook and the posts were mean calling Amy fake and accusing Christy of copying her daughter. Thinking it was best to ignore this woman; Christy locked the caring site down and closed her computer. Amy came first. All she cared about was Amy.

Chad had gotten hardcopies of all of Amy's medical records from all of her doctors and he had gotten all of her testing on CD from every hospital she had ever been too. He was a man on a mission and he had no idea what his mission was. He and Christy spent hours reading Amy's early reports from the neurologist. All read Static Encephalopathy and looking that up they learned it meant unchanged brain disease often seen in autism.

They read every EEG report and were shocked to learn that when Amy was ten months old the neurologist had been so concerned over her EEG that he had advised a video EEG and the nurse had written that the parents refused. How could they have refused when they weren't asked? Chad shouted and he saw his wife withdraw from him when he did. "I'm not mad at you," Chad said and he saw the status encephalopathy over and over again until after the big sleep. The report changed after the big sleep had occurred and the records now read encephalopathy unspecified.

Normal gait, normal strength, normal reflexes, no dysmetria, these were all positive things and the couple settled down and felt confident this was a seizure syndrome. And to add to that, they were seeing and recording these partial complex episodes and showing them to the neurologist and he advised they not yell at Amy in these episodes as they were yelling and pleading with her to see them.

"She's epileptic, that's the one thing I'm certain of," the neurologist said to the parents at the appointment Chad had made. "I don't know if this is autism. She certainly presented early with autism, but now, I'm just not certain." He ordered blood testing for Amy and he had all of his records faxed over to Keesler Air Force Base. "When Amy was tested with genetics in 2003 things were different. We've come a long way in six years; let's get some more testing done."

After the VNS had been placed, Christy started taking Amy daily to the local park near their new home. There was a huge lovely pond with a covered picnic area and there was a water park on the hill and a park with a rock wall on the other side. Every afternoon Christy would give Amy money and they would go buy day old bread and head for the pond. Christy videotaped Amy feeding the ducks and the geese and running from the fowl laughing as the little girl did. Sometimes in the evenings Chad would come with them and they would feed the turtles and the fish at the edge of the pond. They were a family, they were enjoying life and though Amy wasn't like other children, she was still doing well in her new school, better than anyone had predicted. She also had a little boy friend which everyone found adorable as the little boy liked Amy as well.

Amy also had a service dog named Sheltie, and the dog was also Amy's best friend and Christy's helpmate. Early on the dog had learned to predict when Amy would have a seizure. No one understood how the dog instinctively knew the seizure was coming, but Christy could now cook dinner in the kitchen with Amy in her playroom and when Amy had a seizure, the dog came and got Christy. It was impressive to see. The dog was much like Lassie in the movies.

Amy fell. No big deal, all children fall, Christy thought as she helped her daughter up. But Amy had fallen hard and Amy had made no attempt to pull herself up. While holding the video camcorder Christy noted that Amy was swaying in her walk and she lowered the camera and watched her little girl walking.

"That's not normal," Christy said and she knew, all the doctors would blame the seizure medication or they'd probably say it's the VNS now. So Christy noted the change in Amy's walk and carried on living, waiting for the next doctor appointment in Keesler.

Chad took off and drove them to Keesler. The neurologist's office had called and told Christy that they found a duplication of chromosome 16p11.2 in Amy and that was known to cause autism and seizures. Amy's diagnosis was at last made and they referred Christy to the Simons VIP research program. The trip to Keesler was just a sit down with a geneticist to discuss the 16p11.2, but that doctor didn't speak of the duplication in Amy.

This geneticist was the same one that had seen Amy as a two and three year old suspected of having autism and he looked at the girl now not yet ten years old and he shook his head. "I'm confirming the diagnosis of a seizure syndrome. The 16p11.2 duplication does not have the repeat regressions we're seeing in Amy. And she has things going on now that weren't going on when she was little. I see myoclonic jerks now and chorea and nystagmus. Amy's not ADHD now and I see more developmental delays than I see autistic tendencies."

This doctor again went over Amy carefully as he had many years ago and he ordered the parents to the lab. "One of you will have the exact same duplication, because this child's diagnosis is not connected to the duplication. More testing and studies need to be done on Amy. I'd like to keep following her."

Chad and Christy went to the hospital lab. Christy was certain that the duplication would belong to her. She saw Amy fall again for no reason. The child was on her feet one moment and on her face the next moment. "Baby," she had cried out and picked up Amy from the floor.

"I'm okay Mommy," Amy said and patted her mother's back in comfort. "I just fall. I don't know why." Christy put Amy back in the stroller Chad was now pushing as he'd gone out to the car for the stroller because Amy was tired. Christy told him that Amy fell again and he lifted his child up and into her stroller.

"She falls because she's tired and she's tired because of the seizure," Chad spoke with confidence.

"I don't know," Christy worried as they pushed Amy in the stroller. "She's not having grand mals as much now. Mostly they're all absence or partial complex."

"They're wearing her out," Chad spoke in a certain voice. "Remember our last trip to Disney?" Christy did remember that trip. She had left the camcorder running and sitting on the table aimed at Amy on accident and the child had back to back absence seizures obvious on the video and when they realized what was happening and they had used the rescue medication.

"And in Busch Garden's," Christy said knowing that she had been filming Amy when Amy's eyes had darted upward and to the side and Amy dropped with Grover catching her.

"The seizures are wearing her out and we'll figure this out. We have a geneticist now on our side," Chad was feeling better and he planned another trip to Disney World after Amy had the g-tube placed.

Chapter Seventeen

Isaiah 43:1: "But now, this is what the Lord says…Fear not, for I have redeemed you; I have summoned you by name; you are mine."

"That woman that's popular on the internet and in the LGS community has posted again on Amy's caring site," Chad said speaking of the North Carolina woman that they had not even thought of in more than a month. "It was unkind and there are several posts." He sat down on the bed and he saw that Amy was sleeping with the feeding tube running. The little girl was resting shortly after the g-tube surgery.

"I'll remove them," Christy said and went quickly to remove the posts. "I wish I'd never spoken to that woman Chad. She seems to be determined to let me know Amy doesn't have LGS. Who cares what Amy has? She's just a little girl and Amy's not hurting that North Carolina Woman."

Within the hour the woman called her on the phone and Christy looked at Chad aware she had no idea how to handle this situation. "Please, leave me alone," Christy answered the phone and after she said this the woman went on a tirade of how Christy was copying her daughter and there was nothing wrong with Amy. Chad reached for the phone and hung up the phone.

"We ignore her," he said and Christy agreed. This woman was nothing to their life and she never would be. All that mattered was Amy.

"You can't be serious," Chad yelled into the phone seeing his wife withdraw from him and hide in the bathroom. He knew that he couldn't yell in front of her without her going back in time to the nightmare she had survived. Chad threw the phone on the sofa and went to his wife. "The developmental doctor said we didn't consult Amy's primary on the g-tube and they won't approve the formula because they think feeding therapy is enough."

"She malnourished Chad," Christy said looking up at her husband.

"I know," he said and took a deep breath. "Amy's not going to malnourish again. I'll buy the formula."

Christy watched her husband gear up for his motorcycle trip to the base where he worked and she looked at Amy on the sofa asleep. Amy slept a lot. Picking up the phone she dialed the surgeon's office, the doctor that put in the g-tube and she told the nurse at the office about the formula not being approved by insurance. The nurse shouted into the phone and Christy screamed hanging up the phone and bursting into tears. She wasn't cut out for this constant battle to get Amy services and appointments. She was a coward. Christy was afraid of the whole world.

The phone rang and Christy answered in a weak and timid voice. "I didn't mean to yell," the nurse said from the surgeon's office. "I just told the doctor and she's ordered the formula for Amy, it should be there in three days. In the meantime come to the hospital and I'll give you enough for a week."

"Is this a common problem?" Christy asked the nurse as she looked at Amy sleeping and knowing that she'd have to wake her daughter up to go for the formula.

"Believe it or not, this is a common problem and it's a stupid one that doesn't need to happen," the nurse answered and Christy hung up reaching to pick Amy up and get into the car to go back to Pensacola and to the hospital. The nurse met her at valet parking and put the formula in her trunk allowing Amy to sleep and Christy cried the whole way home. Nothing was easy for them. Nothing was easy for Amy. The little girl didn't deserve this; Amy was just an innocent child.

The popular internet woman in North Carolina called again in September and Christy chose to do as she and Chad decided to do and ignore the call. Within a week they found a YouTube site in Christy's name not put up by Christy.

"That's odd," Chad said as he looked at the site in his wife's full name and there were videos of Amy on the site, videos where someone was poking fun at the way Amy talked. "I'll have the site taken down," Chad said and he sent Christy's photo identification to YouTube and told them the site wasn't hers and within a few hours the site was down and Chad and Christy carried on taking care of Amy and now dealing with the VNS, pull-ups and formula in a feeding tube.

The feeding tube was the most wonderful thing that had happened to them. Amy was still in feeding therapy and she was still not progressing with eating by mouth, but the tube took away all worries over the little girl not eating. Amy had gained up to a normal weight and her skin had a glow. Best of all the medications were going in and the seizures were much better controlled. Chad and Christy felt that for the first time in a long time, they had taken a step forward in Amy's health though the primary care doctor refused the prescription for the formula to be paid for through insurance, the surgeon's office was supplying all Amy needed.

While in Disney World, Chad got the call from the geneticist at Keesler Air Force Base. Chad had the 16p11.2 duplication. Chad had enjoyed a twenty-four year career in the military, he had his degrees, the duplication was normal for him and Amy's was identical to his, therefore Amy should be like her Daddy. This doctor felt that he was right, there was something else going on with little Amy Bac.

Little Amy Bac had a secret and she feared her secret was known to her mommy because she kept seeing mommy cry in the kitchen. She would hug her mommy and tell her mommy that she loved her all the time hoping mommy would be okay again. But still, little Amy Bac saw her mommy crying and one day as they went into the surgeon's office for her formula she tipped over again and slammed into the floor and mommy screamed out loud in fear and picked her up and they both cried.

"I don't mean to fall," Amy said hugging her mother around the neck.

"I know you don't baby mine," Christy said to her sweet child. This beautiful little angel that prayed and knew Jesus Christ as her savior, was precious and adorable, despite whatever illness that she had, Amy was precious and adorable.

"I fall all the time," Amy said and stood up only to tip over again.

"Let's get the formula and go to the park," Christy held tightly to Amy's hand confident that by holding the little girl's hand Amy wouldn't fall again.

"We don't have any food for the ducks," Amy said as they reached the park and got out and Christy grabbed her camcorder. Christy had been filming when Amy fell at the surgeon's office only an hour before and she had filmed Amy swaying walk. Something was very wrong with her child and she was scared. Within a few minutes Amy attempted to climb the rock wall and couldn't, Christy became more fearful and Christy knew. Something was the matter with Amy. Something that was autism or epilepsy.

"Don't fall," Christy screamed as Amy attempted to climb the ladder to the slide. Amy had always been a monkey climbing everywhere. Her nickname from Chad and Christy both had been monkey as they'd lived across the street on base from a park with two sets of monkey bars and Amy climbed those bars swift and sure. Now Amy couldn't climb the ladder to the slide.

"Now that I'm retired," Chad said when Christy answered her phone on the drive home, "we can choose our own doctors with no referrals. I have us an appointment with the geneticist in Birmingham."

"Do you think she might help?" Christy knew, she knew what Chad didn't know. Amy was struggling to walk without falling.

"I don't know, but we're going to try," Chad said and after she hung up, Christy called her brother Allen and she confessed to her brother how Amy was falling, tipping over.

"Just like Mama," Allen spoke in a frantic voice. Her brother knew, their mother had died and their mother had died slowly over many years losing skills and abilities slowly winding up in a nursing home for the last years of her life. Her children barely knew her because of the disease that robbed them of their mother.

"Maybe it's the seizure medications," Christy said to her older and trusted brother.

"Maybe she's just like Mama," Allen spoke in a doom and gloom voice and heard his little sister crying. He knew, he knew how she'd been abused and blamed for things that weren't in her control and he wondered, of all the people to go through something like this, why his sister that had already suffered far too much in this life?

The popular internet woman in North Carolina had posted many times on the caring site. Christy ignored the woman and carried on until in January the woman started calling night and day saying into the phone that Christy was a liar and worse. This made no sense, why in the world did this woman care about them? They didn't even know her.

Chad notified the police and showed the officer all the missed calls from this popular internet woman in North Carolina on his wife's phone. The officer informed them that in order to file a report they had to have the calls documented. "Just flip your phone open and close it, the call will register on your bill."

Within hours the popular internet woman called again. Christy opened and close the phone and the popular internet woman would call right back. Over and over again the calls came in registering on their phone bill each time, the popular internet woman wasn't giving up. Chad finally had enough and he answered the phone. He tried in his diplomatic way to reason with the woman. "Just leave us alone and we'll leave you alone." The calls continued through the night and the next day Chad filed a police report and at last the calls stopped.

The trip to Alabama was not what Christy and Chad had thought it would be. A mother that was an advocate came with them as they felt better with a third party ear listening to what the doctor said. Surprisingly the doctor came in and told the couple that she didn't know what more she could do for them than had already been done. The advocate spoke and before the appointment was over tests had been ordered for a suspected mitochondrial disease and both Chad and Christy said the real reason they were here was because they wanted the diagnosis of LGS confirmed.

As they left Alabama, the couple were filled with hopes. They had found a doctor that would soon tell them what Amy had, the doctor would treat the illness and Amy would stop regressing. This had been so simple when for years their lives had been consumed with trying to find help and help was only a few hours away north of their home near Eglin Air Force Base.

Christy found her YouTube site was again copied and again in her full name. The site also put her age as 100 years old and said that she was a fat, ugly and some very dirty word. This made no sense, Christy thought and again she approached her husband showing him what was done, only now the site was attached to an adult website that was pornographic. Within minutes Chad called the local police and the site was taken down. This time YouTube was advised to monitor any site put up in Christy or Chad's full name and the couple again knew that being online wasn't safe.

They had the caring site locked down, only people that were invited could write on the site and Christy only had one group she was in on Facebook at that time. The group was a prayer warrior group. She was still a member of the Yahoo LGS group, but rarely did she post there. Instead Christy had developed a friendship with other mother's and they were her friends online and her Facebook was not public. The popular internet woman in North Carolina wasn't a concern to Christy and after the phone calls were stopped, Christy never thought of her.

In March they went back to Alabama and checked into the epilepsy monitoring unit. Before they even got into a room Amy fell for no reason, she just fell. The epileptic specialist saw her fall and put a yellow band on Amy's wrist that read 'fall risk.'

"How long has she been walking like that?" the epileptic specialist asked Christy and Christy told the doctor only for a couple of months. Amy had the EEG leads attached to her head and was in the bed comfortable and playing. The epileptic specialist kept Amy on her seizure medications and she left the VNS on.

With Amy settled in the room the specialist took Christy into another room and spoke with her about Amy. Christy frowned as the doctor questioned the LGS diagnosis and Christy said that she doubted the diagnosis. The specialist then looked with Christy at videos of Amy at age seven playing soccer and baseball. Christy shared Amy's school work and cumulative folder as well as the neuropsychologist's testing and all of the past EEGs.

"I'll let you know," the doctor said and sent a nurse in for blood from Amy. "I don't think this is LGS. I have a diagnosis in mind for your child. We'll see how this goes."

Christy was filled with hope. This doctor had a diagnosis in mind, that was the best news ever. With a diagnosis came hope of a line to stand in for treatment and cure. Feeling relieved, Christy came into Amy's room and saw the nurse taking Amy's blood and Amy being as Amy always was, good natured and happy. A huge smile lighting up the little girl's face as she colored in her book and watched the Disney channel.

The week was long and hard. Amy didn't sleep much nor did Christy. By day three the epileptic specialist came into the room and said that Amy wasn't an epileptic. Christy was torn between shocked and happy. "How could the other neurologists make such a mistake?"

"I don't know," this epileptic specialist said to Christy. "I'm ordering an MRI and an MRA for Amy and more testing. I'm certain I know what this is." She turned to leave the room, but at the door she looked back at Christy. "You're remembering it wrong. Your daughter never ran nor did she play well. She's always been as she is now. You're remembering it wrong Mrs. Bac. Are we clear on this?"

"I have photo and videos of Amy playing soccer and baseball," Christy spoke up almost feeling angry and Christy never felt angry.

"Then look at them, you'll see, Amy never ran." The woman left the room and Christy hurried and called Chad and told him what the epileptic specialist had said,

"Amy's not an epileptic?" he asked in a raised voice. "After 147 trips to the emergency room in her lifetime with her caught in a seizure? No damn way. And we're not remembering it wrong. We have videos of her running in Disney World and at the park. Amy ran and she rode her bike and she danced in church and she played the piano and she didn't start stuttering until a few years ago."

"It's true Chad, she told me Amy's not an epileptic and we're remembering it wrong. Amy never ran," Christy said to her husband and now she was in tears.

"Listen to me baby," Chad spoke in a firm tone of voice. "I'm leaving here now; I'll be there before midnight. Amy's on three seizure medications and she has a VNS. Not seeing seizures at this time is because they're controlled. We've had control in the past, but it never lasted long. Do not let that woman turn off the VNS or take away Amy's medications."

"She already has Chad," Christy fell apart crying hysterically and wanting to cuss someone out the way her husband did when he was at the end of his rope.

"I'm on my way," Chad said and he made it to his wife in record time with a speeding ticket to prove he drove fast.

"The MRI and MRA were normal," the specialist said to Chad and Christy. "All testing was normal. You'll leave Amy's seizure drugs here,"

"Oh no we won't," Chad used his military voice and he took a step toward the woman. "We've been in the hospital one hundred and forty seven times with my daughter trapped in seizure. We're not leaving here without her medication."

"I've turned off the VNS and the drugs have been disposed of," Chad was told and he looked at his wife in shock. "Your daughter has a medical condition called Alternating Hemiplegia of Childhood. The medication isn't legal in the United States, but you can get it through Canada. Here's the prescription. Amy's episodes are not seizures; they are what is seen in Alternating Hemiplegia of Childhood."

"She's serious Chad," Christy said and sat down taking a deep breath. "Amy's going to be fine once we get this medication."

"This is bull," Chad said and started throwing Amy's clothes into a suitcase.

An appointment was made to follow up with this doctor in four weeks. Christy could see that her husband was upset, but she was relieved. Amy would get well with this drug and their lives would be happy again and Amy would be reading and telling stories and running around the yard with her service dog again in no time.

Christy's hopes and expectations were not met. Within days of returning home Amy was jerking, myoclonic, Christy thought and wished this wasn't happening. Christy also went to field day and she videotaped Amy's walk and Amy was now obviously clumsy to anyone watching her for a brief moment. Within three weeks of their return from Alabama, Christy knew she had to get Amy into a new neurologist.

"I've got the MRI and MRA report," Chad said into the phone to his wife. "The MRA is normal, the MRI is not."

"I don't understand," Christy said ready to burst into tears.

"I also have all the blood tests on Amy," Chad went on speaking. They had gotten the medication for Alternating Hemiplegia of Childhood and Amy had broken out in a rash. "The gene that causes AHC is negative," Chad spoke in a harsh voice. "The woman also tested for Spinocerebellar ataxia type six Christy and Amy's MRI states there is atrophy of the cerebellum."

"Amy's new primary has a copy of all of Amy's MRIs Chad," Christy stood up and pulled on her shoes. "I signed for him to get all records from Alabama too. He'll have this by now. I'm going to try and get worked in to him today. Amy's not due home from school for five hours."

Christy hung up from her husband and hurried to Amy's primary care doctor's office. The man was wonderful and he was going to lunch motioning for Christy to join him. "I have the reports now," he said and looked at her from across his desk as he swallowed a bite of his sandwich. "I can tell you this," he looked through the papers, "Amy does not have Alternating Hemiplegia of Childhood – AHC. I've compared Amy's MRIs that I have on CD and Christy; there is atrophy of a part of the brain that controls movement and coordination. This is not good and I feel confident Amy is having seizures." He wrote a script for an anti-seizure drug and slid it across his desk. "You need to see a new neurologist."

"But her old neurologist,"

"Hasn't been a lot of help to Amy," the primary said looking at Christy. "The man jumped on autism when Amy wasn't clearly autistic and she hadn't even turned two yet. And your little Amy is regressing. I've seen her walk and its ataxic now Christy. This is not good. Go to this neurologist," he wrote a name down on a piece of paper and handed it to Christy. "Do you remember what you told me about your mother?" Christy nodded completely unable to breathe. "You said you were afraid Amy has what your mother had." Christy slowly and carefully nodded her head. "I think you're right. Look this up," he wrote down on another piece of paper – Spinocerebellar ataxia.

"My mother," Christy said and the doctor nodded his head.

"You've known for a long time what happened to your mother Christy and you've seen the signs in Amy. That's why you've been so afraid. I'll call this neurologist and get an appointment for Amy right away. Atrophy in the brain of a child is bad. Trust what you're seeing Christy. You've know for a while that Amy's not all right."

"So the diagnosis of LGS was always wrong?" Christy asked and the primary stood walking her to the door.

"LGS is a criteria a child must meet. Regression and uncontrolled seizures are what doctors look for and that's what Amy's been living with. I'll call you with an appointment time for this neurologist."

Christy took Amy to this new neurologist more than two hours away early in the morning. The man saw how Amy's eyes weren't even and he saw her walk and he witnessed her unresponsive and staring and her pupils dilated and he turned to Christy. "Move to a big city right away," he said and Christy shook her head.

"We just bought our house less than a year ago. We can't move."

"Move," the doctor said. "There's an ataxic research center in Tampa, go, leave as soon as you can. Get to any big city with a major Children's hospital."

Christy left the office and called Chad in tears. "No worries," Chad said. "We've done everything for our little one Christy. I'll put out my application and we'll move. I make enough money to support two homes."

"The specialist in Alabama, we see her next week," Christy cried on.

"And we will, both of us together with our little Amy," Chad said still unaware that his child was now diagnosed ataxic. "We'll move, just wait, it won't be long."

Christy was shocked. The popular internet woman in North Carolina had posted on the internet that Christy had Munchausen's by proxy and was copying her child. There was a fourteen page blog on Amy and both Chad and Christy saw the blog and ignored the thing. They were too afraid for their child to worry about someone they didn't know that didn't know what they were going through.

Chad was offered a job in Los Angeles but he nor Christy wanted to leave Florida. Within the week, he was offered a job at MacDill Air Force Base in Tampa with U.S. Central Command and he accepted the day they drove up to meet with the Alabama epileptic specialist.

"What are you doing here?" the specialist asked in a voice that was awful to hear of Chad and Christy. She never even looked at Amy.

"We have an appointment," Chad answered in as equally an awful voice. "My daughter broke out in a rash taking this drug," he put it down in front of her. "We got it from Canada as you told us to do. We're also seeing what we are concerned are seizures," he didn't bother to tell her that the primary care doctor had put Amy back on an anti seizure medication.

"There's nothing more I can do for you if Amy can't take this medication," she said and stood up and Chad stood up with her.

"Excuse me," he moved to stand in front of the door. "We waited two hours to see you. We drove up from Florida. I have all of Amy's test results and she doesn't have the gene that causes

AHC and you tested for SCA6 after you found atrophy on the MRI of Amy's cerebellum."

"I can't help you," the woman spoke again and Chad moved out of her way while opening the door for her.

"No, you can't help us and you never did. Here," Chad shoved a CD at the woman. "Because of what you told my wife she's spent hours looking at videos and photos of our daughter running. She made a video of Amy speaking normally and running many times. We're not remembering it wrong. We're that little girl's parents and the best source of information for you doctors. If you don't listen to the parents, you won't ever know the child. On that CD you'll see my child ran well and walked normally and her past doctors documented that fact in Amy's records. You owe us an apology. Doctors take an oath to do no harm. That child is a child. She deserved not to be harmed."

Chad picked up Amy and within the hour they'd called the medical director of the hospital and told what had happened to their child. Within the month, Chad, Christy and their little Amy were on their way to Tampa. The plan was to take only what they'd need, rent an apartment, get Amy diagnosed and treated and go home. "We'll be here for about six months," Chad said to Christy as they unloaded their car on a hot June day. "Just six short months and Amy will be well and we'll be home."

Christy got Amy into a neurologist in Tampa and the doctor already had all of Amy's records and testing on CD. She came into the room and saw Amy and looked at Christy. "The records say the child has an abnormal gait and station. When did this happen?" she had Amy walk and saw the little girl swaying from side to side, she also saw the chorea like movements and the jerks.

"The past six months," Christy said watching Amy fall and not even attempt to hold out her hands and catch herself. The neurologist reached in a box for a ball smaller than a beach ball, but a good size and she threw the ball to Amy. Amy didn't even try to catch the ball and it hit the little girl in the head.

"I watched all the videos you sent me on DVD," this female neurologist said and they went back into a private room. "I think epilepsy is the least of your daughter's problems at this point. The brain atrophy is far more concerning. I think she has Spinocerebellar ataxia." There were the two words Christy had heard before. "Let me do some testing and I want her in for an EEG as soon as possible. I saw where the doctor in Alabama took her cold turkey off of the anti-seizure drugs. I'm unsure what is a problem now for Amy because she needed to be weaned off the drugs and frankly, I feel with her past EEG results Amy needs those drugs. Today I'm turning back on the VNS and I want you to go to Quest lab for this testing. Do not hesitate to go to the ER if Amy appears to be in crisis."

Christy took Amy to the lab and had Amy's blood taken. She then went home and helped Amy into a swimsuit and the two went out to the pool and swam. This was all Christy could do. She had to wait for testing. At least the VNS was back on and Amy was on the one seizure medication.

Chapter Eighteen

Psalm 23:4: "Even though I walk through the valley of the shadow of death, I will fear no evil, for you are with me; your rod and your staff, they comfort me."

The whole world had gone mad. Amy was now terrified of escalators, something that she had loved all of her life. She screamed in the elevator and she fell for no reason. She had a busted chin from a fall and by the end of June she was waddling like a duck, not just swaying. Her feet were wide apart and she was crouched and stooped. Christy had opened up the caring site intent on updating it before she went to bed one night and forgot to close the site down. The next morning the popular internet woman from North Carolina called Christy and Christy didn't answer her phone. Within a moment a text came through begging Christy to answer the phone and she did wondering what accusation this woman wanted to hurl at her now and not caring. Amy wasn't all right. Amy was far from all right and Christy was scared for her child.

"Some man is posting ugly on the caring site, you need to see what he posted on your site," the popular internet woman said to Christy and Christy hung up the phone. Let anyone post what they wanted, she didn't care. The woman texted her and she texted back that she had nothing to say and wanted nothing to do with the woman and let that be the end of that.

Before mid afternoon Christy had Amy out in the pool. She then came inside and they made cookies together. By four in the afternoon Amy was talking to Chad, only Chad wasn't home. She then started talking to her friend from back at Eglin and she wouldn't respond when Christy begged the little girl to look at her. A phone call to the new female neurologist and she was advised to get Amy to the nearest emergency room.

"The little girl was taken off her medications too quickly," the neurologist said. "And she has a past history of intractable seizures. Move fast, don't wait. Seizures can kill. Call 911 if you can't handle her alone." Christy listened to the female neurologist and she grabbed Amy up into her arms and ran to the car calling Chad at his office.

"I'll meet you at the base gate," he said to her and she drove to him seeing him jump the gate and run to the car. He got in on the driver side while she climbed over the seat and held Amy in her arms in the backseat. The little girl was non responsive, she wasn't shaking, but she wasn't with her mother and her father in that car. Her pupils were huge, she was deathly still and she looked too pale.

There was no wait at the General hospital emergency room. Chad pulled up and a team came to them getting an IV started and the little girl admitted within moments. Terrified out of her mind, Christy paced with Chad sitting in a chair at the foot of Amy's bed with his head in his hands and leaning forward. Within the hour they were in a room hooked up to an EEG machine.

The night was long, Amy never made a move. She stared and was still and silent. Chad went to the apartment and got Christy's laptop and change of clothes and took these back to her while they waited on the doctor to come in and tell them something.

"I have to go to work," Chad spoke at four in the morning and Christy knew that he had to leave her. "I just started this job. I can't take off."

"We'll be fine," Christy assured her husband and he kissed her for a long moment. "Pray," she spoke softly as he went to the door pulling her with him and he kissed her again.

"Our love will save her," Chad said in a certain voice. "I promise."

Chad left her and Christy decided to look up her caring site. If anything negative or cruel had been posted there, it was gone now. She thought of the popular internet woman in North Carolina and she pulled up the woman's blog and she read the blog. A month or two before she might have cried over what was written there about her, now seeing the ugly accusation of Christy harming Amy didn't matter because the popular internet woman had written about Amy calling the little girl that had never harmed anyone ever stupid, fat and retarded. The popular internet woman posting on this public blog such a thing of Amy seemed beyond cruel as that popular internet woman had a handicapped child of her own. Christy saw the horrible accusations made against her and she could find no understanding. She didn't know this popular internet woman. This popular internet woman was nothing to her life. Why in the world was this popular internet woman spending time posting about her and Amy? And the blog was now more than twenty pages long. Putting the computer down Christy went to her daughter and held Amy's hand praying for her child and for the doctors and waiting for someone to come in and talk to her.

"Christy," Chad said her name into the phone when she answered. "Did you get any sleep?"

"No, and neither did you," Christy answered and saw Amy was too still on the bed.

"That woman in North Carolina wrote some pretty damning things about you on that public blog," Chad said. "I responded to her blog in the comment field and you don't need to see what she's written baby. It's disgusting. The whole thing is sickening." Christy laid her head down on the bed and cried.

"I don't even know the woman Chad. I've not spoken to her in a year. And now Amy's sick,"

"Get some sleep," he told her in a firm voice. "Just lay your head down on the bed and get a few minutes of sleep. I'll talk to you soon."

Christy did what her husband told her to do. Sitting on a chair by the bed, holding Amy's hand, she laid down her head on the edge of the mattress and went to sleep.

"I'm not going to speak against a doctor," the neurologist said as she came into the room. A tall imposing woman with a sour look on her face and Christy frowned as she looked up at the woman.

"My daughter?"

"Should have been weaned off her medication, but I didn't say this to you. We'll wean her back on slowly in the next few weeks. That's all I can do for you, good day." Christy watched the woman leave and another doctor came in, a woman that identified herself as a child psychiatrist.

"I came in earlier and you were asleep," she said as she stood by the bed. "Your laptop was open and I read that site."

Christy knew this doctor was talking about the blog that woman in North Carolina had written and she shrugged her shoulders. "My daughter?" she turned the conversation back to Amy.

"We'll get her back on her seizure medication. And I want to put her on Lithium and Abilify," Christy frowned but didn't argue with the doctor. Christy avoided confrontation at all cost. If she became angry she only showed that anger to those that she trusted and Christy didn't trust many people.

The woman left the room and Christy stood and went to her computer quickly looking to see what Chad had posted in the comment field. His post was sad, she could read his fear for his only child in that post and she hated that he'd allowed that woman to hurt him with her horrible response. A response that stated clearly and in few words that Christy had harmed Amy.

Early on Friday afternoon on the North Carolina woman's blog was a post accusing Christy of Munchausen's by proxy and of harming Amy. By Saturday several people had responded encourage someone to make Amy safe. Christy ignored what was written and Chad as well, but they were both aware that someone was making a blog go viral about them and their child. They were both very aware that the blog was all about Amy, an innocent little ten year old girl fighting for her life.

On Sunday Christy drove home and took a shower and changed clothes. She hadn't eaten all week and Chad met her in the hospital cafeteria with food, but she couldn't eat. Her mother-in-law had flown in and was with Amy. They all knew Amy's situation wasn't good; the child should have been weaned off of her medication. Amy was just ten years old, she should be protected, Christy and Chad kept saying to one another. And they knew, it was their job to protect their child.

Christy came into the hallway of the Pediatric ward and saw the police officer when he came to her grabbing her in a rough manner and pulling her into a room. "We have a report that you've been bringing in drugs and are drugging that little girl to make her appear to be having seizures," Christy was pushed face first into a wall and her body was searched. She could say nothing; she knew the popular internet woman's blog had gone viral. She was thrown into a chair by the large officer and his finger was in her face as he yelled at her and accused her of harming her child. All Christy could do was sit still and wait for what would happen next.

And then Chad was there. He came into the room, pushing the door open when it shouldn't have opened and he had his computer in hand and the blog pulled up as well as the police report for the YouTube site in Christy's full name attached to the pornographic site and the harassment report for all the phone calls. He also had his phone records online pulled up and Christy knew, her husband had come in to save her.

"Mother's don't shrink brains," a female doctor said to the officers in the room and Christy looked up and saw two officers in the room along with the doctor and Chad.

"My wife has never even had a traffic ticket," Chad was yelling. "My daughter has an extensive medical history and she's had many hospitalizations due to seizures. This is wrong. Some internet personality in North Carolina has singled out my family to write about in her fantasy made up story. The only truth in this blog is my wife and daughter's name."

The officer took the laptop from Chad and spent a long half hour reading the posts and the comments and the whole blog. "This is aimed to be ugly," the officer said looking at Christy. "I'm sorry I manhandled you."

"That's what the woman that wrote this blog wanted," the other officer said having read the blog with her partner. "Let's get this family moved into a room where no one knows their name. Someone might see this blog and believe what's written here."

"I've already ordered the portable EEG," the doctor said from the doorway. "We're moving the child now."

"If someone will spend all this time writing this long blog on a stranger, there's no telling what she'll do, if it's even a woman," the officer that had been rough with Christy said.

No one noticed but Chad that Christy was silent. Chad saw his wife shaking all over and he knew that she had been slung into her abusive past. He knew she had PTSD from what had been done to her and today he hadn't saved her. Today she had been hurt when they were already hurting over Amy's health.

Amy woke up and wasn't talking to anyone that was there. She chased bubbles that only she could see. She talked to mermaids that only she could see and the doctors said it was from being taken cold turkey off the drugs. The little girl also ran wild up and down the halls if she were able to escape the room. She fell on her face often. Christy and Chad cried, they cried because they had taken her to Alabama and this was the result of that trip. They cried because the child they had before that trip was so changed.

A month in the hospital with the psychiatrist questioning Christy over that popular internet woman's blog and the couple were glad that soon Amy would be discharged. Christy had no desire to speak of that North Carolina woman nor did Chad. They had to see Amy well, that's all that mattered. Amy was put on Seroquel, Abilify, and Lithium by the doctor as well as one of her anti-epileptic medications. She had the VNS turned up high and Christy hoped that soon Amy would be back to herself.

The neurologist never came into the room again after telling Christy she'd not speak against another doctor. Christy didn't care, the pediatrician was wonderful and explained the seizures and Christy talked often to the new female neurologist that had diagnosed Amy with Spinocerebellar ataxia.

The psychiatrist asked Christy to come to her office and Christy did. While there the doctor diagnosed Christy as suffering from bi-polar disorder, the same as Amy. The woman insisted that was all that was the matter with Amy. She had done a CT scan and she further insisted there was no atrophy in Amy's brain. Christy accepted this and made an appointment to see her later in the week.

Amy was discharged and the little girl, Chad and Christy had was gone. Once home, this child stared all the time, she made almost no noise. She was gone; it was as though there was no one home in the building. To make matters worse, DCFS and the police had been called again. They came to the house and met Amy and offering their sympathy to the little girl's parents, they turned and left within the hour. But that wasn't the end of this Munchausen's accusation.

Again the blog was up and again the blog was encouraging people to contact the authorities as Christy was a danger to Amy. Christy and Chad chose again to carry on as Amy's parents and ignore this popular internet woman's posts. The police had been contacted and told that Christy had taken Amy from her home at Eglin Air Force Base and was burning the little girl with cigarettes. Christy didn't smoke.

This time the police came in and found Amy wasn't burned and Christy was living at MacDill Air Force Base. Poor little Amy had been terrified, the child going between her bed and her reclining chair and hiding from the police until the officer had grabbed Christy in a rough way and the child started to scream. The police were supposed to protect the victims, instead they were terrifying them.

Christy called DCFS herself and she made an appointment to be assessed for Munchausen's by Proxy. In tears she told the social worker that she wanted this to be her fault. If this were her fault they could take Amy away and Amy would be well. The social worker met with little Amy Bac, talked to the doctor and learned of the atrophy in Amy's brain, the new female neurologist going so far as to state that someone had called her office to tell that Christy had Munchausen's by proxy. The caller didn't identify herself and the new female neurologist believed the call to be a hoax.

DCFS sent Amy home with her mother and told Christy that mothers who have Munchausen's by proxy don't turn themselves in. They defend themselves and try and justify what they're doing and make what they're doing real in their own minds. Christy left the office and made an appointment with a top psychiatrist in the county getting in within the week. If she was the cause of Amy's being unwell, she would know soon. She would do anything to save her child, including giving Amy up.

Amy's appointment with her psychiatric came and Christy took the little girl in. Amy never spoke, the child just stared and Christy asked the doctor about all the drugs Amy was on. The doctor said they were what Amy needed. She then gave Christy prescriptions for Abilify, Clonazepam and Lithium. Christy filled the prescriptions at Walgreens pharmacy on the way home where she left Amy with Chad and went to meet her own psychiatrist.

An hour into the appointment with her new psychiatrist and Christy felt better. She had shown the doctor Amy's videos of running and playing. The doctor asked her to come back the next day and bring Amy. Christy, at the door as she was leaving, turned to the doctor with the drugs Amy's psychiatrist had prescribed to her and asked if she should take these medications or wait and take medication this doctor prescribed.

"Where did you get these?" her psychiatrist asked and Christy said from Amy's psychiatrist.

"That's a conflict of interest," the doctor said. "Do not take these," she kept the drugs and put them in her drawer at her desk. "There are bad plumbers in this world Christy, and there are bad Doctors."

The next day Christy brought Amy in to the psychiatrist and the doctor immediately made a phone call. "There's a child psychiatrist at the hospital I want you to see, Christy." She spoke into the phone and within the hour she had an appointment for Amy. "Go home and get Amy's medication and all her medications she use to be on before going to Alabama and take them to this doctor."

Christy did as she was told calling Chad so that he could meet her and go with her to see this new doctor.

Amy was non-responsive still. She was empty, there was really no Amy and this new doctor stood in his office doorway and watched the parents coaxing the child into his office, the little girl wasn't there and he couldn't believe Amy had once been near normal and chatty, a happy child. But he had taken fifteen minutes to watch her videos on YouTube and he felt what he was seeing now was a tragedy.

This doctor watched Amy sitting on the floor and he looked at Chad and Christy. "I see myoclonic, I see dystonia, I see what is certainly an altered state of awareness and we're taking this child off of these antipsychotic drugs in the next three weeks. She's going back on the anti-seizure medication only and we're going to see what we get. The Depakote should help with the dystonia and the Clonazepam will help with the myoclonic I'm seeing."

After talking for an hour with the parents he listened as they showed him the blog the popular internet woman in North Carolina was writing of Amy and he was baffled. "You don't know this woman?"

"Never met her," Chad spoke and Christy nodded her head.

"I spoke to her on the phone nearly two years ago about epilepsy, I don't even know anything about her," Christy saw the doctor nodding his head as Chad told him Christy turned herself in to DCFS for Munchausen's by proxy.

"After all you've been through with Amy not having her needed seizure medication and learning of the atrophy in her brain, I suspect that a diagnosis of Munchausen's would be good with you Mama bear."

"Very very good," Christy said and she relaxed for the first time in months. "I'm seeing a therapist every Tuesday night as well as the psychiatrist."

"A therapist can be supportive and you certainly need that. Let's hope this blogger will find something positive to do with her time." He looked back at Amy. "We start today weaning her off these three drugs. And Mrs. Bac, I was told her doctor prescribed you drugs, please don't take them."

"I won't," Christy said going to Amy and leading the little girl out of the office. They might be okay; Christy thought and held on to Chad's hand, but Amy was changed.

The next day the female psychiatrist that had prescribed Amy and Christy the anti-psychotic medications called and she told

Christy to come in now, that Amy had missed her appointment. Christy called Chad and he came home taking his girls to this doctor with the intent on firing the woman. He walked into the room and listened to the woman saying she was increasing Amy's Seroquil and he had heard enough.

"Why are you drugging my wife and my daughter? Amy has atrophy in her brain, she's epileptic, why give her all these mind altering drugs and my wife as well?"

"Because they both have a duplication of chromosome 16p11.2 that causes severe mental illness," the doctor answered him and he started laughing. In fact Chad was laughing so hard that he fell forward in his chair and laughed for a long minute.

"You're an idiot," he finally said standing up and reaching for his wife's hand and then Amy's hand. "I'm the one with the damn duplication. Dear God, my poor wife. And you prescribed her medications when you weren't her doctor, you were my child's doctor."

Chad pulled his family out of the office never realizing that his doing so would cause Christy to become a victim of again. And all because of some woman in North Carolina that Chad nor Christy knew. A popular internet woman that didn't know little Amy Bac in anyway.

She was in the pool with Amy swimming when they came again, two police officers and a DCF officer. She waved to them and they came out to the pool and met Amy and Christy. The three law enforcement officers saw within moments of meeting Amy that something was wrong with the little girl. The officer saw the little girl jerk and her eyes dart upward and they heard her speech pattern and they left.

And this happened again, they were eating ice cream after dinner watching television and again DCFS and the police were at the door. The report was that Amy was being beaten, and they saw Amy was not hurt and again they left.

And this happened again and again in a short time. The police knew the family, they also knew of the popular internet woman in North Carolina and they spoke to the Sheriff's department in her district and the blog was taken down. The blog would reappear but only for a short time and Christy and Chad didn't care, they were living and life was getting better.

Amy was weaned off of all the antipsychotic medications and back on her epileptic medications by October. She also had a new pediatrician at the Complex Pediatric Clinic in St. Joseph's Children's hospital. The team there were wonderful and when Amy ran in with her smile they met her in the hallway with paints and ponies or both. Amy adored Jo, she thought the nurse Colleen was pretty and begged her mother for blond hair like nurse Colleen, and Lisa was her friend, she loved Lisa most of all.

Christy loved the nurses, their patience and kindness and care of Amy. She loved the medical staff as they were wanting to help. The lead doctor explained the autonomic dysfunction happening to Amy. He explained the cerebellum atrophy and he tickled and teased Amy and the little girl's giggle was back. This man was honestly the best pediatrician in the whole country.

Amy was as she had been before the trip to Alabama except for one thing. Amy was falling more. Amy was tipping over. She'd knocked out a front tooth. She had a black eye and the helmet was no more for the drop seizures, the helmet was for the falls.

Christy took Amy back to the psychiatrist that had weaned the little girl off the drugs and he was shocked when the little girl walked up to him and hugged him and said, "Hi, my name is Amy."

"You gave me my child back," Christy hugged the doctor as well.

"Her walk," the doctor said as he saw Christy and Amy to the door and released them back to the neurologist. "Wide base gait, feet out, stooped and crouched and her shoulders pushed forward. She's much more ataxic than she was three months ago."

"I know," Christy said and burst into tears telling the doctor of her mother.

"You have all the reasons in the world to be afraid," he said and he hugged the crying mother. "Atrophy in the brain is bad, more so when the brain was normal for the first nine years of her life."

Chapter Nineteen

Joshua 1:9: "Have I not commanded you? Be strong and courageous. Do not be terrified; do not be discouraged, for the Lord your God will be with you wherever you go."

Christy was fixing dinner and Amy was watching the Lion King Simba's pride on television when the pounding began at the door. She ran to the phone and called Chad putting him on speaker. "The police are here again," she cried into the phone and saw he had hung up. They had seen that the popular internet woman in North Carolina had her blog on Amy back up again, so they weren't surprised. But this time was like in the hospital.

The huge police officer came in when Christy opened the door and grabbed her by the arm slamming her into the wall. Another officer looked at Amy and the little girl, seeing her mother hurt screamed and ran to the back of the house hiding in the closet as her mother was searched for drugs and yelled at for hurting Amy.

"I never hurt Amy," Christy cried pathetically as the officer shoved her to the floor so hard that her glasses came off of her face.

"You've been hurting that child for a long time," the officer snatched her up from the floor before shoving her into the wall hard again and she cried out as her face hit the edge of a corner of the wall causing her whole face to ache. He was cussing at her, calling her terrible names and she screamed when he threw her again to the floor. This time, Christy was crawling from him screaming for help and he grabbed her up by the back of her shirt and threw her onto the sofa where she hit with a horrible thud before becoming still.

Little Amy Bac heard her mother screaming. She put her hand over her mouth and was crouched down in the closet behind Daddy's suitcase. Every time she heard her mother cry out, she scooted further and further into a corner shaking in fear, wanting to save her mommy, but too afraid to move.

"Come here little girl," the police officer said and Amy screamed covering her head in a further effort to hide. The man reached for her and she sunk her teeth into his arm kicking him hard as he pulled her out from behind Daddy's suitcase. As he got her into his arms and her teeth off of his arm the officer held her high where she couldn't get down. The floor was a long way off and the little girl started hitting the man in the head screaming for her mommy.

"Let her go, oh please, let her go!" Christy pleaded as the officer came into the room holding Amy. "She's just a little girl. She doesn't understand."

"You shut your mouth," the officer standing over Christy said with his finger inches from Christy's nose. "I'll do to you what you've done to her," the officer raised his hand and Christy closed her eyes waiting for the blow when Amy cried out in her stuttering voice.

"Don't you hurt my mommy!" And Christy opened her eyes seeing little Amy Bac fighting the officer that held her.

"My God," a police officer came into the scene of Amy beating an officer in the head and Christy cowering in a corner of the sofa. He picked up Christy's glasses from the floor and handed them to the terrified mother seeing that once she had the glasses on that she knew him. "This family has a stalker online. The child is fine." He reached for Amy just as Chad came into the house and Christy burst into tears.

"Enough of this," Chad said. "This is harassment."

The DCFS agent came into the apartment and saw the family. "We won't be back sir," she said in a certain voice seeing little Amy Bac was shaking all over, the child was terrified. "We're the ones hurting this little girl. Not her mother."

Chad watched the officers leave and took Amy into his arms, his little girl crying. "They hurt my Mama," she said over and over again to her Daddy as Christy sat on the floor with Chad and they hugged their only child.

And all of this had happened because Christy had doubted the diagnosis of LGS. If only they'd accepted that diagnosis and stayed out of Alabama. If only Christy hadn't spoke to that popular internet woman of LGS in July of 2010. They wouldn't be here now trying to survive the accusation of Munchausen's by proxy because all of Amy's doctors knew Amy was unwell. The grocery store clerk that met Amy in the checkout line could see in a glance that Amy wasn't okay. The handyman that fixed the clog in the dishwasher could see that little Amy Bac couldn't stand up straight and her eyes darted upward and she'd lose tone. Everyone, anyone, could see that little Amy Bac was in trouble and her parents were frantic to help her and they only wanted to keep her safe.

Some popular internet woman far away from them in North Carolina had decided that Christy had Munchausen's by proxy and that woman wrote of that accusation often. What no one understood, not even Chad and Christy, was that each time that accusation was made came guilt, guilt because they were older parents, they had lived a good and full and healthy lives and they still were healthy. Their child wasn't living a full and healthy life. Their child was unwell in many ways from eating to walking to drinking a glass of water. Why were they healthy and this beautiful, innocent child so ill?

Christy and Chad knew their whole situation and they had taken down the caring site. They had opened up a prayer page for

Amy and on that page almost weekly posts appeared by people with the first name of Davis or the last name of Davis, often no profile photo on their Facebook or a profile photo of a threatening looking television character and the accusation on the prayer page that Christy had Munchausen's by proxy.

Christy had a blog with no written words on the blog, only photos of their many Disney trips. The reason she had the blog was because her computer crashed and she lost all of her photos. Keeping those photos on a blog she wouldn't lose them if her computer died. The blog was called 'the happiest place on earth' and that blog was found and attacked. Comments in the comment field stated that Christy was the Pied Piper of Hamlin and leading doctors and the medical community over a cliff with her lies of Amy being ill. There were posts by other mothers of sick children calling Christy terrible names and these comments were posted daily for months. Chad locked the site down so that no one could post public on the site and within hours, Christy's YouTube site was attacked.

For days curse words calling Christy the ugliest names anyone might think of were put up on Amy's videos. Those videos were only on the site because Chad was gone from home so much in his military career that Amy grew up on YouTube for Daddy to see. Within the year, that site would be closed down as well, a site named 'girlchristian' that was harming no one and only depicted the love these parents had for their child.

The internet was not safe for little Amy Bac or her mother. Christy couldn't join an epileptic group online without the rumor of her harming Amy being spread in the group within hours of her joining. The assertion made by strangers that Amy was fake was far and wide from a caring site to YouTube to Facebook to blogs written of the innocent little child. The parents were living and dealing with private emails from people they didn't know hurling the accusation that Amy was fake and only retarded enough to act and worse, using scripture from the bible to expose a lie, the lie being little Amy Bac.

"These people don't understand," Chad said as he changed his wife's email for the fifth time and closed down the YouTube and caring site. "You want this to be Munchausen's by Proxy. If that were Amy's diagnosis, then she would be well."

"My therapist says that this is about more than that Chad," Christy sat on the floor holding Amy in her arms and on her lap. "I'm older, I should be the one that's sick like this. My mother was sick like this and she died too soon. I watched my mother die and leave this life due to something that looks just like what's happening to our Amy. This is my fault. Amy's just like Mom. And Amy has this and I don't. It should be me falling Chad. It should be me that's battling seizures. It should be me that's being poked fun of by that woman in North Carolina for the way I walk, not our little girl."

"Oh baby," Chad left the laptop on the floor and hugged his wife with their child hugging them both.

"I'm scared Mommy," Amy spoke in a shaking voice. "That man scared me pushing on you and yelling really loud."

"That won't happen again," Chad said in confidence.

Christy would learn on Tuesday that the DCFS situation was at an end. The officer had called the neurologist and spoken to her in detail of Amy's situation with Chad and Christy's written permission to do so. The neurologist spoke to Christy and was outraged over what had been happening. DCFS had to investigate, Chad and Christy knew that and they opened their lives and their home willingly to that investigation each time a call was placed. There are children in this world that are true victims of violence, if anyone knew that, Christy Bac knew that. Those children needed all the protection the law could afford. She wanted that protection for her own child most of all. But Amy wasn't being harmed by Christy or Chad. Little Amy Bac was being harmed by a horrible and tragic disease, a disease that no law enforcement officer in this world could protect the child from.

Christy's therapist offered understanding of the popular internet woman to Chad and Christy. Every time Christy posted a video to YouTube that showed Amy's condition was worsening or of a suspected seizure happening in the video, the popular internet woman posted of Amy being fake and Christy lying. If Christy joined an online group, within hours the rumor of Christy copying other mothers or faking Amy was put out. "Can't you see?" the therapist asked Amy's parents. "She looks bad when others see Amy is real and you're not what she's stating you are. She has to ruin you or she'll look like the one that's lying. And the woman is probably very sorry she ever posted about you and Amy. Now, she doesn't want to look bad so she's attempting to destroy you."

"So what do we do?" Chad asked

"Have your own internet presence," the therapist advised. "DCFS knows the truth of Amy and of Christy. Stand firm and strong, that woman is the one wrong. Join groups Christy, post videos and photos of Amy, open up your site and let this woman do whatever she wants. She's nothing to you and certainly nothing to Amy. Let people see the face of total innocence. That's your face Christy – and Amy's."

Christy was in the grocery store the next day when her phone rang. The child psychiatrist that had prescribed her and Amy the drugs informed her that she'd missed her appointment with Amy. Christy explained that she hadn't missed the appointment, her husband Chad had cancelled the appointment and they wouldn't be back.

"I'll have you and Amy both Baker acted by end of day if you don't get in here now," Christy took her groceries to the car and put them in the truck. "I'm reporting you for Munchausen's by proxy syndrome right now to DCFS."

Christy hung up and called her own psychiatrist, the doctor laughing into the phone. "That doctor can't Baker act you and Amy, she would have to have seen you both within twenty-four hours and deemed you and Amy a threat to yourself and to others. You've not seen her in weeks. Go home and rest, I've contacted Department of Children and Families and explained in details your case. They won't bother you again. And Christy, you're a loving mother that's trying to help her daughter. Go to Disney World and enjoy Amy. Forget that awful doctor. She'll be dealt with; she prescribed drugs to her patient's mother and diagnosed the mother incorrectly of the duplication of 16p11.2."

So many ugly people in the world, Christy thought as she went to the school and picked up her little girl. And gossip is easy to believe. Christy couldn't fault the psychiatrist completely; the woman had been swayed by that hurtful blog. That was sad that people believed something cruel and ugly written online. All Christy could do was hope this was behind them.

Amy was back. The little girl was giggling and talking and happy. She loved school and had many friends, she was very popular though now the public school system had her in a school that was very small and only very handicapped children attended. Christy felt it was the wrong place for Amy, her daughter could still read some and Amy knew simple math, but the teacher assured her that Amy was in the correct setting educationally and everyone there was so wonderful that Christy was happy. And best of all, Christy was allowed to volunteer. Within the first year, she knew every student by name and all the teachers as well. Life was good.

In October of 2011 Chad and Christy took Amy to Houston, Texas as part of the 16p11.2 research program with the Simon's VIP. They spent a week there and the neurologist and geneticist listened to Christy and Chad as they told of Amy. The team there stayed late watching videos of Amy run and jumping rope and riding her bike. The team sat on the floor and played with Amy. They listened to her attempt to read and they tested Chad and Christy as well.

A week there and the team met with them, the neurologist had already talked to Chad and Christy and told them that Amy's reflexes weren't right, that she had chorea like movements and myoclonic jerks. Everything the couple had heard in the past, they heard again. The neurologist saw the MRIs that had been done and they were compared by the radiologist at Texas Children's Hospital.

"With the normal cerebellum changing to show atrophy over time," the neurologist had spoken in a kind and gentle way, "we can diagnose a neurodegenerative disease."

That day it became official, Amy had a progressive degenerative disease. Christy and Chad were urged to go home and apply for a Make-A-Wish trip. The rest of the 16p11.2 team came in and said, "hold on to your chairs folks," and they told Chad and Christy that Amy was not autistic. Amy was globally delayed with behaviors. She might fit the autistic diagnosis but Amy was not autistic and whatever was going on with her was not due to the 16p11.2 duplication.

Christy pulled up her email as she waited for Chad to finish with the doctors. As he had the same duplication for Amy he was getting his test results and learning that his IQ was very high, he was in the brilliant range. Christy could have told them that information. In her email she frowned seeing something from that popular internet woman in North Carolina. Usually the woman emailed her that her job as a Christian was to expose liars; Christy dismissed the emails and she knew that she'd dismiss this one as well.

"With your daughter's brain having atrophy, I mean with her brain dying," Christy read these words wondering what this woman meant. She read the rest of the email and went back into the room where the doctors were knowing that she had only written in her caring site journal of Amy's brain atrophy, how did that woman in North Carolina find out about the atrophy? The caring site was locked down.

"Excuse me," Christy spoke and the neurologist looked up at her and smiled.

"Did you need something Mrs. Bac?" the doctor came around the desk and Christy nodded her head.

"Is my daughter's brain dying? Is that what atrophy means?" Christy heard her voice shaking and she saw Chad coming toward her.

"Amy's brain isn't dying," Chad pulled his wife into his arms as he said this.

"Actually Mr. Bac," the doctor said giving the parents a look of intense sorrow. "Atrophy like Amy has overtime is indicative of the brain cells dying."

"My God," Chad said leaning into his wife and Christy held him close.

"Go home; take a Make-A-Wish trip while your daughter can still walk."

"Do you mean she won't be able to walk soon?" Christy whispered and the doctor touched her hand.

"Overtime if this continues to progress, yes, she'll lose the ability to walk."

"Will she die?" Chad asked and pulled Christy closer in his arms.

"We don't know that Mr. Bac. Go home; take a Make-A-Wish trip with your daughter. Have all the fun that you can while you can."

Christy walked away from the doctor and reached Amy sitting in her Safari tilt stroller. The child was asleep; the chair tilted all the way back. Amy was weak and they knew that she was, but the couple kept pushing her to do all that she could. Amy was in PT and OT and ST privately and in school. They wouldn't give up on Amy and they knew, Amy wouldn't give up on them.

"All for one and one for all," Christy said wondering how that woman in North Carolina found out that Amy's brain had atrophy.

The FBI agent kept calling and Christy thought it was a hoax. Chad thought so as well. Since he worked at U.S. Central Command, Chad had connections and he used those connections to verify the men calling his wife were with the FBI. The man on the caring site that the North Carolina woman had called Christy about months ago had threatened to harm Christy and Amy. What the man had done was a Federal Offense and they wanted Christy to help in seeing him put away. This was ironic, someone could really harm Christy and Amy's life and nothing happened to them, but some man almost did something to harm them and he was going to jail. After talking with the FBI of what the man had done, Chad and Christy knew they had to make certain that what he had done to them never happened to another family and they agreed to testify.

Christy had spent hours trying to find out how the popular internet woman had learned Amy's brain had atrophy. She had only emailed her prayer partner that information, they hadn't even told their family. She went to Amy's caring site and looked up the woman's name that was her online prayer partner and email in the file. Within seconds, Christy saw there were two women using that name as her prayer partner and coming to her caring site. What did she know of this online prayer partner she'd met? Christy asked herself and she emailed the woman with the email address different from the one that was her prayer partner for the last year.

Within fifteen minutes of emailing the woman with the different email address Christy was given a phone number to call. The woman was a neighbor and friend to the woman in North Carolina. That North Carolina woman had convinced her friend that Christy was a stalker. She now realized that her friend, the North Carolina woman, was using her name to stalk Christy.

Feeling this was even more bizarre than it seemed, Christy contacted the FBI agents and told them what was going on. The neighbor said she would sing like a bird and she had sung. She had told Christy everything the North Carolina woman was doing. Christy's therapist had been right, the woman didn't want anyone knowing that little Amy Bac was real and that she, the popular internet woman, was wrong.

Another email came in from the North Carolina woman and Chad sat down with Christy to examine this woman's posts and emails, typical engineer mentality, Christy knew and she smiled while snuggling next to her husband and seeing Amy sitting on the floor with her Nintendo DS. The little girl wasn't the gamer that she had been, she was now only playing games for toddlers and often she would get frustrated and cry over the game, but Amy didn't give up trying.

After an hour and a half looking at this woman's public posts, comparing the dates Chad found that if Christy posted on the caring site, which was locked down, of how Amy was doing, this woman would post contradicting what Christy had written. If Christy put up a video on YouTube and it was obvious the change and regression in Amy, this woman would post negative of Amy often implying or writing outright that Amy was only mildly mentally retarded enough to act.

"This woman has a following of people that want to hear this garbage she's posting," Chad said to Christy. "To her, this is some sort of game. For us, we're seeking help for our daughter. We're trying to find that one doctor that will ask us, 'why'd it take you so long to get here,' and that one doctor has a treatment. She posts public and it's tearing us apart because what she is posting is false about our little Amy."

"So we just go on with our lives ignoring her?" Christy spoke in a way that let Chad know she didn't want anything to do with this internet woman. This woman was nothing to Christy's life. All Christy cared about was Amy.

"The photo of Amy's side by side MRIs," Chad said and the couple posted that photo on their blog. Anyone with eyes could see the change in the MRI. The cerebellum was the little flower shaped thing at the back and base of the skull. Amy's cerebellum had filled up the area in the early MRIs until the Alabama MRI. The cerebellum was obviously much smaller than it had been even to the naked eye. "Now, we link our blog to the caring site, our Facebooks and YouTube channel. Anyone believing this woman will come to those sites and be led here and see the side by side MRIs with Amy's name and the dates on the film and know, Amy's not fake or a lie or anything else this woman is saying."

"I don't want this woman in our lives," Christy cried as Chad held her and he said the truth.

"She's not in our lives. She knows nothing of the fear we're in." Chad looked at Amy struggling to play her game. 'I don't think anyone has any idea what is happening to us. Not even the doctors. We've lost the little girl that we had and we've lost her in more ways than one." He turned Christy in his arms and held her close. "We're Amy's parents and I love you and you love me. This is our world. Let the woman say what she will of us because that defines her, not you and I baby. You and I are just fine."

This was the night of November fifth and within hours their blog had over a thousand hits and comments of sorrow for what they were going through. The tide changed the night of November fifth and sixth for Chad and Christy Bac. Now they were popular internet bloggers and they were blogging the truth of a little girl that had been the subject of gossip and rumors. They found support in the posting of that side by side MRI. They no longer stood alone. November sixth of 2011 would always be a day they remembered. A day when the truth of little Amy Bac became known and the lie made to be just what it was – a lie.

Amy's PT was pushing Amy hard. The little girl didn't know what to do. She wasn't happy with PT but mommy said she must go. Amy knew something was wrong with her, she asked her parents often why she kept falling. Everyday mommy made her practice walking a curb at school and everyday she fell or slipped or nearly crashed herself. But mommy believed in her, mommy was certain that she could walk that curb and Amy did try for her mommy, because she loved her mommy so much.

"It's a good thing I have this helmet on," Amy said to her parents when they reached to pick her up after a fall. She looked at mommy and daddy and she saw that they never fell. Mommy was clumsy but Daddy, he wasn't and mommy had Meniere's disease. Amy thought that she had Meniere's disease as well and Amy said so many times.

Amy often heard mommy crying, mostly she heard mommy crying after PT because that lady in the room that pushed her hard was always saying mommy had low expectations of Amy and that mommy baby'd Amy. She didn't understand what these things meant, but she knew mommy was crying over these words and she wanted to tell that lady not to make her mommy cry no more.

Amy went home and told Daddy one night about the woman and she heard mommy crying even more to Daddy and this time mommy was saying it was her fault Amy fell all the time but Amy didn't know why it was mommy's fault because mommy didn't fall, she fell. After a few minutes of hearing mommy crying that it was because of mommy that Amy was stumbly, little Amy Bac ran to her mommy saying, "I love you mommy. I love you. Don't cry no more." And mommy hugged her close while Daddy looked mad at mommy.

"That woman in North Carolina and her accusations have gotten to you baby," Daddy yelled. "You want that stranger with no education to be right instead of top doctors in our country."

And Amy was scared; she was scared because Daddy was mad. And then Daddy had her and mommy in his arms and he was making everything all right. And Amy felt better. Daddy was going to fix things.

"I broke my arm," Amy said as she came out of PT and to her mother holding her arm, her words stuttered and slurred.

"She did not break her arm Mrs. Bac," the PT said and Christy met the woman's eyes. "Do not baby her. She's just seeking attention."

Christy went very still – too still. She had been told in the past that she made molehills into mountains by a man that hit her often. She'd been told that she was seeking attention and her mother died seeking attention, her mother Sara died in a nursing home seeking attention. Christy threw her face into her hands and she cried, her poor mother had been falling like Amy and Christy, as a child heard her mother being called fake and an attention seeker. Everything that woman in North Carolina was saying of Christy and this PT was saying now of Amy had been said of poor dead Sara. How did these people know these words were destructive to Christy? Saying these things to Christy slung her into a past of horror and pain and humiliation, a place where no one needed to be.

Little Amy Bac held her arm and saw mommy crying again. She wouldn't complain of her arm again, mommy might cry worse. She didn't want mommy to cry and over and over and over again as they walked to their car, Amy told her mother that she was sorry.

"You've done nothing to be sorry for baby mine," Christy said and helped her child in the car. The PT had told her to ignore Amy's pain and her arm would be better soon. On the drive home Christy kept looking in the rearview mirror seeing Amy's face and she knew, she couldn't ignore her baby.

"What the hell!" Chad screamed loud and long when he came home and found Amy hiding in her little special alone place and Christy frantically searching for the little girl and telling him about PT and the fall and how Amy was seeking attention. "I'm gonna seek some attention," Chad picked Amy up into his arms and started for the car. "I don't care what that PT said, Amy's going to the emergency room and getting her arm x-rayed." He saw the relief flooding his wife's face and he stopped and closed his eyes. "You've been bullied all your life," he said patiently to his wife. "You think these naysayers are right and they're not. Baby, trust yourself, if you think something isn't right, it isn't right." He pulled her into his arms with his daughter held close against his chest. "And her arm damn sure better not be broken."

Amy's arm was broken in two places, her wrist and her elbow, the cast was high up on her arm. She didn't heal in six weeks, it took little Amy Bac over eleven weeks to heal. And the woman in North Carolina was finally leaving them alone. Ever since the November night they had posted on their blog the side by side MRIs of Amy's where you could clearly see the changes in Amy's cerebellum, the North Carolina woman was at long last leaving them alone.

Christy stuck with the current PT waiting for the doctor to find Amy a new PT. She never left Amy in the room alone with the PT. Christy would see that Amy wasn't hurt again.

"A woman online that helped us to see the mitochondrial specialist in Atlanta wants us to meet her for lunch," Christy said to Chad on a Saturday evening. "She is in town at Disney World and I'd like to thank her for her guidance."

"Then we'll go to lunch," Chad smiled knowing they'd go to Downtown Disney while there and he would get Amy another Princess gown. His little girl lived in her Disney Princess gowns.

They pulled up to the restaurant at the time they were to meet this woman and the woman wasn't there. Christy called her phone and the woman sounded shocked. "You mean you're really here?" Christy laughed and Chad did as well because the woman was on speaker.

"Where else would I be?" Christy teased and the woman said she'd be there soon.

"I'm starving to death," Chad said as they waited and Christy waved seeing the woman hurrying toward them. They hugged real quick and Christy felt that she was hugging a new and dear friend and she had met the woman online on Facebook.

"She's real," the woman said of Amy as the little girl walked between her parents in the new way Amy walked, swaying back and forth.

"What do you mean, 'she's real?'" Chad asked looking the woman in the eyes and the woman began talking the minute that they sat down.

The North Carolina woman, this new friend told them, had insisted that Chad and Christy wouldn't meet her. The North Carolina woman had said the couple would never allow anyone to see and know the truth, that Amy was a fake and a copy of the North Carolina woman's child. But she could see, this new friend; that Amy was very real and she went on to tell them that the popular internet woman had lost her own child for Munchausen's by proxy. Chad and Christy didn't want to hear this gossip, they wanted know nothing of that popular internet woman; she was not important to their life.

"We don't want to hear this," Chad spoke in his military voice. "That woman means nothing to us and never has and never will. Her personal life is her business and she needs to mind her business. Amen the end." Christy could only nod her head in agreement. "We never want to hear of that woman again."

After they'd eaten Chad pulled his family to the car and buckled Amy in meeting his wife's eyes. "Block that woman from your Facebook and from our phones right now. If she'd tell us gossip about that North Carolina woman, you can bet your sweet butt she's on the phone now talking to that North Carolina woman about us."

Christy did as her husband ordered her to do and she did so gladly. Seconds later that woman was standing by their car and looking in the window at Amy. "For shame on that woman picking on this little child. I'm so sorry I believed her. Forgive me."

Chad and Christy did forgive this woman they'd had lunch with because they knew that was the Christian thing to do, and they blocked her because the changes in Amy were too hard to accept. Having Amy stalked on the internet and referred to as stupid, retarded, fat and worse was just very wrong. Too many people believed gossip and lies. Little Amy Bac deserved better than to be the subject of gossip.

"That woman had no intention of meeting us for lunch today," Christy said to her husband.

"No, she didn't," Chad agreed. "Because she believed gossip and for shame on her."

Chapter Twenty

Matthew 6:34: "Therefore do not worry about tomorrow, for tomorrow will worry about itself. Each day has enough trouble of its own."

By September of 2012 Chad had his family safe. DCFS and the local police knew that they were victims and they were now being protected instead of persecuted. The FBI knew that they were victims and was watching out for them. The woman from North Carolina was leaving them alone at long last and had been since November the sixth of 2011. They were watching Amy hoping the little girl would get better and aware that the latest MRI showed the cerebellum atrophy again. The MRI was no worse, and it was no better. They wouldn't use Make-A-Wish with Amy stable, they'd not take away the chance of a trip from another child with their little girl stable. They also knew that if this was Spinocerebellar Ataxia, it was very slow progressive. They had years before things would get worse, they thought and Amy's doctors agreed.

The neurologist wanted them to be seen at the Ataxic Research Center in Tampa but to do that, Chad and Christy had to get a referral from the neurologist they'd met at the General hospital months ago. The appointment time came and the neurologist came in saying that she wouldn't see them. They told her they just wanted a referral and nothing more. It had been more than a year and three months since she had seen Amy last and she moved to examine the child.

"Her strength is good, but her reflexes aren't normal." The doctor said and then stated that she saw chorea and myoclonic and nystagmus. She gave the referral and for that they were thankful.

Seeing the doctor that dealt in ataxia, Chad and Christy were hopeful that at last they were seeing the right doctor. Again they'd brought all the medical records and MRIs on CD a week before the appointment along with videos on DVD of Amy playing and near normal so the doctor could know how Amy was only two years ago. The appointment was short. The doctor came into the room and had a family tree made for Christy with the affected members. Christy asked pointedly if Amy might have what her mother had and the doctor said that it was possible.

A few weeks later Christy and Chad were told that Amy didn't meet the criteria for the program and Amy was only seen there one more time. Broken and frightened that every door they tried to go through was shut in their face all the couple could do was live in a state of uncertainty for their child and for themselves.

Chad knew they had no nest egg, their savings was depleted. They had moved from their new house and between the rent on the apartment and the mortgage back at Eglin, they had little left set aside. They had come here intending to stay only a few months, get Amy diagnosed and go home; that wasn't going to happen. And worse, Chad saw that their daughter was now walking crouched, stooped, her feet wide apart and she swayed often stumbling and falling into the wall.

Amy never made it far now, only thirty feet at most. And this was a child they had on film running up the monorail at Disney World. His little girl at age two had walked with a bucket balanced on her head and his wife had recorded his child doing that. His little one had danced around their living room and she had sang in church with no balance or coordination problems. And now she couldn't walk down a hall in a normal way, she walked as though she might have if she drank a bottle of wine.

"Just like Mama," Christy burst into tears as they saw Amy swaying and holding onto the wall. "Just like my Mama," Chad heard the worry in his wife's voice and he wondered what her child's future held remembering that Christy's mother had died from her disease.

"I'm going to deploy to the Middle East with the company I work for," Chad said as he put down his briefcase and reached for his wife. "I need to do this Christy. The house at Eglin isn't selling; we need to build our savings back up. We've used so much going to Atlanta to see that mitochondrial specialist and paying out of pocket. We went to Alabama and that cost and Children's Nemours in Jacksonville and we've been to every Children's hospital in this area and the co-pays on all the testing. I need to get ahead baby. We don't need to add to our worries."

Christy knew Chad was right about the money and the co-pays on insurance. Amy had all the nuclear and maternal mitochondrial DNA tested. Amy had whole exome. And the testing for the Spinocerebellar ataxic genes had been twelve thousand dollars. They'd had the CGH microarray done as well. Every genetic test that could be done on Amy had been done with no findings that explained what was happening to our little girl. Their savings was gone, they had the huge mortgage back at Eglin and Christy couldn't work as Amy required full time care. The little girl couldn't bathe herself, brush her hair and the only thing she could do to dress herself was pull her baggy night shirt over her head.

Chad and Christy had left no stone unturned. They'd done everything they knew to do. Amy could no longer scramble eggs or heat her hotdogs up in the microwave. She was no longer able to play on the bowling team or be on the swim team. Two weeks before the base pool closed Amy had nearly drowned and Christy with her, the lifeguards having to pull them both out. There was no soccer game or baseball game; there was nothing now except for Amy's love to My Little Ponies and the Lion King. The little girl had gotten so bad that if Christy had a pot boiling on the stove for noodles, Amy would stick her hand in the pot. Every minute of the day Amy had to be watched.

"How long will you be gone?" Christy knew that no matter what, she would support her husband. In their marriage they'd been a team. They'd never fussed or argued, they always found a common ground for the good of one another and for the good of Amy.

"Six months," he said and with those words Christy and Chad began making plans for her to live without him, for him to be with his little one every second that he could be with her in the coming weeks and securing power of attorney in case the worst happened.

Christy watched Chad put their estate plan in the strong arm box the night before they left for one last trip to Disney World, their final few days to be a family before he left for the Middle East. They stayed in Shades of Green and spent three days in the park. On the last day they took Amy to get her hair done like a Princess in Downtown Disney and the time of Amy's hair appointment came and went. The little girl was already dressed in her Princess gown and she was excited and fearful that they had forgotten her.

"It's a long time mommy," little Amy Bac fretted in her stroller and Christy did all she could in reassuring the child that her turn would come soon.

Chad was watching all the little girls going back to get their hair done and Amy's appointment was well past. He had stepped up to the counter to say something when a family of three little girls was taken back and those girls had no appointment. Suddenly a woman came out with several other women and they were yelling loudly, "Make way for the Princess Amy." Within seconds Amy was being wheeled in her stroller up to the front of the store and put in the window where everyone could see her getting her hair, nails and makeup done.

"Mommy," Amy cried out and Christy look to see her child was crying real tears. "Daddy, they're making me a real Princess." Chad turned and reached for his wife pulling her into his arms. Christy was crying and he was wiping the tears that fell freely onto his face away. "Don't cry Mama, I'm a Princess now. Look," Amy pointed out the window at all the people looking in at her and she smiled. "All my life, all I wanted was to be a Princess."

Chad took a taxi at four in the morning to the airport leaving Christy standing outside the sliding glass door that overlooked the pool of their apartment building watching him go far away from her. He was worried about her. He was afraid for Amy. And he knew that his wife wasn't strong. Chad knew that her past had made her weak and that she had suffered. He didn't want her to suffer ever again. His plan in making this deployment was to keep her safe and make her safe forever financially.

Christy watched her husband leave that cold early December morning and she knew, she was on her own with Amy. The six months seemed in that moment to stretch on and on into forever but Christy had a plan in mind. By the time Chad returned home, she would have Amy diagnosed. She had heard of two doctors in Orlando, one was a geneticist and the other was a neurologist, both were said to handle difficult cases and she intended to see that Amy saw both doctors.

The time was only eight in the morning, Christy had Amy dressed and ready for school when the phone rang and she lost her breath when she heard the realtor's voice. They had a full offer on the house. Chad hadn't needed to go to the Middle East after all, and his plane had just taken off. She couldn't even tell him of the offer but she did accept as she hurried Amy into the car and to school.

Within the week she had Amy into the geneticist and the doctor had gone over all the testing. She wanted to refer Amy to another doctor and Christy had heard of this doctor at Children's National in Washington, DC. "I'll need to wait until my husband returns in six months," Christy spoke to the doctor as Amy hugged a Disney character that was visiting the children's hospital.

"I think it'll take five to six months to get into this doctor. I'll make the arrangements and Amy should have another MRI before you go up to Washington, DC."

Feeling good about this doctor's plan Christy took Amy and they went to Disney World for a week staying again in Shades of Green. Amy announced that her favorite ride was the bus ride from the resort into the park. So one morning all they did was ride the bus, Amy's smile covering her whole face.

The day after Christmas, with Chad's power of attorney, Christy sold their home in North Florida. They were now out from under that huge debt. When Daddy came on Skype while Christy was selling the house they both laughed that their nest egg would grow fat again in the five months Chad was gone as Christy was living on his retirement and all of his earnings were going right into the savings account. Chad had also made smart moves. When he retired he paid off all their credit cards and they never used credit cards again. If they didn't have cash to buy what they wanted, they didn't need what they wanted to buy. The couple were feeling upbeat, soon they'd see this specialist at Children's National and have a diagnosis and a treatment for Amy

In early February the primary care doctor talked to Christy about Palliative care. Christy felt this wasn't needed because Amy was stable. The little girl was no better, but she was no worse so Christy refused the Palliative care and instead the primary talked to her about the changes in Amy over time and if anyone knew of those changes it was Christy. Palliative care didn't mean that she was giving up on Amy, the doctor said and he urged her to think over Palliative care and after speaking with him, she gave him her word that she would consider that as an option.

Little Amy Bac was scared. She was scared because her mother was scared. She heard her mother telling the doctor of how Amy's eyes hurt in the sunlight. The doctor had come and shined a flashlight in her eyes and Amy fought not to cry as the doctor turned back and said to her mother that her pupils were sluggish. Amy didn't know what that meant, but she knew that her eyes hurt in the light. On the way home from the doctor, she saw her mother pull into the Walmart and get out of the car. Within a few minutes mommy was pushing her in her stroller into the store and when they came out, little Amy Bac had on My Little Pony sunglasses and her eyes didn't hurt anymore.

Christy was watching Amy closely and she wasn't happy. Amy's walk had changed again, the little girl was walking like an old old woman and Amy was holding onto furniture. One morning she found Amy sitting on the floor and she knelt down and asked the child if she had fallen.

"No mommy," Amy said in a tearful voice. "I have a problem," the child said and reached to hug her mother, the hug turning into a clinging hug.

"What is it baby mine?" Christy asked pulling her child onto her lap and rocking Amy in a sitting position on the floor. "You can trust me, tell me anything. I love you, I love you with all my heart and all my soul and all my life."

"Look," Amy said and showed her mother her leg.

"Amy," Christy whispered her little girl's name seeing Amy's foot and leg quivering. This isn't right; Christy pulled Amy up into her arms and went for the camcorder videotaping this quiver. Within fifteen minutes she had the primary care doctor's nurse on the phone and an appointment for early afternoon.

The quiver was not only in Amy's feet and legs, the quiver happened in Amy's arms and her hands as well and she showed the doctor as Christy sat in stunned silence that her child had kept this fear and concern inside. Amy was a chatterbox but there were some things that Amy couldn't talk about and Christy was quickly finding that out about her little girl.

"Palliative care," the doctor said to Christy. "Amy has a neurologist, an endocrinologist, a cardiologist, an orthopedic surgeon, a GI and a host of problems. She needs one doctor to oversee all of her care Christy," and the mother knew Amy's doctor was right. With Chad on Skype they made the choice together as a couple to enter Palliative care and the doctor was very supportive, very kind and he guided Christy though what she needed to do for Amy's overall health.

Chad called from his iPad to Christy's iPad early in the afternoon. After months of waiting Christy was finally in with the neurologist that knew ataxia that was in their area. He was a Pediatric Neurologist and Chad and Christy were very hopeful that he would offer advice and direction or even a medication that would help Amy as she was now struggling to walk even twenty feet on her own.

The doctor watched Amy walk seven steps down his hall and turned to Christy sitting in a chair nearby holding the iPad so that Chad could see Amy's walk. He had been gone for over four months. "Damn," she heard her husband swear in a low voice. "She's gotten worse."

"Well, you both can calm down," the neurologist said with a happy smile and patted Amy's head. "I know ataxia and this won't get any worse." Christy heard Chad curse again and she turned off Skype thanking the doctor for his time and helping Amy into the stroller, Christy left the office hoping against hope this doctor was right. He'd certainly said what she wanted to hear.

"She's gotten worse in the past four months," Chad yelled from the iPad when Christy connected with him again via Skype. "We need some medication or a treatment, Christy. We don't need to be told this won't get worse. Every month, this is worse. We're seeing that baby."

"I don't know what to do Chad," he heard his wife crying. "I don't know how to fix this." And her greatest fear was, that no one else in the world knew how to fix this either.

"It's time we talked about a wheelchair for Amy," the Palliative care doctor said as he came into the room for Amy's routine visit.

"No," Christy said and met the doctor's eyes with her own seeing that he was serious. "She can still walk."

"She's tired Christy," the doctor patted Amy on the head. "She needs support. Wheelchairs aren't advertisements for those that can't walk. They're for those that can walk but fatigue and are ataxic like Amy is. It's taking all of her effort and energy just to stand. Here, try standing like she does," and the doctor crouched and hunched forward making Christy do the same. "In seconds your thighs are burning and you back is aching. She needs the chair."

"I'm not ready for this," Christy said shaking her head.

"I'll see you in a month," the doctor said and Christy nodded her head knowing that Amy's tremor was getting worse. "We'll revisit this discussion in one month."

Little Amy Bac wanted to cry. The PT had told Mommy that she could walk around the building for ten whole minutes without stopping. Amy heard Mommy say that Amy had never left that building to walk around it, the place was on a busy street and Mommy would never allow Amy that close to traffic. "Scared of fast cars," Amy said as she looked at the PT and Mommy and Mommy was crying. The PT said it was Mommy's fault for not pushing her to make her walk and Amy thought that if Mommy pushed her to walk, she'd really fall down bad and she fell down bad without Mommy pushing her.

Amy fought not to cry seeing her Mommy cry when the PT made a noise and told Mommy that she needed to make Amy walk and gave Mommy tickets to the fair ordering Mommy not to park in handicap. "You need to walk Amy," the PT bent down and looked Amy in the eyes and Amy blinked hard to keep from crying. "You're fooling your mother by being lazy." Amy saw the PT looking at Mommy again and the woman said that Amy was manipulating Mommy and Amy didn't think she could do that to mommy because she didn't know what the word meant.

Things got worse for Amy when her Mommy burst into tears and grabbed her up running from the building. Later she heard Mommy on the phone crying harder and the speaker was on. Mommy was talking to the new doctor that Amy liked a lot and that doctor was upset with Mommy saying that he had just heard from the PT that Amy could walk ten minutes without stopping around the building. Mommy turned off the phone and Amy went to her mommy patting her back.

"It's okay Mommy, I'm here."

Christy grabbed her child and held the little girl close as she hugged Amy. "I'm making a molehill into a mountain," she cried and pulled Amy onto her lap. "And tomorrow we're going to the fair with the camcorder and you and me are going to figure this thing out."

Amy woke up on the morning of July 9, 2009 slurring and stuttering her words. By March of 2011 she was falling, yet before that time, the little girl was playing sports and piano and dancing. She could read and write; listen to stories a teenager would read and tell about the story she heard read to her back in detail. She had run everywhere and now she struggled to stand up straight.

Something was the matter with Amy and Amy knew that something was the matter and mommy wanted to fix things for her. Her mommy wanted to make her better and Amy wanted mommy happy. Amy knew, her mommy loved her best of all.

Christy didn't park in the handicapped area at the fair. She didn't take Amy's Safari tilt stroller out of the trunk of the car. She didn't even take Amy's hand. She held the camcorder ready and prepared to prove to the world that she was making a mountain out of a molehill. And Amy fell twice just trying to reach the gate to enter the fairgrounds. As they entered the gate, Amy was leaning on her mother and her face was blood red. Christy knew, the world wouldn't have proof today that Amy's mountain was really a molehill, because there was no molehill, there was a mountain and Christy was more afraid than ever.

Amy's lips turned blue, she was shaking all over. Her eyes darted upward and to the right and she fell down. This was not good. This was a nightmare and within a few moments, Christy had Amy on her back and was piggyback riding the child to their car. The camcorder and the camera had captured the true state of Amy's condition, whatever that condition might be, and Christy wished with all of her heart that this wasn't happening. She wanted that woman in North Carolina to be right. No one would ever know the damage that woman in North Carolina had wrecked into Christy's life with the accusations that Christy was making her child ill.

The Palliative care Doctor watched the fair video and photos on Christy's iPad. He closed his eyes several times and shook his head. The PT had not been truthful with him. With Chad on Skype the doctor took Christy's iPad and went into another room and talked to Chad. He told Chad that he knew all about DCFS and that woman's blogging of Amy and the accusation of Munchausen's by Proxy. He told Chad that Christy wanted to have Munchausen's, something Chad already knew.

"That's treatable," Chad said in a slow sad voice. "I wish this were on Christy too; then Amy would be well."

"Damaged," the doctor said to Chad. "Your wife has been damaged and she's suffering worse because she knows Amy's not all right. Christy is the one now dressing Amy and bathing the girl and fixing her hair and brushing her teeth. All of Amy's needs Christy is meeting and things change every single day. I'll get Amy a new

PT and Chad; you need to talk to Christy about a wheelchair for Amy. The little girl needs the chair."

"But you agreed with the PT when she said Amy could walk," Christy said to the Palliative care doctor when he brought her iPad back into the room that she and Amy were in and he talked to her again about a wheelchair. Chad was no longer on Skype.

"I'm sorry Christy," the doctor said and put a hand on her shoulder. "I was wrong. I messed up."

No doctor ever had admitted to messing up, Christy thought as she looked down at Amy sitting on the floor playing with her ponies. "I'm not ready for this," Christy said and reached to help Amy back into her stroller.

"You're not ready," the doctor said, "but Amy is."

The very next morning as Christy was bathing Amy; Amy lost her balance in the tub and fell. Christy held her child, twisted her body and Amy fell on top of her with Christy hitting the edge of the tub and cracking three ribs. And still the wounded mother, wounded by wild, careless and false accusations, refused to allow her child to go into a wheelchair. Amy was going to get better. Christy was going to push until Amy did get better.

Chapter Twenty-One

1 Peter 5:6-7: "Humble yourselves, then, under God's mighty hand, so that he will lift you up in his own good time. Leave all your worries with him, because he cares for you."

The night was pitch dark, the hour very late as Christy stood outside the second story apartment she and Amy had moved into only three months earlier as the apartment they were living in was being treated for termites. She looked beyond the darkness and she saw a car pull up, a taxi and she lost her breath seeing her husband coming toward the stairs. Amy's service dog rushing to greet Chad.

"Oh dear God," Christy prayed and fell into Chad's arms. "You're home, it's really you."

"I've nearly died without you," Chad put his arm around her as they went inside the apartment that he hadn't seen before. "Where's my little one?"

"Asleep," Christy whispered and led him to the bedroom where Amy was sleeping in their bed. Due to the seizures Amy had slept in their king size bed with her parents most of her life.

"Amy," Chad bent over his child to wake her up seeing Christy with the camcorder on. "Little one, I'm home."

"Daddy?" Amy came awake slowly calling for him. When she opened her eyes and saw him she cried out and hugged him. He was home, Chad had come home to his child and to his wife and to his dog and he vowed never to leave them again. His deployment was over. He was retired and he belonged with his child now and for the rest of his life.

"My God," Chad spoke in a shocked voice as he came around the corner and saw Christy standing in the kitchen at the sink.

"What?" he heard his wife asking him and he shook his head hard.

"Amy," he went to where Christy stood and saw Amy scooting on her bottom into the bedroom. "She can't stand up straight anymore, can she?" he asked the question he already knew the answer too.

"We're going to Children's National to see the neurologist there next month. Amy's having an MRI ten days before we leave." Christy handed her husband breakfast and they sat down and talked, Chad doing most of the talking.

"I think it's time to do the Make-A-Wish Christy," he spoke in his military voice that she knew that she would do as he said. "This isn't for us, it's for her," he nodded toward Amy. "I don't know if whatever this is that she has will kill her or not, but it's certainly destroying her quality of life."

"I know you're right," Christy said to her husband and if it was for Amy's good and would make Amy happy, then Christy knew that it needed to be done.

"Back when she first started to struggle and lose ground we agreed we'd give her all that we could," Chad said and held his wife's eyes with his own. "We have a nice nest egg now; she gets all that we can give her."

The MRI was done at Arnold Palmer's Children's Hospital. Chad had brought over all her past MRIs on CD and he spoke with the radiologist personally that the past MRIs would be compared and we'd know without doubt if there was changes. Chad asked three times if the man was going to do this and the radiologist took Chad and Christy into a backroom with rocking chairs and swore to them he'd compare the MRIs.

"No more mistakes," Chad said firmly to his wife as they sat waiting not so patiently for Amy's MRI to be done. "And three days in Disney World."

After Amy's MRI was complete Chad drove his family to the Caribbean Beach resort. They stayed in a waterfront room and Christy pushed Amy around the resort in her Safari tilt chair and the little girl was thrilled. Amy loved sliding down the slide and her Daddy took her up again and again and again. In the evenings, her parents took her out and they raced their remote control cars, Daddy always won and mommy always wrecked. Amy tried to chase after the cars but she could only manage two steps and she fell. The little girl knew she needed to stay sitting down.

Chad rented a boat and took his child out riding on the water. Amy loved the ride and within the hour he and Christy rented a paddle boat and working hard, they made Amy laugh and giggle with their playing on the lake. This was how they were supposed to be. They shouldn't be worrying about Amy's health, they should be playing and having fun all the time that they could.

They left before dawn heading north on I-75. Their destination was Washington, DC and Children's National Hospital. Chad drove the whole way and Christy let him while Amy slept in the backseat. Their little girl was sleeping more and more. She was up to four hours a day napping and ten hours a night sleeping, some nights she would sleep twelve hours. Amy was twelve years old now as well and no signs of puberty, but she had grown some in the past year so Christy wasn't concerned.

They reached Washington, DC early the next afternoon after having spent the night in Virginia. Chad had them checked into their downtown hotel and within the hour he and Christy were walking, pushing Amy in a used Quickie wheelchair toward the memorial wall for the Vietnam War. Amy was taking a nap and Christy noted that even in this chair, Amy was falling over to the side. She kept thinking of the doctor urging her to consider the wheelchair and here Amy was in a wheelchair and it was no support to the child.

Chad hailed a cap for them to go home before dark. Amy was tired and fussy and Christy was as well. They'd gotten their photo made in front of the white house and had lunch in the park. Despite the heat of the day, the wind was blowing and they'd enjoyed being outside.

"The A/C is broken in our room," Chad said to his wife as they entered the hotel.

"Amy can't take this heat," Christy said as both parents knew Amy didn't sweat. After explaining their problem to the front desk clerk they were moved into another room and Amy was tucked into bed within the hour, fast asleep as their appointment was at seven thirty in the morning.

Little Amy Bac knew that she hardly ever was fussy and she tried never to cry. She wanted to make mommy and daddy happy so she smiled all the time and she knew they liked her smiling. Here in this big hospital she knew that she was tired and droopy, she wanted to go home, but it seemed important to mommy that she be here so she tried to smile and sit up straight.

A very beautiful doctor came into the room with a pretty nurse and they talked to mommy and daddy. Amy lay on the bed resting because the car made her really tired and she'd been in that car a long long time. She just needed some sleep and she might feel better. Her eyes closed and she listened to the voices of the grownups for a minute, but only for a minute and she was asleep.

"You know that your daughter's brain isn't right," the doctor spoke these words while looking at Chad and Christy heard her husband's voice and his words.

"Amy has cerebellum atrophy," Chad said in a clear voice and felt Christy take his hand.

"The MRI has changed Mr. Bac," the doctor said slowly almost carefully. "Amy has whole brain atrophy now."

"No," Chad said looking at Christy. "Amy has cerebellum atrophy."

"I'm sorry Mr. Bac," the beautiful doctor said. "Her whole brain is involved." The doctor left her chair and woke up Amy. The good natured little girl sat up and attempted to read a chapter book, but she couldn't. She was able to show all her numbers and letters and count to one hundred. The doctor and her team, several people were now in the room, wanted to see Amy walk and gladly, to please them, Amy stood and walked.

The head nurse watched and took notes and asked Christy and Chad many questions. She then moved to Amy and asked Amy many questions. The nurse noted the movements Amy made and alerted the doctor and the parents watched the doctor watch Amy's jerks. "She's epileptic," the neurologist spoke as she thumbed through Amy's printed records and saw Amy's EEG reports. "The ataxia and the atrophy in the brain are very obvious," the doctor turned back to the parents. "This is certainly a form of myoclonic epilepsy that is progressive. Here's the genes that need to be found." The doctor wrote some genes down on a paper and handed it to Christy. "A skin biopsy would be helpful as well in narrowing this down."

"We had whole exome done," Chad spoke up and the doctor turned her attention to Amy's daddy.

"I'm aware of that Mr. Bac," she spoke as she came closer to him. "But whole exome skims the surface of the genes, things can be missed. These genes," she pointed to the paper Christy held, "need to be targeted." The doctor looked back at Amy and shook her head. "She's precious," she spoke slowly. "I'm sorry this is happening to her. I watched several of her older videos playing sports on YouTube, she was very good."

Chad and Christy left the hospital late that afternoon crushed and broken. They had a diagnosis, progressive myoclonic epilepsy – wasn't that Lennox Gastaut Syndrome?

Reading the Arnold Palmer Children's Hospital written report of Amy's MRI made both Chad and Christy know, whatever Amy had, their little girl was getting worse. "Global brain volume loss," Chad spoke several times as he held the report. "All I know is this is bad."

"I have an appointment for Amy's monthly checkup with Palliative care," Christy said as she helped Amy put on her shirt and then reached to brush her child's hair. No one realized that Amy was now like a two year old; she could no longer dress or undress herself. She couldn't tie her shoes. She couldn't brush her hair or her teeth any longer. The little girl was back to drinking out of sippy cups and eating what food she would eat with a large and deep spoon.

The little girl was dependent on her mother for all of her care. Even eating cereal was a challenge to keep the food on her spoon though the feeding disorder was awful now and Amy had limited herself to only four foods. Her constipation was a nightmare to deal with and she'd started having cycle vomiting six months earlier.

"Christy," Chad approached the subject carefully. "The wheelchair we bought used isn't the right one for Amy. Even the doctor in DC said so. She needs more support due to fatiguing. Talk to the doctor today."

"I don't want this," Christy cried and Chad rushed to pull her into his arms seeing Amy looking at her mother. "I want that woman in North Carolina to be right," she sobbed against her husband's motorcycle jacket. "I want Amy to be well, Chad. I want that woman to be right and all of this is my fault."

"That woman was wrong baby," Chad held out his hand and Amy scooted on the floor and pulled herself up holding on to her Daddy's hand before she hugged her mommy. "Just talk to the doctor today." Chad hugged his child close and wondered if anyone could understand the depth of their grief over Amy's regression. He knew one thing for certain, that woman in North Carolina had no idea how badly she had harmed him and his wife and he felt if the woman knew what she'd done, the woman would be glad.

"Amy can still walk," Christy helped Amy to her feet from the wheelchair that she and Chad had bought online and she showed the doctor how Amy could walk holding onto her hands.

"She needs a wheelchair," the head doctor of the complex clinic said and Christy shook her head hard.

"If that child can walk to the car from this office then she doesn't need a wheelchair," the doctor was firm in his speech, yet gentle. He saw the hurting mother let go of her child and he saw Amy, for her mother's sake holding onto the wall and walking down the hall. The little girl sat down on the floor and looked up at her mother.

"I just need to rest a minute," Amy said trying to smile at her mother.

"Order the chair," Christy burst into tears.

"We'll get with the PT," the doctor said and Christy lifted her daughter up putting the child in the wheelchair that was the wrong type that she and Chad had bought online.

Amy had left her lunchbox in the car. The little girl only ate a few things and Christy was careful to keep those foods at hand that Amy liked, they were prepared for the child at all times. She pulled into the school parking lot and jumped out of her car hurrying inside with the lunchbox.

"That mother is handicapping that child by putting her in that chair," Christy heard the teacher aid saying this and she stopped still outside the guidance counselor's office.

"Amy can still walk," the teacher's voice was the next one Christy heard. "She just needs to stop and rest every few feet. We can provide a chair for her to rest in."

"I agree," the guidance counselor spoke and Christy wiped the tears off of her face.

"Amy's doctors don't agree, nor does her PT," Christy spoke up in a voice filled with pain.

"Mrs. Bac," the aide said and Christy handed the woman Amy's lunch box.

"I don't understand why everyone blames me," Christy cried on. "Amy came into this school and day one she walked the balance beam in PT. That was nearly three years ago. Now she's struggling to walk and it's my fault? I've done this?" Without another word Christy left the office and went home to find her day wasn't going to get any better.

"Excuse me," the apartment manager called out to Christy and she turned around hoping this woman wouldn't talk too much, she didn't feel like talking to anyone or listening to anyone. "Mrs. Bac, I saw Amy attempting to walk down the stairs this morning. That child cannot manage the stairs. If she falls and gets hurt we could be sued."

"You want us to move into a downstairs apartment?" Christy gave the woman her attention and forgot what was said at Amy's school only a few minutes earlier.

"No," the woman said. "We're releasing you from your lease. You need to vacate the apartment in two weeks."

"In two weeks?" Christy couldn't believe this was happening.

"Your child is at risk," the woman very nearly yelled and Christy burst into tears. "She doesn't walk well. She can't manage those stairs. She's going to break her neck. We're asking you to move."

"It's not my fault!" the mother screamed and ran from the apartment manager up to her second floor apartment.

Mommy always told her that prayers and faith after a good soaking cry will save you, little Amy Bac thought knowing mommy had cried, prayed and told Amy to have faith. With Amy buckled in the car she and her mommy went in search of a house to rent. In three days they saw over twelve houses, all that mommy referred to as dumps and Amy thought that she liked the way mommy said the word dump, it made her feel tickled.

On their way back to the apartment Amy saw a yellow house with a sign in the yard and she pointed and called out "Mommy," really loud and soon after mommy stopped the car, they had a new house to move into. A house with no stairs so Amy wouldn't fall down and get hurt, the little girl thought with a smile on her face. Little Amy Bac had spent months terrified of coming in and out of that apartment and Mommy had given her piggyback rides often, but no more. She was going to be safe in this new house, this house that was on the ground.

The yellow house on Van Buren Drive wasn't their own home, but it was the first house that Chad and Christy with Amy had lived in since they had left Eglin Air Force Base. The school bus came to the house so Amy didn't have far to walk. She held on to her mommy and made it up the bus steps until October when her wheelchair was ready and her wheelchair was wonderful.

Christy took the tray of Amy's new wheelchair and decorated the top of the tray with My Little Pony stickers. The chair was a pinkie pie pony pink and Amy loved that it was hers. "Now I can go anywhere I want mommy and I won't get tired ever again," Amy spoke in a cheerful voice and Christy found that Amy was right as they went out together shopping.

"Everything you need in a grocery store is at the very back," Christy laughed as she pushed Amy. "All we could reach were magazines and candy when you were walking baby mine. But now," Christy pushed the chair down the store aisle, "now we can get the sandwich meat and the chicken breast and even a watermelon."

Christy was able to take Amy to see movies again. Christy took her daughter out to Chinese. They took long walks around the lake that separated their home from the base. The wheelchair had set both mother and daughter free and the dog too as Amy's service dog, Sheltie was going with them everywhere. A few months after moving into the house with no stairs the Make-A-Wish foundation had Amy come and meet the dolphin, Winter at the Clearwater aquarium. Amy was thrilled and the chair made this possible. Amy's wish had been to meet Winter and Hope and here she was kissing Winter and waving to Hope and no parents could ask for more than seeing their child as happy as little Amy Bac was that day.

Christy and Chad had also learned that Amy had one gene that caused Batten disease. They were waiting on permission from their insurance company to have this gene investigated to see if this would be Amy's diagnosis. Both of Amy's parents were very aware that Batten disease is a progressive myoclonic epilepsy and they prayed their journey to diagnosis was at an end though Batten disease was not the end that any parent would ever want for their child. Batten disease is always fatal, the life of children with this devastating diagnosis is stolen a piece at a time just as Amy's life was being lost a piece at a time.

Before their Make-A-Wish Disney cruise, the insurance company informed the couple that they wouldn't pay for the testing of the gene. Now out of options they went on the cruise determined to have fun with their daughter. Everything now was about making the most of every minute.

"I'm going to take Amy up the AquaDuck," Chad said to his wife seeing her sitting with her leg propped up. Christy had twisted her ankle dressing Amy in the pink swimsuit. She sat and watched her husband push, pull, drag and carry Amy up the steps laughing at Amy crawling as well. That was her girl, always pushing forward, nothing held Amy back.

Christy heard Amy before she saw her daughter, Amy's scream of joy loud and long and filled with just what Christy and Chad wanted to hear. But within minutes the scream of joy turned into a cry of pain. Jumping up despite her swollen ankle, Christy ran to Chad holding Amy and within a few minutes the family was down in the lower decks with the doctor X-raying Amy's leg. The good news was that Amy's leg wasn't broken, but it was huge, more swollen than Christy's.

Wrapped up tight and in her chair with ice on her ankle Amy carried on with her mother hopping along behind the wheelchair holding the chair for support of her own injury. "Some trip this is turning out to be," Chad said while shaking his head and Christy laughed giving him a hug.

"We're here, we're together on the Atlantic and Amy's stable despite this injury. We're together."

Amy loved the live on stage shows; she loved the fancy dining rooms and even attempted to eat a little. She spent hours on the balcony of their cabin looking out at the water while mommy drank coffee and read books to Amy. The trip was relaxing and just what they needed and the injuries weren't their focus. They were a family. The Three Musketeers. All for one and one for all.

Chad had a voicemail on his phone and they knew what they were hearing wasn't good. The company he worked for was letting everyone go. Chad was without a job. On the drive home Christy held his hand. This wasn't the end of their world. Chad was retired from the military and they'd made smart moves, they could easily live on his retirement, but they wouldn't be able to pay to have that gene sequenced to see if there was more than one Batten disease causing gene.

Little Amy Bac knew just what to do to help Daddy when she saw that he was upset. She bowed her head and she prayed and she told Mommy it was all okay now. Mommy unloaded the car and unpacked while Amy watched Winnie the Pooh and Daddy talked on the phone. Soon Daddy was smiling and Daddy was smiling because he would be starting a new job.

"God is good," Christy kissed Amy on the cheek and the little girl leaned into her mother. Amy knew what her mother had taught her was true – God answers our prayers.

Amy was invited to the premier of 'A Dolphin Tale 2' and sat in the section where Winter kids sat. She was thrilled to be there and had met the girl that played Hazel in the movie having her photograph taken with the young actress.

Life was good in the house on Van Buren Drive for little Amy Bac. They had a wheelchair van and she and her mommy were out and about all the time. The bus picked her up at the door and she no longer had to worry about the steps leading up and onto the bus, she was lifted up in her wheelchair with no threat of her falling ever again.

Amy loved the wheelchair. For Amy, the wheelchair represented freedom. They went to Disney World again every weekend and one Tuesday morning her mommy was acting silly and making faces at her and Amy laughed when mommy told Amy that today was their 365th day in Disney World. Mommy and Amy had spent a whole year of Amy's life in Disney World.

In early July Amy's dream came true. Her father bought tickets to the My Little Pony convention and dressed in her favorite pony clothes, Amy was taken to the convention. For Christy this convention opened a whole new world for her daughter Amy. All of the young people had something in common with her daughter. They all had a love of ponies and they all liked talking of ponies. Amy fit in with her peers and Amy was loved and cared for by this wonderful group of loving people.

Chapter Twenty-Two

Psalm 27:1: "The Lord is my light and my salvation—whom shall I fear? The Lord is the stronghold of my life—of whom shall I be afraid?"

Mommy was crying again, Amy knew by the noise coming from the living room. Was it because mommy was sad that Amy was sitting on the floor and not even trying to stand now? She wanted to keep trying to walk, but it was so hard. Even at school the teachers weren't making her try and take a step or walk. Instead, someone pushed her chair all the time now. She didn't want mommy to find out the truth because mommy would be sad. But the truth was, going to school made Amy hurt and she wanted to stay home more and more each day.

Mommy's crying had changed and Amy held still and heard Mommy on the phone with Daddy. "We've had all these tests Chad and they've not found a gene that would cause this. No doctor can figure her out and this woman in North Carolina has seen Amy's records." mommy stopped talking, Amy heard mommy crying harder and she was afraid. She didn't like it when mommy cried hard. "I'm going to cuddle with Amy," the little girl heard her mother say into the phone and Amy crawled to her bed laying down and soon mommy came and climbed in and they cuddled and mommy sang all the pretty little ponies song until Amy went to sleep.

"Christy," Chad said his wife's name into the phone. "I want you to email that woman back. I know we made an agreement to always ignore her, but I want you to say, yes, we'd like to see what you have."

He looked at the email his wife had forwarded to him from the woman in North Carolina, an email written by that woman in North Carolina that stated that she worked for an insurance processing company and that she had proof Amy was fake and she asked if Christy wanted to see that proof. In the email it was obviously a threat, the woman wrote that others saw this information when processing the insurance claims and very easily, Amy's medical records could be exposed to the world.

"She's left us alone for so long now," Christy said into the phone as she did as Chad instructed and emailed the woman the one sentence stating they wanted to see what she had on Amy to prove Amy was fake.

"She writes that she has proof Amy isn't receiving services," Chad spoke thoughtfully as he went over the email carefully. "If she's seen anything of Amy then she knows Amy's real. This is just a threat. I'm going to google her and check out her Facebook and see if there's any information on her."

"Amy's asleep again," Christy cried into the phone. "Chad what if it is me? What if I'm doing something wrong? I'm not forcing Amy to walk; I did put her in the wheelchair."

"She can't walk but a few steps and she can't leave the house without that chair. Don't let this woman get to you, that's what she wants. She's tortured us and tormented us for years calling Amy fake and worse accusing you of Munchausen's. This is all about her Christy, not you or me or Amy. She's the one that is doing this." Chad went silent and Christy saw in her inbox that the woman had emailed her back.

"Chad, she's emailed back that she has to check with her legal department before she can share what she has. But now I know she's seen Amy's medical information." Chad was silent for a long few minutes and Christy sat still waiting to see what he would say when he finally spoke.

"There's a major insurance processing company in Concord, North Carolina. She has a Google site with that place listed as her employer. She also has on her Facebook that she processes Amy's insurance company here in Florida. And Christy, she had a LinkedIn site. Take a screenshot of those sites baby."

"So she's going public with Amy's medical records," Christy burst into tears not wanting people to see the many things happening to her child's health.

"Baby," Chad spoke in his calmest voice. "She's HIPAA certified."

"What does that mean?" Christy sat up after taking screenshots of the sites with the North Carolina woman's information of where she worked in North Carolina.

"That means that it's against the law for her to have done what she's done by emailing us and saying she's seen Amy's records and will share them with us to prove Amy's not getting the medical treatment that Amy's getting. Don't worry, on Monday morning I'll make some calls. In the meantime, we're taking Amy up to the cemetery to decorate the graves and just get out of town for a few days and we're not going to let this woman hurt us. She doesn't know us baby. We don't know her. Who can figure out why she's done all that she's done? We're complete and total strangers to her and yet she's written about us as though we're people she knows and what she's written has held no truth. The only thing in her postings of us that are true is our names. What makes me upset is it's not my medical records she's threatening to expose, nor your medical records. It's our little unwell girl, a twelve year old child's records that are being threatened."

"I never thought of it that way Chad," Christy cried into the phone.

"That's because you want this to be your fault, then Amy won't be sick. But like that doctor said years ago when this woman made the accusation of Munchausen's, 'mothers don't shrink brains.' You're innocent Christy. You've done nothing but try and protect Amy. That woman has done all she could to tear a little sick girl down. That's not right and that's on her. Not on us. Amy is her victim."

Chad came home early bringing dinner with him. Amy slept all afternoon and through the night. At six in the morning on a Sunday morning they left for the cemetery with flowers and angels and some bleach to clean away the mildew on the headstones. And to be together as a family, that's all they wanted, just to be together as a family.

On Monday morning as they were driving back into Florida, Chad made the call to the insurance processing company in Concord, North Carolina. The gentleman he spoke with was doubtful in what Chad told him, the man just didn't think this sort of thing were possible. Chad pulled off to the side of the road and he forwarded the two emails to the man and verified that the man had received them.

"This isn't legal," Chad said in a clear and certain voice. "I've spoken to a woman at the Department of Justice. People that process insurance claims are bound by HIPAA to never speak of what they see. If this woman were processing her own mother's claim, she couldn't tell her mother."

The man in Concord told Chad he had the emails and the situation would be resolved right away; there was no reason to involve anyone else. Chad got back in the car and as they stopped to have lunch in Gainesville, Christy received an email from the woman in North Carolina, she stated that they had no right to look her up, that her LinkedIn site was for business reasons.

"We stalked her," Christy said realizing that now she knew something of that woman and she didn't want to know anything of that woman.

Chad shook his head as his phone rang knowing they wished that woman would let them alone. He answered the phone before he leaned his head against the side of his seat. "She lost her job to be mean about a little girl that is very likely dying. She has to be mean to us when we're falling apart. Amy's the love of our life. She's the neatest kid." He was crying and Christy was crying with him. She had climbed over the seat and was holding onto him. "She ran baby," he sobbed hard. "Amy ran and she was happy and she kept us up at night and now she's sleeping all the time. And that woman posted that Amy's fake. No one wants Amy to be fake more than we do. We want this damn disease to go away. We don't even know what it is so if there's a treatment or a cure, we have no line to get in."

"Amy's holding on," Christy said as she looked back at her little girl curled up with an American girl doll and sound asleep. Amy use to read to her dolls and have tea parties and now she slept with the dolls. "Let's just go home," Christy pulled Chad back into the car. "We need to keep looking for a house to buy. We need a forever home with Amy. Once we get a forever home she'll perk up. We'll paint her room pink. Amy loves pink."

Christy put all her efforts that were left over from caring for Amy into finding a house for their family. She took Amy out to little communities in the Tampa area and the two sought out that perfect forever home. "We have to have a pool Amy," Christy said to her daughter as they pulled up in front of a house that Christy knew was just what she had in mind. Chad had looked at the house and shook his head; it was on a corner lot and he didn't want a corner lot. But once they entered the house and saw the pool and the backyard he changed his mind and the master bedroom had a huge walk in shower and handicapped rails, the perfect room for Amy with a front bedroom that was the same size. Chad and Christy could have the front room and Amy this large and lovely master bedroom.

They went home and discussed the house and Chad called the realtor, but the house was sold. The housing market was recovering and they knew, if they found something they liked, they needed to buy fast.

Christy laid in the bed and on her iPad she found the perfect home. Travertine tile floors, a swimming pool enclosed, granite counters in the kitchen and bathrooms, a stone sink and a huge garage for two cars and storage. She woke up early the next morning and she went up to see the house and after walking through, she knew that it wouldn't work out, she couldn't get Amy's wheelchair through that house.

Late the next afternoon, Chad and Christy had toured eight more houses and turned them all down, they went to another home and it was perfect, everything they wanted, but it wasn't near the expressway so Chad could get to and from work with ease.

"This place looks just like the one that Amy's wheelchair wouldn't fit in," Christy said and turned to face the realtor.

"Same floor plan, same size home only that home we looked at yesterday was packed full of furniture. I couldn't even walk through the place." The realtor saw Christy going to the door.

"I think we've already found our home," she said to Chad and they went back to the house with everything they wanted and seeing the house was much bigger than they knew, they put in an offer. "They have a dining table that will seat twelve Chad. There's room, there's plenty of room for the three of us."

The offer was accepted on the new house. With their lease up on the Van Buren rental house, Chad and Christy boxed and packed everything up and put it in a U-Haul. "Our last move baby!" he called out to his girls and Christy agreed with him.

"We're getting too old to move every other year like we have been," Christy laughed and hugged her husband before getting in the van with Amy to go to the closing of their new home. "Twenty-one months in the apartment outside of MacDill base, seven months in the apartment with stairs and now fifteen months in the Van Buren home. It's time for us to put down roots."

"And for me to have a pink room," Amy said with a smile. What Amy didn't know is that the painters were at their new house now painting her room pink. Tonight they would be settled. Tonight Amy would be sleeping in a pink bedroom.

"And we're going to grow old together Amy Bac," Christy said in a teasing voice and heard her daughter giggle. Amy was stable; all they had to do was keep Amy stable.

The first months in the new house were fun. Disney World was much closer and they went often to have dinner with the characters and to Mickey's Halloween party where Christy met several other families of children with rare diseases. She also was faced again with a mother that only planned to meet them to prove what the woman in North Carolina was saying of Amy was true. The woman met Amy and then hugged Christy and to Chad and Christy both she said, "your child is real. I was so certain Amy was fake because of what that woman posted."

Chad pulled Christy away from the woman and he told her to not come near them. "This is disgusting. These women of handicapped children listen to some woman calling a little girl fake and they believe this woman and come here to prove Amy's fake. Well Amy's real. Amy's always been real," the last words Chad very nearly screamed and Christy again fell apart in tears.

The gossip of little Amy Bac needed to just stop. The gossip of little Amy Bac never should have been started.

"Chad. we have to stay focused on Amy. She's all that matters," Christy said and her husband agreed turning and giving Amy his attention.

"We didn't dress up and come out here for nothing," he pushed the chair fast around the Magic Kingdom and Christy ran to keep up with him, Amy laughing loud that she was running again and this time she was running in her chair.

Christy and Chad felt certain the North Carolina woman would leave them alone if they just continued to ignore her. She had posted something public about Amy and several people spoke up to her negative post and she retaliated by posting that Christy was making everything up and doctoring emails to make this North Carolina woman look guilty. Chad and Christy saw these posts and all they could do was shake their heads and carry on as they had been.

Christy had been busy making the house perfect and taking Amy to the new therapies near their home. Amy was now in aqua therapy and able to spend time in the pool even in the winter. Amy also loved the water. The first year in the house was happy and full of love. All the neighbors knew them; they'd made friends and every day Christy took Amy for long walks and best of all, the ducks came right into the yard. Amy could sit in her chair in the front yard and feed the ducks.

The day before Amy's MRI, Christy took her child to Dinosaur World and they walked the whole area. Amy was able to feed the huge goldfish and see all the wildlife while Christy was able to enjoy time with her little girl before their appointment in the morning. Chad was going with them and again he had Amy's last MRI on CD to give to the radiologist. Everything would go smooth and easy Christy thought. Tomorrow would be done soon and they'd see that Amy's brain was stable and together Chad, Christy and Amy would grow old.

"They made a copy of the MRI from Arnold Palmer's Children's Hospital," Chad said as he climbed into the car and looked back to see his little one was asleep still. Christy had her laptop open and the CD of the latest MRI inserted in the drive. "Do you see any difference?" Chad asked and Christy shook her head.

"To the naked eye, the cerebellum looks the same but I'm a mom, not a doctor," Christy said and she saw Chad looking at the images on her computer screen. "I'll come back for the written report in two days," Chad said as he backed out of the parking space.

"It'll be stable Chad," Christy insisted. "It just has to be unchanged."

Even hearing his wife's words Chad felt no comfort. Amy had been able to make it from the front door to the car when they moved into the house. Now the little girl couldn't go but four or five steps at most. Chad was afraid of the newest report of her brain, but not so afraid that he wouldn't have a copy in his hands as soon as possible.

"Atrophy of the whole brain, the cerebellum," Chad spoke into the phone with his wife on the other end of the phone line. "Thinning of the brainstem and the corpus callosum," he added and he heard Christy gasp as they both knew. The MRI had changed again.

"The Orlando geneticist said she'd get us into the NIH," Christy said to her husband. "I have every record except for that latest MRI report in this huge envelope ready to go out. All of Amy's medical records are on DVD or CD. I'm going to the geneticist's office the minute you get home."

With Amy in the van, Christy started the drive in the early afternoon. The Orlando traffic was a nightmare but she made it through on toll roads and reached the geneticist before end of day. "I even have the postage on this," She handed it to the geneticist and saw the woman quickly go through everything before smiling at Christy.

"Good job mama," she said handing the package to her nurse.

"She's not your Mama," Amy cried out and then giggled. "She's my mama."

They made it, Christy held up the letter as she jumped up and down. They were accepted by the NIH and were due to go up in only a few short months. Kissing Amy she felt certain now they would have a diagnosis and hope for Amy. She closed her eyes and knew that she needed this diagnosis; she needed this for her mother who had died too soon and undiagnosed. She needed this for her brother and her sister and even possibly herself as she held a diagnosis of Meniere's disease. And she needed this so that she could quiet the hurt the North Carolina woman had caused her with the accusation of Munchausen's by proxy.

"I know you need this," Chad said and pulled her into his arms. "It's natural for mother's to blame themselves. And what's been going on for years by a total stranger has really done us both in. But now, we're going to the top research institute in the United States, they have to figure out something for Amy, that's what they do."

The trip to the NIH was grueling on Amy. They had to take the train from Orlando to Washington, DC. They had a sleeper car and Amy laid in the bed while Chad and Christy sat on the floor. The little girl was very uncomfortable and a twenty-four hour train ride was never for a moment comfortable for her.

After managing the train station and then finding the cab in freezing temperatures, they were on their way to getting checked in and starting what they feared would be a long hard week on Amy and then another train trip home, another long train trip home.

Amy was as she always was. She rarely complained though her mother and father could see the pain in her eyes and on her face. She was miserable and the minute they were checked into their room, Christy had Amy tucked up in the bed with Spongebob on her iPad.

The NIH was like a military institute. It was up and running, everything in a certain order. Chad and Christy were thrilled to see their nurse was the nurse that had worked at Children's National Hospital and had seen Amy in 2013, just three years ago. Amy was still walking and able to read some then and to count to one hundred. Now, everything was a struggle for Amy.

The nurse was thorough and took them from test to doctor and back to test again. The first day they never stopped moving and Amy was worn out even though she'd been in her chair most of the day. By the end of the second day Christy and Chad both were wishing they hadn't come here. Amy had failed a tilt table test, a sweat test, something was found wrong with her brainstem and finally a doctor came in and she sat down and said to them while pointing at Amy,

"This is not autism." Chad and Christy had already learned that with the 16p11.2 team at Texas Children's Hospital in 2011 but neither said this. Instead they listened how Amy was severely and globally delayed in all areas though Christy sat alone in the room and read Amy a story about a duck and Amy loved the story and hugged her mommy.

How did we get here? Christy asked herself as more doctors examined Amy. A neurologist tried to get Amy to walk and the little girl took a few steps and fell, Christy catching her. This was too much for her daughter, Christy thought and by Thursday night all they wanted was to go home and let Amy rest. Amy was tired now.

Friday came, the longest week of Chad and Christy's life and they had to stay another two nights before they could leave for home. By this time Amy's eyes weren't even, she was struggling with sitting up for more than a few minutes; she couldn't hold her head up but for a minute at most. Her gut issues were a major problem. She had the feeding disorder and the choking and the jerking and chorea like movements were all the time.

They left the NIH behind and decided to just live. The team in Maryland was as unsuccessful in arriving at a diagnosis as all other doctors had been in the past. Their last hope had faded away. The only correct diagnosis they'd had in all these years was the early one of Lennox Gastaut Syndrome.

Chad and Christy came home thinking of the specialist in Washington, DC at Children's National, she had said progressive myoclonic epilepsy – Batten disease and the couple paid to have the gene tested and two more genes were found but the genes were not known to cause the disease. Was this their diagnosis? Amy fit this diagnosis of Batten disease the best. The mothers of children with Batten's disease were all facing what Chad and Christy were facing. Slowly losing their children and these brave and courageous mothers took Amy in as one of their own and the support was all anyone could ask for.

Chapter Twenty-Three

Psalm 55:22: "Cast your cares on the Lord and he will sustain you; he will never let the righteous fall."

In the spring the local Children's hospital had a prom and the event was on Amy's birthday. Happy and excited, Christy bought a beautiful gown and together she and Amy went to the hospital where the staff at the complex pediatric clinic helped get Amy dressed. The little girl's hair was done, a crown and makeup put on and Amy looked like a living Princess. This was the night of her fifteenth birthday and in the wheelchair she danced with her mommy and she laughed at the decorations and she enjoyed every moment of the evening.

Christy felt the night was magical. If only Chad might have come, she fretted. But her husband had to work and taking the chair onto the dance floor, Christy danced with her daughter for hours before she put the little girl in the van and took Amy home. Photos taken with her service dog, Christy undressed Amy of the gown and tucked the little girl up in her bed laying down next to Amy and doing what they had done every night since they moved into this new forever home. They watched Lassie episodes on YouTube.

"Did she have fun?" Chad asked as he peeked into the room when he arrived home from work.

"She loved it Chad," Christy sat up in the bed. "This was the best night of her life."

"I'm glad," he came in and kissed his girls goodnight. Amy and Christy were in the master bedroom and he was now in the guest room. Amy had grown and there just wasn't room for all three of them in the king size bed. "By the way," Chad spoke as he made to leave. "The NIH report is in."

"No diagnosis?" Christy asked him and he shook his head.

"None." He put the report in the window seat and Christy left the bed with Amy sleeping and she read the report.

The nurse that knew them from 2013 had told them that Amy's MRIs had been read wrong and Amy's brain was unchanging. She'd always had the atrophy. Chad and Christy were waiting for the report to come in and confirm what the nurse had told them because no doctor had said this to them. They had also been told Amy didn't need one of her medications and after careful thought, they'd started weaning Amy off the medication and preparing to meet the doctor in a month.

The report was too long. Christy couldn't read this. She put it aside and told herself their local doctor would talk to them and explain. In the meantime, Chad had made up a list of every radiologist that had compared Amy's MRIs in her life and if this information of Amy's being stable atrophy were true, a whole lot of someone's had made mistakes. Chad meant to speak to them all as he was the one that had been in charge of getting on disc every MRI done on Amy when it was done.

This journey had been a nightmare Christy thought. They had met wonderful, supportive and caring medical personal along the way. And a couple that hadn't been so wonderful or supportive. You can't let one or two bad apples in a barrel of a thousand apples spoil the whole barrel. The truth was, almost every doctor that saw Amy wanted to help her. And doctors are human just like all of us.

After talking it over, Chad and Christy decided that they'd done all they could, now it was time to just love Amy.

Amy's doctor came to the house on a sunny Saturday morning and he saw Amy's toes were discolored and Amy was crying of zappy pains. The doctor showed Chad and Christy the NIH report and he highlighted and explained the report to them. Amy had generalized neuropathy; she needed the drug they were weaning her off of. The medical test confirmed Amy's diagnosis. So the medication was restarted.

Carefully and with kindness, the doctor opened up the report. He talked of every test explaining it to the parents. He showed Chad and Christy the MRI scans and anyone could see the cerebellum changes in each MRI scan. He showed them the black areas in the scan where before there had been white.

"The black is spinal fluid, there should be white there, the white is Amy's brain matter, but there isn't white there because sadly Amy's brain is dying."

He drew out Christy's family tree showing the many members that had multiple sclerosis and Christy told him that the nurse said Amy couldn't have what her mother had because Christy didn't have the disease.

"Penetrace variable," the doctor wrote on the NIH report. "You don't have to have the disease to pass the gene onto Amy." Chad and Christy listened to him as he explained each test. He then sat on the sofa and drank a soda that Christy gave to him and they talked of how there had been mistakes made and he hoped that the mistakes were now corrected. He also talked to them of the woman in North Carolina. "You've been on an emotional journey," he offered them comfort. "She's your little girl and you love her. To have someone picking on your child, well that's hard to take. Parents of healthy children don't want their kids picked on."

"And the accusations aimed at Christy," Chad spoke up reaching for his wife's hand.

"Horrible groundless accusations with the intent to cause harm. Why someone would want to harm a stranger no one can even understand." The doctor saw the couple before him clinging to one another and he knew, they were a team, team Amy. He just hoped that Amy held on for a long time.

"We have to pray for her," Christy said and heard Amy calling for her. Chad walked the doctor to the car and told him how grateful they were, they would forever be grateful that he'd given them today.

On October sixth, 2016 with the home health aide on duty, little Amy Bac took her last independent steps in their forever home. Even standing in the pool was nearly impossible to do. She could stand and she could pivot and she tried to take steps, but never again would she have the independence of walking around her own home.

That following weekend, with the help of the home health aide and her husband, Chad and Christy moved Amy from her front bedroom to the master bedroom overlooking the pool. Her hospital bed, her feeding pole and oxygen tank, and a soft chair for Christy to sit in were all in place in the larger room with Amy's toys in the window seat. For many hours Amy lay on that floor and played with her toys while watching TV. Amy was now comfortable and Christy slept on a blowup mattress each night right next to Amy's bed.

More time was spent having dinner with the characters in Disney World. They tried to go to the Magic Kingdom for a full day but Amy was too weak. Sitting up for more than an hour was hard and at school she was having to nap. She was also catching every virus that hit the children in her room and spending more time at home than at school. So at the end of the school year in 2016 Amy was placed on hospital homebound and she able to get the rest that she needed.

Chad took his family to the All Star Music Resort for four days in January of 2017. They had spent four days in the fall in the Art's and Animation Resort. He was trying to give to his child all that he could while Amy could still sit up. Staying in the resorts made it where Amy could sleep in the room and if she felt up to going to the parks, they could drive over, stay a few hours and go back to the hotel room for Amy to rest.

The first day they had breakfast with Lilo and Stitch then went to their room and slept. The second day they spent four hours in the Magic Kingdom. Amy wasn't able to transfer onto rides but Chad and Christy tugged and pulled her onto her favorite rides, Winnie the Pooh and Buzz Lightyear. On the third day they spent only three hours in Epcot and then went back to the hotel. Chad and Christy very aware that their fun Disney lives with Amy had come to an end. The hurt was deep; this had been their lives since Amy was a baby. This disease, whatever it was, had robbed them of everything except their precious daughter.

One week after they returned home Chad had some testing done. He was diagnosed with cancer and the cancer was bad. The couple knew they had to go back to Disney World with Amy one last time. Christy knew that she might lose her husband before her daughter. The morning before Chad was scheduled for major surgery they went to Disney's Hollywood Studios. Amy would see Frozen on stage and meet all the characters that would sign an Olaf toy for her. They would see the Star Wars area and Princess Sofia and finally Doc McStuffin before they bid the parks farewell never dreaming that their lives were going to change forever in less than twenty-four hours.

Christy had all of her attention focused on Amy and now her husband was in trouble. The complex pediatric clinic helped arrange for nursing for Amy and Chad went into surgery. Nine hours later Christy met him in recovery and they learned that the doctor felt she had gotten all the cancer.

The next morning before Christy could get Amy settled with the nurse, Chad went into a crisis with pulmonary embolisms. Rushed to ICU, Christy got to her husband and they knew he wasn't going to have an easy recovery. Amy was holding her own at that time and Chad was in for the fight of his life.

After the embolisms, Chad developed a blockage. For more than three weeks he tried to get better and nothing worked. Christy was spending the day at the hospital with Chad for eight hours and the rest of her time was with Amy.

Little Amy Bac was horribly confused. Daddy had gone away and hadn't come home. Mommy had always been here with her and now Mommy was gone a lot, but then Mommy would come home and they'd watch Beauty and the Beast and everything was all right until Mommy left again. The nurses were all right the little girl thought to herself, but she wanted Mommy and Daddy. Amy wanted to go have dinner with Winnie the Pooh again.

Christy came home one night a month after Chad's surgery and saw that Amy was frightened with her gone. She climbed into the hospital bed and slept the night holding Amy and telling the little girl that she was loved and Daddy would be back soon. But that wasn't true. The next day Christy reached the hospital and Chad wasn't well. Testing showed a problem and the doctor said they'd have to operate in the morning.

Home with Amy for the night, Christy barely slept. She held Amy again sleeping in Amy's bed and prayed that Chad would be all right. She was afraid, more than afraid. At three in the morning she left the bed and checked to make certain their estate plans were in order. If Chad died, she'd be all Amy had in the world. They'd saved and planned for Amy's future. The house would be paid off if Chad or she died, over a million dollars in life insurance policies going into trust for Amy's care and then the savings. Amy would be secure with nurses and a court appointed guardian if anything happened to Chad and Christy. Chad had seen to everything, Chad

had made them responsible parents that cared for their child even in death.

The nurse arrived an hour early and Christy hurried to the hospital. Chad was now in critical condition. After surgery he went into septic shock and he was placed on life support. It was their eighteenth wedding anniversary and Christy had forgotten all about the date. Later she would learn that Chad's cancer had spread and that he needed chemotherapy, but the oncologist told Christy that he couldn't have the treatment, he was too weak and wouldn't survive chemotherapy.

Several days passed before Chad was stable. He wasn't getting strong fast. Days turned into weeks and Christy was dealing with his fragile health as well as Amy's. Chad had a drain, an ostomy bag, a TPN line and he was so weak that he couldn't sit up. Amy was now choking on water, her eyes weren't even and she was also a diabetic.

With Chad in the hospital, Christy took Amy to the St. Joseph's Children's hospital prom. The complex pediatric team again helped Christy dress Amy in a poofy ball gown and Amy's hair and makeup were done again this year. Amy looked more beautiful than the year before, but now Amy couldn't sit up straight. She couldn't dance in the wheelchair as she had the year before. She was tired. She was weak and her mommy was terrified for her well being.

Amy turned sixteen on the night of the St. Joseph's prom while her father continued fighting for his life. Amy's sweet sixteen birthday was wonderful because of St. Joseph's Hospital's prom, had it not been for that prom, the special birthday would have passed unnoticed.

Chad came home for a few days but he wasn't able to make it at home. He was back in the hospital fighting infection and fighting his inability to eat. A GJ tube was placed and Christy hoped that would turn the corner and it helped, but there was no cure for Chad.

Over the summer he relearned to sit up and to walk and to try and eat. He gained weight despite vomiting all the time and every time he was sick Amy would say, "Poor Daddy."

More surgery in October and again in November and Chad was still far too weak. But by Christmas Christy's focus was on Amy. Her little girl didn't realize that Santa had come to see her. Amy seemed lost in her own world and distant from everyone. St. Joseph's hospital gave the family a generous and loving Christmas yet there was no joy in Amy as her mother opened her gifts. The little girl that they had the year before had screamed in joy over a My Little Pony, but this year Amy barely looked at the ponies she was being given this Christmas.

"This is sad," Chad sat in a chair weighing one hundred pounds less than he had the year before and looking like he would die far sooner than Amy would.

On the second of January, Chad went back into crisis and Christy rushed him to the emergency room. He was re-admitted to the hospital and for thirty-one days he did not come home. For thirty-one days Chad fought for his life while a crew came in to remodel Amy's bathroom and make it handicapped accessible. Christy was torn with staying home with Amy and going to Chad. As she'd spent much of the year with her husband, she chose to be with her daughter and she would soon forever be thankful for making that difficult choice.

Chad came home in horrible condition in February. He had to relearn to stand, to sit up, to hold his head up. He was being fed through a feeding tube and more than a year had passed since the initial surgery to remove the cancer. He wasn't strong enough for the chemotherapy and the oncologist told Christy the cancer would more than likely come back as stage four.

All of February and March passed with Christy not leaving the house except to go to the pharmacy or grocery store. She sat on the sofa in the living between Chad and Amy. Their lives had dramatically been altered as Chad entered his battle with recovery and Amy seemed to be fading away.

While Chad relearned to sit up, Amy lost that ability to sit and the child reclined in the bed all day. She loved watching Spongebob. She loved listening to her shows on her iPad but she never asked to go to Disney World. Amy was content at home in her bed and she had two full time nurses that loved her and cared for her.

Christy and the day nurse took Amy to the new My Little Pony Movie and the new Beauty and the Beast movie. Amy had been happy to see her favorite actor, Chris Pine in Wonder Woman. She loved going to the movie and the ice cream parlor next to the theater. She loved going to the complex pediatric clinic where they had a coffee shop with chocolate muffins and a man gave her a penny for the wishing well. In May they went and Amy was measured for a new wheelchair, her old wheelchair was no longer supportive, she had lost too much. She couldn't even hold her head up for a minute.

Chad was able to walk to the car and he had his own wheelchair. With the nurse he and Amy went to see Jurassic World and the Incredibles Two. On August third a movie Amy had been waiting to see had finally come out. Christopher Robin. Chad and Christy packed her up in her old chair that wasn't supportive enough, Christy dressed her in a cute outfit and with the nurse and an aide they all went to the movie. Amy loved Christopher Robin so much that the family went again the next night. Amy was thrilled.

Something odd happened to Amy on the night the movie first came out. She had to paint. She wanted her paper and paint brushes were out all the time. Day after day, almost every single hour of the day, Amy had to paint. She was so insistent over painting that Christy left orders with the night nurse.

"If Amy wakes up at three in the morning and she wants to paint, she paints."

Chad was still battling to eat but the feeding tube was helping him become strong. Amy was changing and it wasn't good. On the twentieth of July she developed a breast mastitis and the doctor treated it with an antibiotic. Two weeks later Amy developed an ingrown toe nail, not a good thing for a diabetic and she had to see the foot doctor. He dug the nail out and she started another oral antibiotic and an antibiotic ointment as well. Two weeks later the toe was still infected and another round of antibiotics was needed before the infection was finally cleared up.

By September the first Amy's ordeal with infections was finally over, but Christy was concerned about another problem. Amy would tell the nurses that she had to go to the potty. A big ordeal to get Amy out of the bed and into the chair and rolled over the toilet and then Amy would sit there for thirty minutes or longer and not go to the bathroom. Treated for a suspected UTI for ten days and still the condition was not clearing up.

Christy was concerned. Her daughter wasn't able to urinate often or well and there were other changes happening to her daughter. Amy drank almost all the time, the little girl had diabetes insipidus, Amy was chronically thirsty, but now, Amy rarely asked for a drink. Amy was also taking a long time to eat the only food that she was eating at this time, cheese grits. Usually Amy bothered her mother and her nurse to heat the grits up at least twice at mealtime as she liked her food hot, but now, Amy wasn't asking for her food to be hot and Amy wasn't eating.

On the morning of September sixth Christy went into Amy's bedroom and saw her child smile. The smile wasn't like one Amy had always given to her mother and Christy realized, her daughter looked different. Amy's facial features looked slack. Taking a photo Christy went to the phone and called the complex pediatric clinic. An appointment was made for the eleventh of September and certain that Amy couldn't sit up in the van at this time, Christy made arrangements for an ambulance to take Amy into the hospital for the appointment.

"She looks bad," Christy said to Chad and he shook his head.

"She's just tired and she needs to urinate and she'll be fine," Chad said while still struggling to eat and looking very ill himself. "She's pulled through other crisis' baby; she'll get through this one too. She's like her Daddy. In a few weeks she'll be eating her cheese grits again and drinking a ton of her strawberry crush."

"I pray you're right," Christy fought not to cry and saw that Amy's nurse was as concerned as she was. "I want a photo of us together," Christy said and she pushed Chad in the room having the nurse take their pictures. The photos were awful. Chad was skin over bones and Amy couldn't even sit up. This was bad and Christy stayed up all night long writing and reading and praying and afraid. She could lose them both. She could lose Chad and Amy. She could be left behind.

The ambulance that was to take them to the hospital was late. By the time the EMTs arrived Amy was worn out and couldn't stay awake. They put her in the ambulance and Christy rode in with them, the private duty nurse was with Amy. Together at the hospital with the EMTs they all went upstairs and their appointment with GI had been missed as the ambulance was late. Amy would not have to wait and be worked into an appointment and the wait was over three hours. Christy knew, there was no way that Amy could wait on this stretcher in the hallway for thirty minutes let alone three hours. The little girl was pale and taking each breath as though she had run a race, Christy had to speak up. Amy needed help.

Christy went to the complex pediatric clinic across the hall and she was told there was a wait to be seen there as well. She saw the orthopedic surgeon down the hall with Amy asleep on the stretcher and he asked the nurse where her mother was and Christy hurried to him, the doctor reaching for her hand and pulling her close. This doctor had seen Amy in March, Amy had been sitting up for the appointment and interacting with him, now Amy looked near death.

"I can't believe this change in Amy," the orthopedic doctor said in a very concerned voice. "Christy, if there's anything I can do for you, any way that I can help Amy, please don't hesitate to contact me."

"I don't want to lose her," Christy fell apart, the tears falling freely.

"I remember when she broke her arm and I first met her," the doctor gave Amy's frightened mother a supportive hug. "She walked into my office and told me she would only let me put her arm in a cast if the cast was pink."

"That's Amy," Christy laughed past the tears. "She always has to have pink."

"Christy, the doctor has a room ready for Amy," the nurse with the complex pediatric clinic came and told the frightened and worried mother.

Amy slept on never moving or even indicating she heard what was going on around her. This was very much not like Amy; the little girl had to hug everyone that was near her. Amy had to be a part of all conversations.

"She's sleeping a lot," Christy said as the doctor came into the room they were in and sat down. All of the loving and familiar nurses of the complex pediatric clinic had come in to see Amy before the doctor arrived and Christy was crying. It felt as though they were all saying goodbye to Amy instead of Amy being here for an appointment.

"Her oxygen is low," the doctor said and the EMT had the tank hooked up and Amy on oxygen for the ride home. "When children with these type of disease start downhill, they can sometimes fall fast. Amy's falling fast."

Christy knew. She had known for days. Amy was sleeping all the time; she wasn't even trying to eat her cheese grits. She would lift her spoon up and then drop the spoon on her bib unable to reach her mouth. Several times Amy had choked on her drink in the evening and the choking had been frightening. And the painting, for days Amy had been painting, but now the paint brush laid on the tray untouched. Amy wasn't even waking up to ask for her toys.

"Do you think I only have another year left with my daughter?" Christy asked the doctor, the private duty nurse looking at her and the pediatrician shook her head.

"I think you only have a week or two left with Amy," the doctor spoke in a kind and gentle way. "You might not have that much time."

She didn't fall apart but Christy cried. Everyone in listening distance knew that a mother was losing her child by the crying. The doctor was among the best to be on Amy's team, Christy trusted this doctor completely.

"Amy's excited for the new Lion King movie due out this summer and Dumbo in March. She has to live to see those movies. She's planned on that," Christy cried as the doctor gave the mother all the understanding in the world.

"I'll let hospice know to bring out more oxygen tanks and a bigger unit," the doctor hugged Christy and cried with Amy's mother. As they left, Christy saw there wasn't a dry eye among this loving and awesome group of medical personnel that had been for eight years what Chad and Christy referred to as 'Amy's dream team.'

"We love you Amy," Lisa said as they passed by her and Lisa gave the child a final hug.

"You're a strong girl," Margo whispered to the child and hugged the mother.

"Call if you need us," Debbie squeezed Christy's hand and touched Amy's cheek.

"Thank you," Christy turned at the end of the hallway and she was hit with the reality that she wasn't just losing her daughter; she was losing the love, the support, the kindness and the care of this wonderful group of people. "A journey no one should take alone," Christy whispered as she turned to follow Amy's stretcher to the elevators. "I was never alone while here in Tampa. We might not have been diagnosed, but we were cared for."

Christy came into the house and she and the nurse got Amy settled into bed. The pulse ox was delivered and the nurse hooked it up to Amy's toe. The oxygen tank came next with the capability of giving Amy more oxygen than the old tank. Within a few minutes, the hospice nurse was in the house followed by the hospice nurse that could write prescriptions.

"We won't increase any medications at this time," the nurse said seeing Amy's oxygen levels. "This happened fast, she's never had levels this low."

"She's not able to eat and she's only drinking a little," the hospice nurse that knew Amy well said as the hospice social worker came in.

The Bac home had always been busy, now it was frantic and overrun with the medical team. Chad came in from an appointment of his own and he saw everyone everywhere and Christy told him what the doctor had said. "No," was the only word he said to his wife as he hurried around the corner into his little girl's room. "Hey you," he said and Amy cracked her eyes open and reached for him.

"Daddy," she said as Chad hugged her and she looked a little like herself. "Did my toys come yet?"

The toys Amy was referring to were the toys of Pooh, Piglet, Eeyore and Tigger from the new Christopher Robin movie. Chad had ordered the toys from the Disney store in July but they were back ordered and every single day Amy asked if the toys were coming yet.

"The won't be here until the end of October," Christy spoke in a broken and frantic voice and Chad stood up from his daughter's bed.

"She wants those toys," he said and left the room followed by his wife.

"Chad, she's dying. They're saying she only has days left."

"If that," the head hospice nurse said to the parents seeing both Chad and Christy spin around and face her. "Even on oxygen her levels are in the low 80s. She's leaving us."

"Should we call Chad's parents?" Christy asked and the social worker with hospice stepped forward.

"I'll call for you," the social worker said and Christy gave her the phone numbers knowing Chad's parents would believe the hospice worker about how serious this was rather than taking the word of a frightened out of her mind mother.

"I have to find those toys," Chad said and left the room not seeing that his wife had fallen to the floor and was crying hard. Christy could do this now because Amy was in the room with the nurse.

Before the day nurse left, she and Christy rearranged Amy's room so that Christy could sit in a recliner next to the bed at all times. The nurse had a chair at the foot of the bed and Chad had one at the side. There was enough room for another chair at the foot of the bed for company if needed and Christy soon realized that chair was needed.

The home health aide came into the room as Amy slept and together the nurse, Christy, Chad and the aide spoke of a ball gown for Amy to have on in the coffin. This was important to Chad and to Christy because Amy had always been a Princess and loved her Disney Princess gowns. Calls were made, hospice stepped in to help find the perfect gown, David's Bridal shop was consulted and by the end of the week, a nine hundred dollar pink ball gown was hanging on Amy's bedroom door for her to see when she woke up, which she wasn't awake often and when she was awake, she only was awake for a few moments.

The private duty nurses were wonderful. The day nurse had been with Amy more than a year and a half and she became

Christy's rock in many ways. Hospice was coming in every day and Amy's oxygen was a big problem. One hour her levels would be in the low eighties, the next hour the levels would drop into the love seventies and at times even into the sixties. Over the weekend her levels went into the fifties in the middle of the night. The hospice nurse came and said they were at the end, the private duty nurses that loved and cared for Amy were called and by four in the morning they were all by her side. By five in the morning, Amy's oxygen levels were up in the upper seventies.

Within a week of seeing the team at the complex pediatric clinic the seizures hit and they hit hard. Every second Amy was jerking from myoclonic seizures. An increase in medication, adding on a medication, nothing helped. Amy jerked around the clock both awake and asleep with the private duty day nurse crying in an agony for the child, "she's going to jerk herself to death."

Chad's mother came and bid farewell to her only grandchild by her eldest son. A lot of tears; a lot of hugs were given. Amy loved her Nana very much; the two had always spoken of My Little Pony's together. Before Nana left, Chad told his mother that he had found the Christopher Robin movie toys on eBay. A guy in Orlando had them and Chad paid three times what they cost at the store and he didn't care. He could get the toys for Amy today. So mother and son took a short trip and when they came home, they had Amy's Pooh toys.

Tragically during the night Amy had gone blind, it appeared that her retinas had ruptured. Chad handed Winnie the Pooh to his daughter and held the stuffed toy against her face while Amy's loving and long term private duty nurse told Amy what her daddy was holding against her face. All Christy could do was stand outside of her child's room and cry.

Chad had been trying to relearn to eat for over two months. Every day he'd gone to Burger King for chicken nuggets and he always brought home some for Amy as they had been her favorite food for years. Amy was no longer able to eat, but he came back with a chocolate milk shake for her and she was able to drink a little asking for more the next day. Early the following morning, Christy woke and pulled out the magic bullet making Amy one of the chocolate milk shakes Christy had made for Amy all of her life. She went into the room and held the cup to Amy's lips; the little girl couldn't wrap her lips around the cup. Reaching for a spoon Christy put some into Amy's mouth and it dripped out.

Several moments of panic passed as Christy called the private duty nurse, it was the nurse's day off and she answered the phone explaining quickly that the milk shake wasn't staying in Amy's mouth and Amy wasn't swallowing. The nurse told Christy to not give any more of the milk shake to Amy. "She can't suck or swallow anymore Christy; she's now one hundred percent dependent on the G-tube."

"Oh God," Christy prayed and knelt by the bed with the phone still in her hand and she prayed for her daughter, she pleaded with God for more time, she wasn't ready to lose Amy.

Chapter Twenty-Four

"Be strong and courageous. Do not be afraid or terrified because of them, for the Lord your God goes with you; he will never leave you nor forsake you."

Amy hung on to life by sleeping almost all the time. Her parents kept her favorite cartoon playing around the clock, that show was 'Winnie the Pooh.' The neighbors stopped by to visit, Amy's best friend next door came in and told her that he loved her and Amy told him that she loved him too. He left the house in tears still clinging to the hope that the angel that lived next door to his house would live on. Amy was still a child; she should have her whole life ahead of her.

Chad had become the strong one. For more than a year and a half Christy had been holding him up while he recovered from the cancer surgery and she had been taking care of Amy and now Chad knew, it was Christy's turn to be weak and she had earned this right.

"What if that woman in North Carolina is right and this is all my fault?" Christy asked this question as she paced the living room early one afternoon with the hospice team sitting at the dining table. "I need that woman to be right," she threw her face into her hands crying hard and the hospice nurse came and hugged her.

"No one will ever know what that complete stranger has done to this mother," the nurse said as Christy cried hard. Chad and Christy had taken their blog, the happiest place on earth, a blog that only had happy photographs of their family in Disney World, and they had posted screen shots of some of what that woman had written of their child. They could do nothing more to stand up to the woman, they hadn't wanted too. And they had tried very hard to forgive this stranger that had hurt their lives when their lives as parents had been falling apart.

"The woman was playing a game," the social worker spoke as Christy cried on. "She thought it was fun to post all those things of Amy on the internet. And what she did had consequences that she never felt, but that this mother has been made to suffer for years and will suffer all of her life."

"She never said she was sorry," Chad spoke as he took hold of his wife. "And sadly others have joined in with that woman bashing Amy. We opened the caring site up for a week and the guestbook on the site was attacked with horrible comments saying Amy wasn't real. As though watching our only child together die was not enough hell to face."

"Maybe she'll post that she made a mistake when Amy's dies," the hospice nurse said feeling sorry for these hurting parents. "Maybe she'll email something to try and make up for all the damage that she's done."

"I hope so," Chad said still holding his wife. "But if she does or doesn't, as Christians, Christy will forgive her. Amy would want us to forgive because Amy loves everyone, even people that are mean to her."

Amy held on to life. The seizures had total control and nothing was stopping them. The jerks were unreal and yet, the jerks were all too real. Amy could no longer suck or swallow; she was able to see out of the lower part of her eyes only. She couldn't stand up and pivot onto the toilet chair and she was in diapers full time though she wasn't needing to be changed due to a lack of urination despite the tube feedings. Her speech was slow and hard to understand, as her body was shutting down. Nothing was working right for Amy and Christy never left the little girl's side sitting in the recliner by the bed and praying constantly silently in her head. The round the clock nurses caring for Amy's medical needs while Christy was what she always had been – Amy's mommy.

Into the month of October, Amy held on. She could still speak when she woke up for a few moments, but she only was able to speak a word or two. She couldn't hold her paint brush if she had tried. She couldn't operate her iPad any longer because she couldn't point at anything and hit what she pointed at. Her arms were jerky if she tried to reach for something and she couldn't grasp anything. She couldn't hold her head up straight, her head was flopped to the side.

Her hospital homebound school teacher came often and read to Amy, the teacher's heart was breaking as she had been with Amy for two years and loved the little girl very much.

Chad and Christy's home was always busy. The hospice team was in and out much of the day. The private duty nurses were around the clock, the nursing agency not leaving Christy alone with Amy for even a moment. Amy was too fragile for only her mother's care. Amy's past health aide came and spent a day, the woman left in tears knowing this was the last time she'd see a girl she thought of as a baby sister for the final time alive.

Christy held Amy's hand while the long term day nurse fixed Amy's hair and the hospice health aide came in and bathed Amy. Everyone worked hard to keep the house clean and the dogs fed and Amy's dogs never left her side. Amy had a lap dog, a yorkie named Poppett and Poppy stayed in Amy's arms almost all the time. Sheltie, the Shetland Sheep dog that had been Amy's service dog for ten years stayed by Amy's side sometimes pushing Chad and Christy and even the nurse aside as the dog laid on the little girl as worried over the seizures as the parents.

Another long night passed with the hospice nurse coming in as Amy was in crisis. The nurses all agreed Amy was at the end and yet Amy clung to life. She told one of the night nurses that she didn't want to die, her mother Christy hearing her words and running from the room to break down in tears.

They knelt by Amy's bed as parents and they prayed. They held her hand and they prayed more. The nurses took videos of the family together knowing that soon there would be parents without their child for all the rest of their lives on this earth.

Christy was feeling some hope. The doctor had said on September eleventh that Amy had only a couple of weeks left to live and they were now into October and it was the tenth, a Wednesday morning and Amy wasn't stable, but Amy was holding on.

The private duty long term day nurse came in and got Amy's medications together putting them in the g-tube while Christy held Amy's hand and worried more than ever. Amy was looking at her mommy with a look of fear and Christy kept asking Amy to talk to her and the child wasn't talking. Amy always talked. Amy loved to talk. But now, all Amy could do was stare at her mother.

"Christy," the private duty nurse touched the mother's shoulder. "She's lost the ability to talk. And her head is rigid and stuck to the side. I can't get her neck to straighten up."

"My baby," Christy cried and climbed into the bed with Amy holding her little girl tight and close. "God please help my Amy, please God."

The worst was happening. Little Amy Bac was dying. There was no doubt now, and all hope was gone. The hospice team ordered the tube feedings to stop, Amy was chocking on her own secretions and she bloated. Fear of aspiration was at the forefront of the problems that were now taking over the Bac home.

Little Amy looked at her mother, those huge brown eyes looking into her mother's eyes and the child never went back to sleep that day and night. Her eyes stared into her mother's eyes as her mother laid in her bed with her holding her close as she did when Amy was a baby.

Christy kept saying over and over that she loved her girl. She sang to Amy her favorite songs and she clung to each second wanting these seconds to go on forever. Chad sat by the bed with his head hung down. He had been so certain the cancer would take him before this unknown murderous disease took Amy from this life.

"We're losing everything," he broke down and sobbed having to leave the room. And Christy, Christy held on to her baby and prayed.

At four in the morning the moaning started. The parents called hospice and the doctor came and saw and told Christy to pull on clothes and call 911, they couldn't leave Amy in this pain and Amy was obviously in pain.

The long term private duty nurse and Chad followed the ambulance into the Children's hospital; Christy sat with Amy holding her little girl's hand feeling this wasn't really happening. It was as though Christy were out of her own body looking down on Amy and herself from above. Admitted and taken to a room Christy kept seeing what appeared to be rain falling all around them and she reached out trying to touch the rain.

"You've not slept in days," the nurse said to the mother and Christy heard the words, but she saw that rain and she knew all the angels in heaven were crying and that was the cause of the rain. She even used her phone to take a video of that rain, and she saw the rain in that video, but no one else did.

The nurses and the doctor from the complex pediatric clinic came into the hospital room and were as they always were, loving and kind and broken hearted over Amy. The little girl never slept. Her mother stayed in her bed and her Daddy beside her bed holding her mother's hand. The private duty nurse left in tears and the couple knew their lives as Amy's parents were changed forever. Their lives which had been full of medical personnel and teachers and therapists for the past four years was at an end. Everything they'd done to try and save their only child was at an end. The end would be in some cold room in a hospital and they had fought like hell to not have this be their end.

Several seizure medications were given and the jerking slowed, but the jerking never stopped. Amy was put into an ambulance late that afternoon and with her mommy still clinging to her hand, she was taken to the hospice house. Her last trip alive was being made, her mother's crying loud in the ambulance as Christy's hot and heavy tears fell on Amy's face, the child reaching and patting her mother's back in a caring way.

In their own room Christy took a quick shower. Chad came in with their bags that Christy and the nurse had packed in case this happened. In case they couldn't stay home with Amy. The directions from BrainNet was taped on the wall above the bed as Christy and Chad had made the difficult and gut wrenching choice to donate Amy's brain to the research program hoping against hope for a diagnosis at long last. They had to know what was murdering their child.

Christy pulled Amy's hospital bed over to the bed that was for parents and she lowered the beds to the same level climbing on the crack and pulling Amy close. She ran her fingers behind Amy's ear as she often did and cooed to her baby and prayed out loud. She wasn't ready to let go and she felt Amy wasn't ready to leave her yet. The two laid side by side facing one another and Amy's eyes never closed. All night the little girl looked at her mother and her mother looked at her into Friday morning.

Chad sat in a chair and stared straight ahead. Christy prayed to God to forgive her all her sins and to please allow her into heaven with her child. Around four in the afternoon she wrote a public post on Amy's Facebook prayer page, the post meant for the North Carolina woman that had done so much harm with written words to Christy.

"You took a huge interest in my daughter Amy Bac for years. I thought you'd want to know that Amy is dying. We did all that we could to save her. You should know that Amy has been an awesome and amazing child. She loved her Daddy and Mommy more than anything and we cherished every second we've had with her. God bless and keep you and may we all be like Amy and do only good in our lives. God loves you and He would want us to forgive you, Amy would want us to forgive you and to love you. In Christ's name we pray for you always. Love Christy, Amy's mom."

A comment was made to this post within minutes, a comment by the North Carolina woman's female family member. "I find it very problematic that you're posting as if your child is dead when in fact she is not. This reminds me of a similar case to Amy's. Gypsy Rose Blanchard."

Chad would look up Gypsy Rose Blanchard with Christy later that evening after the long term private duty nurse came to visit and bring some things the parents needed from home. Gypsy Rose was a little girl whose mother made her fake illness for money and gifts. Gypsy Rose escaped her mother by stabbing her mother to death.

The rumors that Christy was harming Amy would continue long after Amy's death. The agony that Amy died would far out outweigh the hurt that the woman in North Carolina had seen Christy suffered with that North Carolina woman's internet popularity.

At six thirty four Christy made her final video of her daughter. Laying on the bed, Christy told Amy that Amy had blessed her life in a million ways. "I couldn't save you baby," she very nearly whispered. "But you saved me." She covered Amy's face in kisses and prayed a silent prayer. "You'll see an angel soon baby mine. The angel is coming for you. Take hold of her wing Amy. And when you see my mama and my grandmamma, please, tell them I love them. They'll take care of you until I get there and I won't be long. I won't be far behind you Amy."

"Oh God," Chad gasped from the other side of the bed. "Little one, I love you. I love you."

The seizure started at six thirty-six. The shaking and jerking were awful to see. Amy was making a noise, the noise wasn't right, it sounded like no noise Chad and Christy had ever heard. Christy refused to move from the bed. The nurses came in and they gave drugs. The doctor came in and more drugs were used. The seizure wouldn't stop until another drug was given. But the seizure, it wasn't at an end, Amy was just in a drug induced state.

At dawn the doctor came in and sat down. For two hours he talked and explained that they were trying to make Amy comfortable. He made it where Chad could hit the morphine pump every twenty minutes with one hundred percent certainty that this was safe to do. The parents didn't want Amy dying by an overdose and the doctor assured them this was safe for Amy's size.

Chad put on the soundtrack to the movie Christopher Robin, the song 'Evelyn goes it alone,' was on repeat and Christy clung to her child while Chad set his alarm to go off every twenty minutes. Amy didn't wake up. Amy didn't move. Christy prayed and prayed and by nightfall Amy's fever was one hundred and six with nothing taking the fever down.

The hiccups hit just after dark that Saturday night October the thirteenth. The hiccups were body jerking and worse than the seizures. The nurse ran for the doctor and within a few moments a drug was given intramuscular that put Amy into a deeper sleep.

The seizures continued despite the drugs, nothing was working, Amy was paying a horrible price in leaving this world and Christy's sobbing prayers weren't being answered. She remembered the abuser she hadn't been able to escape. She remembered her fear and nothing from her past, no pain from her past that she'd suffered could compare to this – to losing Amy in this way.

"Damn seizures!" Chad said in a horrible voice and moved to the side of the bed holding tight Amy's hand. "Seizures started all of our problems, and seizures are going end her life."

The last eye contact Amy had with her Mommy and her Daddy, that brief few seconds of looking at them, was when the seizure took complete control and in that final second, there was a panic in little Amy Bac's eyes that no one should have seen, a panic Amy shouldn't have known.

This completely innocent, adorable, precious, darling girl was held captive in the seizure. She was non convulsive as her mother held her. She was totally unresponsive. More drugs were given and nothing helped. All the parents could do was wait. Hour after hour, minute unto minute, Chad and Christy prayed and they prayed more.

Chad left and went for food and drinks seeing his wife ate something. Christy sat by the bed or laid in the bed with Amy. She held Amy's hand and the day passed, the night passed, another day passed. On and on time went around them, the same song from the Christopher Robin soundtrack playing in the room. The song had no end, Amy's life, the parents pleaded for a miracle, wouldn't end.

"Find a new normal baby mine," Christy pleaded of her daughter and as the jerking got worse, Amy's skin changed colors and Christy changed her plea, "open your eyes one last time, oh please, look at me one last time. Don't let me remember the last time you looked at me, I'll be haunted all of my days."

Amy didn't open her eyes. Chad put Winnie the Pooh in her arms and the doctor came back in with the room dark, the parents never laid eyes on the doctor in the light, they had no idea what he looked like, nor had he seen them. But his kindness and his caring they'd cling for days to come.

"Amy will soon find and know peace," he spoke in a kind voice. "You two will suffer from her death forever in this life. She's passing in the worst way I've ever known."

The parents were held captive, they were helpless as Amy was again making that awful noise that wasn't really noise and the shaking and jerking were back. Another drug given; another drug failed. The noise went on and on and on from Amy and all the parents could do was every twenty minutes hit the morphine pump button.

Sunday came to a close and at ten thirty six in the night the jerking began again, the noise coming from Amy finally stopped. The little girl's fever was too high, her skin was molting, the nurses said and another drug was used intramuscular to try and help. At eleven thirty six Amy opened her eyes but her parents knew she couldn't see. If Amy could see, she wasn't seeing her parents. She was looking beyond them. Christy broke into horrible tears as Amy gasped for a breath and within a few seconds, the sweet child patted her mother on the back, a pat meant to comfort.

"Don't go," Christy begged as Amy looked off in the distance. "Don't leave me. I don't want to live without you." Chad stood up and came to the end of the bed laying on the lower half of his daughter's body.

"I can't live this life without you little one," he cried and saw Amy gasp for another breath.

"Amy, oh Amy," Christy sobbed and again the child reached out and her fingers brushed against her mother's nose. A last touch between them, all was now lost.

Amy gasped, went still and she was still for a long time only to gasp again and go still again. The gasping went on for eight full minutes. The next gasp was short, too short. "No!" Christy screamed and grabbed her little child holding Amy close. "Take me with her God; please don't leave me here without her!"

Something's the Matter with Amy

Chad cried out as he watched Amy gasp the short gasp in his wife's arms. His wife was screaming, no clear words that he could understand, she was screaming over and over and over again and Amy was gone. The nurses had all run into the room and they stopped and cried with the parents, only one left and she went to get the ice to put Amy's head in.

Amy's brain was going to Beth Israel hospital at Harvard. Amy's head had to be kept cold until the pathologist could remove her brain. Still crying the parents watched the nurses pack Amy's head in ice. Her eyes open in death, Christy reached out and carefully closed Amy's eyes before she kissed Amy's cheeks and lips and then looked at every inch of Amy's face memorizing the beauty that was her child.

Four hours passed before the man from the funeral home arrived. Frantic that Amy be kept cold, Chad and Christy followed him in his car to the funeral home where Amy was put in a refrigerator. At five in the morning they reached their house coming into their forever home without their child for the first time. Christy saw Chad fall into bed crying himself to sleep while she stared at the sun coming up outside.

At six thirty she called the mortuary and Amy's body was on its way to the pathologist's office. There was the assurance that only a small part of Amy's waist length hair would be removed in order for the pathologist to get the brain. Another call was placed forty-five minutes later. Amy's brain was in a cooler on its way to the airport and at nearly eleven in the morning another call came in that Amy's brain was safe and on its way to Beth Israel.

She had done all that she could do, Christy thought and at noon she sat alone on the sofa knowing that she had Amy's room to clean. There was almost no time to clean as the truck came to take all the medical equipment away. The bed, the feeding tube and the pump, the oxygen tanks and the compressor, the pulse ox machine

– everything that had been used to keep Amy alive was taken away. The child's bedroom looked raped.

"They might have given us a few days," Chad said as he sat down at the dining table.

"Another post has been made on Amy's page. This one says that I murdered my child and should burn in hell." Christy removed the post and hit the ban button on the person that made the post not even looking to see who the person was.

"I'm sorry," Chad said with his face in his hands. "We tried so hard to save her. We only wanted to save her."

"I wish that woman in North Carolina had been right!" Christy screamed and she screamed these words over and over again until she was hoarse, her husband holding her and crying with her. The woman in North Carolina had stated all over the internet that little Amy Bac was fake, that little Amy Bac didn't have epilepsy. And the truth was – little Amy Bac died in a seizure that knew no end other than to steal Amy's life away.

Their little girl was lost to them, only the memories were left to them. And the pain, the horror, the agony and reality – that they were left behind.

Chapter Twenty-Five

Mark 5:36: "Jesus told him, 'Don't be afraid; just believe.'"

No one called. No one came to visit. Christy didn't eat and she barely slept. Chad's crying could be heard in the house. Often he would look up and find his wife gone, she was walking; she was walking far and wide trying to escape the house.

The funeral arrangements had all been made before Amy's death. Chad had taken care of all three of them years ago. The couple went in and they chose a catered event with the tables decorated in pink flowers and Princess tiaras. Christy's cousins came in to help and to be supportive, but the couple was lost. The last 8 years had been spent caring for and trying to save their daughter. And the truth was, Amy had stable times and the little one often found a new normal. They'd hoped and prayed for Amy to live until she was at least in her late twenties.

But Amy was gone. And the parents feared the funeral would be small. All they had was Christy's two cousins which were God sent and Chad's parents and brother. They ordered several large pink flower arrangements and they decided to decorate the coffin in Amy's favorite toys, Winnie the Pooh and those toys would be buried with her.

Living as though they were in some sort of daze, dressed the part of grieving parents in their funeral attire, Chad and Christy went to the funeral home hoping Chad's former co-workers would attend so the room wouldn't be empty as it was a large room.

"Amy's beautiful hospital homebound teacher is coming," Christy said to Chad as he parked the car and they got out knowing that their child was missing from the car and their child shouldn't be missing from this car. No wheelchair to get out and put together. No Amy to lift up and ease over into her chair. No g-tube to manage or oxygen to fret over. No smile that lit up their whole world from their daughter was to be found.

With Christy's cousins they walked into the funeral home. Chad's parents and brother were waiting for them. Christy left them all and went inside the room to her daughter's coffin; her crying could be heard as she saw all the flowers. All around the room – everywhere were flowers. "Pink," Christy said to her daughter's body as she fell forward and kissed Amy's too cold cheek.

"I love you baby mine," she said on a sob and turned to see Chad beside her, his hand taking her hand as they looked at their daughter.

The ball gown, the makeup, her hair done and the beautiful tiara on her head made Amy look years older than she was. Amy had never achieved puberty, she'd never developed and she always held a baby look about her. Now she looked like a typical sixteen year old only asleep in a coffin.

Chad put her Christopher Robin plastic handheld toy inside one hand and pooh in the other hand as Christy put on her pinkie pie my little pony ring and her Disney Princess necklace. The parents turned and saw friends they'd made on Amy's Facebook page coming into the room. They hugged and were relieved, the funeral had guests.

The food was being placed when Christy stepped out of the room. She was only gone for a moment and when she came back

Something's the Matter with Amy

she saw every private duty nurse Amy had ever had was in the room. Amy's former and current teachers; the PT and the OT and the ST from the past. Therapists that had supported Chad and Christy through Chad's cancer and all of Chad's former co-workers. Every table was full, food was being eaten and the minister was ready to speak when Amy's best friend Krystal came running into the room and into Chad and Christy's arms, couple screaming over and over again the child's name.

"Oh God brought Krystal! It's Krystal!"

Everyone was seated, everyone was talking kind of Amy when Christy felt something touch her shoulder and she turned to look and a friend from the past, one of Amy's advocates was standing behind her. Screaming in joy that the woman was here, feeling loved and supported, the women hugged and they cried and they hugged more.

The staff of the complex pediatric clinic filled up a table. Friends from Facebook, many friends they'd made on Facebook filled up several tables. And in the back of the room sat the doctors, Amy's medical team was here, even the hospice social worker.

This was humbling. This was for Amy. Their little daughter had touched so many lives. Amy's loving and gentle ways were captivating to one and all. If only the child were here, if only the little girl could see the beauty that her life was. A life well lived, but a brief life that ended too soon. Far too soon for her parents who were now left alone without her.

The Reverend stood and spoke, his words bringing a comfort that was needed. Christy stood and went to the podium and looked out at the packed room and the support and love these people gave Amy in life and were giving the parents of Amy in death.

"I want everyone that can to come forward and share a story of Amy. Amy loved stories." She started off with her own memory of Amy; of the time Daddy had put Amy through a window at the age of only two when they locked themselves out of the house.

Amy had run all through the house and hadn't opened the door. Her parents had stood at the sliding glass door pointing and telling her to let them inside, to unlock the door. Twenty minutes later, Chad pushed Christy through the same open window they'd put Amy through and it was mommy that unlocked the door.

Everyone had something funny to remember of little Amy Bac. Every nurse told of how awesome she was and the joy she gave. Lisa, from the complex pediatric clinic spoke of her and Christy shoving immobile Amy into a huge, puffy ball gown similar to the one that Amy wore now for the hospital prom on Amy's sweet sixteen birthday only months passed.

Chad stood up and he told of the turtles. In mid August a turtle had been in the front yard. He'd brought the turtle inside and shown it to his daughter and Amy loved seeing the thing. Later, when Amy was fighting for her life in September, the hospice nurse had opened the front door and a turtle came into the house. The turtle was at their front door. And the day before they went to the hospital Chad had found a turtle on the side of the road and put the thing in the lake near their home. Amy always knew that her Daddy loved turtles, they had several for pets.

The funeral came to a close. Everyone left with hugs and prayers said. Christy's cousins stayed and cleaned up. And Christy stood over the coffin and cried her child's name over and over again. Chad finally came and pulled his wife away.

The cousins left. Amy's parents never saw Chad's brother or parents again; they'd gone straight to their hotel. Alone, Christy went to bed and cried herself to sleep.

Sunday passed slowly. Christy walked six miles in the morning and another six in the evening. She packed a suitcase as she and Chad were taking Amy to be buried in the cemetery. They went to bed early as they had to be up at five in the morning. The dogs were not going with them, their neighbor and dear friend was dog sitting for them and they were aware that the dogs were suffering the loss of Amy too. The little lap dog cried all the time. Every time Christy left the house the little yorkie waited at the door and when Christy came home the dog darted past her looking for Amy in the yard and sluggishly returning to the house when Amy wasn't found. The service dog laid in a corner of the room and looked at Chad and Christy, but she never moved. The dogs were suffering grief as well.

The cargo van rented, Chad and Christy climbed in and reached the funeral home before seven thirty. The director was there with the doors open and waiting. The parents carefully transferred their child's coffin into the van then went back and got all of the flowers putting the flowers in the back of the van surrounding Amy's coffin.

"I cannot believe we're doing this," Christy cried as Chad pulled onto I-75. They had taken this road north to Virginia to see a neurologist, to Washington, DC to see a neurologist, they'd taken I-10 to see a neurologist and geneticist in Houston, Texas, and they'd taken the train to the National Institute of Health in Bethesda, Maryland. All the trips they had made with their little Amy, parents trying to save the life of their only child while some popular internet woman in North Carolina posted that Amy was fake and a lie and blogged hurtful words of the most innocent of children.

"Our last trip with our child," Chad said seeing and hearing his wife crying beside him.

The trip north was made in almost total silence. Five hours as they drove well aware they'd never take another photo of their child again. Christy would never brush Amy's teeth again. She would never again brush her little girl's hair. Christy had taken care of all of Amy's needs since Amy was eleven years old. The round the clock job of being there for her little girl was at an end.

"I never minded," Christy cried to Chad. "I can close my mind and see us in St. Joseph's Hospital at a table, her eating a muffin and me drinking coffee. I can see us on our way to her therapy Chad and the tree that bloomed pink on the side of the road that she loved to see every time we were going to therapy."

"And us in Disney World," Chad said as they pulled into the Burger King and Christy jumped out of the van and into her older brother Allen's waiting arms.

"We lost her Allen," she cried against his shoulder seeing her cousin Melanie hurrying to her and hugging her closer than Allen had.

"They're ready for us at the cemetery," Chad said to the family and he and Christy returned to the van taking Amy's body the last half mile of this earthly journey.

The cemetery was old. Where Amy would be buried was the oldest part of this place. Christy's Great Great Grandfather had bought the plot in the eighteen hundreds. Her mother was here, Amy would lay right next to Christy's mother and on the other side of Christy's mother lay Christy's Grandparents and behind where Amy was going were Christy's two great grandparents. One day Chad and Christy would be on the other side of Amy, their headstones ready to be placed to secure their final resting place beside their only daughter.

Christy spoke the words from the bible as the funeral personnel lowered Amy's body into the vault and into the child's body's eternal resting place. Chad threw in the first handful of dirt; Christy went to her knees and cried. All that was left now were the endless soaking tears of a broken hearted mother, a mother without her child.

Chad and Christy were what they had always been... Amy's parents. Even without her, they were still what they always had been – Amy's parents...

January 2019 – 12 weeks after Amy's death:

Amy's brain is in the hands of a neuro-pathologist and a top geneticist in the field of research at a major University. The study of Amy's brain continues along with testing. What Chad and Christy know twelve weeks after Amy's death is that Amy's brain was losing cells over time. Her cerebellum, the part of the brain that controls coordination and movement was very damaged. The MRI had shown the atrophy when Amy first started falling years ago, the MRI showed that Amy's brain was dying. The MRI had been correct.

Little Amy Bac lost the ability to run and play and ride her bike. She lost the ability to brush her hair and cook the foods that she had once loved to eat. She lost the ability to eat and to drink and even to talk and breath. Amy lost everything including her life slowly over time, and all to a disease with no name. A disease that had taken Christy's mother and was suspected of taking six other family members and possibly affecting three more.

Chad and Christy await the test results on Amy's brain hoping for a diagnosis at long last. After speaking to the geneticist of the cell loss in Amy's brain, Christy had to look at Amy's death certificate, something that she hadn't been able to do. The certificate reads – 'hereditary ataxia.' Inherited from Christy and in the death of her child, Christy's mother Sara was at last diagnosed.

Two more hurtful public posts accusing Christy of killing Amy have been put on Amy's prayer page as recently as two weeks ago. Christy does not feel the hurt of this accusation any longer. Her pain is in the loss of little Amy, her precious Amy Bac…

To learn more of hereditary ataxias you can go to the National Ataxic Foundation website or you can google Spinocerebellar Ataxia. You can read of the rare seizure syndrome on the Lennox Gastaut Foundation website. Amy's prayer page is still open and will be devoted to raising awareness to these very rare and horrific diseases that can happen at any time in a person's life and for which there is no treatment or cure.

The real hero doctors in this country are the ones that are researching these diseases, finding the causative genes and moving forward in hopes of obtaining a treatment.

www.ingramcontent.com/pod-product-compliance
Lightning Source LLC
LaVergne TN
LVHW021232080526
838199LV00088B/4326